FOREWORD

The first time I met Lu Shengli was at my master Luo Shuhuan's house in 1975. At that time he had just returned to Beijing from military service. To take a break after years of highly physical work, he wanted to try something different. Chinese calligraphy is very good for calming the mind as well as the body, so at the time he was studying calligraphy under Master Luo. After that initial meeting, for about a year we did not see much of each other. At the end of that period, sufficiently recharged, Lu Shengli returned to martial arts practice for good. We learned and practiced together all the time, and have remained close friends ever since.

Lu Shengli started his martial art training at age ten. He studied several different styles, amongst them Shuai Jiao (Chinese wrestling), Shaolin Quan, and Tongbei Quan. Since he practiced so hard from such an early age, his basic *gongfu* skills are extremely solid. While he was in the military he also received hand-to-hand combat training. It was around the time we started to meet regularly that he began his training in internal martial arts. Master Luo liked the fact that Lu Shengli always practiced diligently and was quick to grasp the underlying principles, so later on Master Luo introduced him to his own teacher, Grandmaster Wang Peisheng. That gave Lu Shengli the opportunity to receive intensive private training with Grandmaster Wang. For many years, he went to Master Wang's house two to three times a week. His initial focus was mainly on Bagua, then it included Taiji, Xingyi, weapons, and *qigong*.

In 1984, when the political climate changed and traditional rituals were permitted again, Lu Shengli and I were inducted as Master Luo's formal indoor disciples in a traditional ceremony. At this time, Grandmaster Wang gave Lu Shengli and me special permission

to immediately open our doors and accept disciples of our own. This was a huge honor, reward for our hard work, as we were the first ones in our generation allowed to do so.

Lu Shengli is a deep thinker, very serious and meticulous. He firmly believes that the truth can come only from real experience. In his training, no one can convince him of anything without showing him both the theoretical basis for why something works a certain way, and actual skills following those principles in real life. With each skill he invests a large amount of both physical and mental energy. On the physical side, he often repeats a movement a thousand times without stopping. On the mental side, he analyzes each skill in detail and verifies his thinking using real-life situations.

For many years, regardless of the weather, he practiced outside every morning, starting at five o'clock. His level of skill progressed very quickly. For this reason Grandmaster Wang Peisheng later picked Lu Shengli as his assistant to teach martial arts. In 1993, when Grandmaster Wang came to the United States to conduct his first workshop, he chose Lu Shengli to accompany him.

Traditional Chinese martial arts are more than just fighting skills. The skills themselves are deeply rooted in the traditional Chinese culture, especially the philosophies, and cannot be separated from it. For this reason, when teaching martial arts in the West, I have always encouraged my students to visit Beijing, because practicing these arts in their native environment can provide you with more of the authentic, correct feelings that are integral to their understanding. The need to understand traditional ideas in Chinese martial arts practice cannot be overstated. Each time my students go to Beijing, Lu Shengli takes care of every detail of their training and living arrangements. Because of the genuine care he has shown for all of these students, everyone admires him for both his martial arts skill and his character.

One of the biggest obstacles for students of the internal martial arts is the transition from training to fighting. It is not uncommon for people to practice internal martial arts for many years, and to

still not understand fighting principles, or how to apply their skills. Many people either cannot fight at all, or fight using basically external skills. After many years of practice, Lu Shengli recognized this problem. So starting from the mid-1990s, he began to think about how to address this issue. The results of that extensive research are presented in this book.

Under Grandmaster Wang Peisheng's instruction, Lu distilled his vast experience into this new form. In truth, this book describes much more than just a form; it includes principles and training methods as well. It is Lu's hope that learning this form will enable people to understand internal martial arts more clearly. He has since received feedback from many people, and by all indications has succeeded in this goal with many others.

When I returned to Beijing in 1997, Lu Shengli showed me this form, and we discussed the principles and skills involved in great detail. At that time I asked him to write a book on it, but he said he was not ready. He wanted to spend more time conducting research. I know Lu Shengli well, and it is simply not in his nature to show the world anything until he has judged it to be completely satisfactory according to his high standards. So it was not for another two years, with further encouragement from Grandmaster Wang, that he finally wrote this book. Still he hesitated, wondering if it was ready for publication. When I went back to Beijing in 2000, I took a copy of his manuscript home with me to the U.S. I told him I don't care when he publishes it in China, but that I will go ahead and translate it for publication in the United States right away.

I started this effort as soon as I came back. My student Susan Darley helped me translate and edit the entire book. My other students— Peter Capell, Paul Keane, David Ho, Paul Cote, Strider Clark, and Vincent Sha—also contributed in various ways. I am grateful for all their hard work in creating the English version of this wonderful book. Here I also want to give special thanks to Mr. Jess O'Brien— his help really made the publishing of this book a lot easier.

Since cultural backgrounds are very different between the East and the West, many traditional principles and concepts are very difficult to translate. For many concepts and words, a direct one-to-one translation is not possible. So in this book we always try to give plenty of examples and employ several different ways to illustrate the same idea in the hope that together they will form a coherent picture of what the original idea in Chinese is all about. Although we did our best, I still find instances where the translations can be confusing, especially for beginners.

When you read this book, keep these things in mind. When you run into some points and doubts arise, don't stop there and try to figure everything out immediately. Move ahead and read the other examples and explanations we provide on the same concept. And do the same thing for each concept, going ahead and reading all the related concepts on internal martial arts we present in this book. Then, after you have read the whole thing and spent some time practicing, return to these individual points. You will find them easier to grasp now that you have a good overview of the whole context.

This is one of those limitations of human language. There are certain things that cannot be fully conveyed by language alone, fully understood from reading a book. As with any high-level skills, the only way they can be learned is face-to-face teaching and diligent practice. True understanding can only be gained from hard practice and deep reflection. Ultimately this book offers a good reference for your practice.

I am happy that, with this book, more people have the opportunity to gain a deeper understanding of traditional Chinese martial arts, and I hope more practitioners can benefit from it. I truly believe this valuable art belongs not to any one group, or even any one country, but to the whole world.

—Zhang Yun
Pittsburgh, Pennsylvania, 2005

FOREWORD

I am once again honored to introduce yet another wonderful book on the theories and techniques of the Yin Cheng Gong Fa *gongfu* system. This form and the master that developed it hold a very special place in my heart. I had the fortunate opportunity to study with Lu Shengli and be a witness to the unfolding of this innovative approach to utilizing internal martial arts skill in real combat. Lu Shengli was a major force in my life and helped me understand not only martial arts skill, but how to look inward and grow toward becoming a better human being. Looking back to my training days with the mighty Lu Shengli instills memories of happiness, laughter, and brutal workouts complete with tears.

It was the spring of 1993 and I had been studying with my master, Zhang Yun, for about four years. Master Zhang sent me to Beijing to study with his *gongfu* family. His older gongfu brother Lu Shengli took the primary responsibility of taking care of me and my training while I was there. I can remember very clearly the first day that I met Lu Shengli when he picked me up from the airport. He was not tall, but then I am 6' 3" and stood out in the Beijing airport. His demeanor was very polite and humble. He smiled every time we made eye contact, which made me feel comfortable in my strange new surroundings. He carried himself with an air of great energy and nobility. He was accompanied by another man who translated for us. He took me back to his home where I met his wife and daughter. I was then treated to a fantastic Chinese meal, Beijing style. Then with the help of the translator, we discussed my training schedule and living arrangements.

That night I settled in the dormitory of the university where Lu Shengli worked. Six in the morning came quickly and I was awak-

ened with a loud knock on my dorm room door. Lu Shengli was head of security for the university and had sent one of his officers to wake me up. I headed to Lu Shengli's home, where he had cooked breakfast for me. As we ate, he explained in detail these special foods he prepared and their importance in my training. After breakfast we headed down to the training hall to begin our six-hour daily practice. The translator was already at the hall waiting for us. Lu Shengli began by asking to see what I had been learning with Zhang Yun in the U.S. He watched intently as I demonstrated some Tongbei, Taiji, and Cheng-style Bagua. He then asked if I understood the movements and their applications. I replied that I had only a basic understanding and that many movements I could not use at all.

He then turned to the translator and said something in Chinese. The translator's expression suddenly changed to a look of nervous discomfort. I asked him what Lu Shengli had said. He then stated that Lu Shengli wanted me to attack him with any strike I wished. I was hesitant at first, as anyone would be if asked to punch his new teacher. However, after throwing the first punch and having Lu virtually disappear, coiling around me to reappear behind my shoulder, I began to realize his great skill. Repeatedly I tried to punch him, and he would simply move to one side and then suddenly change direction and appear on the other side.

After several of these amazing evasive movements, he decided to demonstrate his hitting ability. After dodging, coiling, and almost slithering around the punch with blinding speed, he suddenly changed directions and lashed out with a whip-like chop that seemed more like a knife than a hand. Before I had time to react he had already changed directions once again and was striking the other side of my body. Where the first strike had been at my neck, the second one hit a pressure point on the back of my lower leg perfectly. Now his stance was so low that his tailbone touched the floor, yet he was able to move from that posture with great speed. The shine that radiated from his eyes was so intense they seemed to burn red,

giving me the feeling that my death was a blink away. Then just as quickly as his angry-tiger intensity appeared, it went away and the pleasant smile and sparkle in his eye were back. It was as if he had a switch that simply turned it on and then turned it off.

This attribute—to quickly switch between moods—made knowing and living with Lu Shengli very interesting. Oftentimes I felt as if he were the kindest and most harmless man around. To see him interact with his neighbors and even total strangers was pleasant, as he was downright chivalrous and charming. However, after many training sessions and being witness to a few real-life combat situations, I came to know a side of him that few people would ever see. This was a side that, when a situation called for it, would be powerful, ferocious, and terrifying. In Chinese this is described as "li hai," one of the first words I learned there. Ironically, the word that I learned to describe one of his personal attributes would be the same one that he used to describe his combat skills.

After living with him and traveling around the neighborhood, I began to notice that Lu Shengli was well known. I also noticed that the people had great respect and affection for him. I was soon to understand why. On many occasions I followed him to fights or arguments between various individuals. He was not only called on professionally for disputes within the college where he worked, but by citizens on the street. Several of the restaurants near the college had problems with people coming in, eating, smashing up the place, and refusing to pay. Most of the time, the police would take so long to respond that the assailants would cause damage, not pay, and leave without getting caught. These owners as well as many others would call Lu Shengli, and he would come in time to help them.

Just as remarkable as his fighting skill was his ability to talk to people and defuse seemingly hopeless arguments. Sometimes just his presence would change the demeanor of those intensely fighting or arguing. There was no more dramatic example of this than the night I was awakened at about three o'clock in the morning by a

knock at my door. It was one of Lu Shengli's security guards. Through a halting exchange I managed to understand that he wanted me to follow him. As we made our way across campus, we could hear screaming and arguing coming from the walkway in front of us. As we got closer, we could see about a dozen college students fighting with each other right in front of the campus security building. The fighting was savage—they were hitting each other with sticks and rocks. The three guards on duty were young and looked terrified as they simply stood on the sideline watching.

A thick fog hung in the cool air of early morning. When I looked down the long walkway through this fog, with the streetlights shining dimly overhead, I could see a dark silhouette approaching from the distance. As it got closer I could tell by the figure's confident and gliding steps that it was Lu Shengli. As he came closer I noticed that many of those fighting also realized who the dark figure approaching was. Many simply stopped fighting and began to quickly walk away. Sticks dropped and shouts softened to whispers. Soon just a few individuals remained engaged in pushing and yelling at each other. As Lu Shengli stepped into the streetlight his identity became unmistakable. Those remaining calmly stopped and bowed their heads as he approached. I do not know what he said, but his voice was calm and quiet. Everyone spoke quietly, and the blood and anger that had moments before filled the air simply was no longer there. From this moment I realized how much this one man impacted everybody and everything around him in so many ways. I was glad to be his *gongfu* nephew and his student.

The following days were filled with long and brutal hours of hard basic training. I would spend most mornings stretching and doing basic pile stances. I then would rehearse the Xingyi Five Elements, Cheng Bagua basic circle walking, the Taiji form, and *qigong* for several hours more. I was very fortunate to learn Liu-style Bagua from Lu Shengli. In our *gongfu* family, Lu is considered the best representative of this style. For many years he learned it privately

from Grandmaster Wang Peisheng himself. This deadly art was used only for combat and quick annihilation of the opponent. With Lu Shengli I trained Monday through Saturday and had every other Sunday off; the other Sunday I spent all day training with Grandmaster Wang Peisheng. Lu Shengli had carefully arranged every hour of my day with training routines where he watched every movement I made. His persistence and attention to detail were constant, and his demands for repetition and focus relentless. Many nights I would return to my room in tears, exhausted and completely challenged to my limit.

Lu Shengli has spent his entire life cultivating his gongfu skills under the tutelage of some of Beijing's most famous masters. Even more impressive is his ability to understand each of the styles along with their characteristics and spirit. He can simply flow from one technique to another in the middle of a full-out attack, as if he had rehearsed that sequence a thousand times. Sometimes a movement looks like Taiji and then suddenly blends into a Bagua technique. Dozens of techniques from many different disciplines seem to effortlessly be at his command at any moment he wishes. In the beginning I simply was impressed and could not understand this ability.

As my time with him increased, he began to explain his methods and why they worked. One truly remarkable skill Lu Shengli possesses is the skill of "ting jin" or listening force. His sensitivity is highly refined—he can immediately touch you and know what your intent is and where your force is going to go. This enables him to know your next movement and respond effortlessly, or even take the time to choose his response. Each time, his movements were executed with perfect timing, speed, and accuracy. Once I would initiate an attack, I instantly felt dazed and unbalanced. To watch him do this to another person is simply beautiful, as it all seems to be so effortless for him.

This first visit to Beijing was just the beginning of my training with Lu Shengli. At this time he mentioned that he was develop-

ing a form of many useful movements from his fighting experience. I practiced many of these movements and tried to use them interchangeably, as I had watched him do. The movements he has chosen are brutal and clever. They all seem to be outstanding representations of the styles they were selected from. They are skills that often present themselves in a fight and are easy to apply. He was always quick to point out that I still had to develop my basic *gongfu* and internal force, as without that, these skills simply become rigid, unconnected external techniques. I used his methods to continue my training and took them back to the U.S. with me.

My second trip to Beijing took place two years later. This time Lu Shengli had finished developing his form and the ideas behind his training methodologies for it. From all his years of training and experience, he had taken sixteen specific postures, which included about thirty skills that he felt were the most useful in a fight. The skills also were selected because he felt that when practiced together, they would help an individual improve internal force and fighting spirit. These skills, when linked together, have a very smooth and powerful flow to them. Lu Shengli understands the difficulty so many face in developing their skills into useful and effective applications. Oftentimes a master may have tremendous basic skills and a strong root. To try to move him can take two or three men, and then it is not done easily. However, when the speed and power of a violent attack come his way, he falls to the flurry of a fast and heavy hand.

From years of research and personal experience, Lu Shengli began to ask himself what methods could improve this transition from having internal force to being able to use it effectively in combat situations. Lu Shengli would also call upon his grandmaster and mentor Wang Peisheng. He had a very close and personal relationship with the grandmaster and would question and test his ideas with Master Wang's extensive expertise in combat. In this way Lu Shengli created a remarkable method that so many can now bene-

fit from. He provides a bridge to many traditional concepts with easy-to-understand training methods. These methods are rich in detail, handed down by Wang Peisheng with an added clarity that comes from Lu Shengli's personal experience and research.

Lu Shengli evaluates his form constantly. He continually strives to improve and refine each skill. When I returned to Beijing the last time, I was amazed to see that the form was even more detailed and advanced. For example, when he taught "Ba Wang Dou Jia" (Ba Wang shakes his armor), he explained the application of the skill with great detail. He talked about how to look at and feel the opponent, how to get the first touch by intercepting and grabbing the hand, how to angle the body and turn, and how to release the force at the right time with right direction. All these details made the skill even easier to understand and apply.

It is a common adage in the internal arts that movement is used only to achieve the concept of having no particular skill; that any movement is skill. The practitioner uses form as a tool to train the mind and body to realize this concept. However, many still cannot reach this level, especially when tested under true combat conditions. Lu Shengli's form and concepts guide the practitioner in that direction effectively. When practicing this form you can feel the comfortable, flowing movement of your force. It feels familiar to internal practitioners since it contains so many components of Taiji, Bagua, and Xingyi. When the actual skills are practiced and used according to Lu Shengli's ideas, they seem to be easily executed and effective, realizing the principles of relaxing, following, and releasing the force at the right time and right direction.

Thus, there are many other individuals who admire Lu Shengli's form and his innovative approach. With Grandmaster Wang's encouragement, Lu Shengli started to write down his ideas and personal experiences. And then Master Zhang Yun translated these notes into English. On my most recent trip to Beijing I helped Lu Shengli shoot photos to accompany the translated text. I truly believe that

this book will help many practitioners improve their understanding of the internal arts and fighting concepts.

I am confident that the steadfast internal practitioners will in time come to deeply appreciate the detailed concepts and knowledge presented here, the results of cumulative experiences thoughtfully compiled by such a talented master. Lu Shengli is definitely a rare example in today's world. He is a warrior trained in ways long forgotten and largely misunderstood by modern society. Upon meeting this quiet and humble man, one cannot help but to liken him to a knight or a samurai. Yet he is thoroughly modern in his rigorous approach to training, in combining the best of the old and the new. He carries a skill handed down from a truly impressive lineage of some of China's greatest masters. For those not fortunate enough to have met the great Grandmaster Wang Peisheng, there is comfort in knowing that an essential part of him survives today in this most remarkable practitioner of true Chinese *gongfu*.

—*Strider Clark*
Pittsburgh, Pennsylvania, 2005

PREFACE

Traditional Chinese martial arts are an important and highly valued component of Chinese culture. They have deep roots in philosophical principles and include the development of high-level skills. The branch of Chinese martial arts known as Neijia Quan, or internal martial arts, attracts many people with its subtle combination of physical skill and philosophical principles. Although many people study internal martial arts, only a few really understand the essence of these systems and as a result, only a few achieve true mastery. There are several reasons for this state of affairs. One important reason is that in the past, many masters taught Neijia skills only to a select group of private students. People who trained in public classes were shown only external postures and were not taught the uses of these movements nor the principles on which these movements were based.

Past generations of masters refrained from teaching their skills to the public at large because of a widely shared belief that such knowledge could be dangerous if given to ill-intentioned or irresponsible people. In such cases, it was feared that high-level martial arts skills might be used for destructive purposes. So, martial arts knowledge was carefully guarded and taught only to those deemed worthy of using it for beneficial ends. Because of this traditional wariness, Neijia groups have been said to control their "doors" very strictly. The resulting risk that Neijia skills might be lost was considered preferable to the risk that a malevolent person might learn martial arts skills and then use them for evil intent.

Although the effort to keep martial arts knowledge limited to a relatively small group of practitioners was well-intentioned, it prevented many good people from learning the skills they sought. As

it became more difficult for succeeding generations of practition-ers to learn internal martial arts skills, those who possessed such mastery were increasingly unwilling to share their knowledge with others. Thus, an originally honorable idea eventually became a con-servative force limiting the spread of valuable knowledge to gen-uinely interested people.

Another reason that Neijia skills are not well understood, even by many practitioners, is that these skills cannot be understood directly and clearly. If a master doesn't really want to teach from his heart, it is almost impossible for a student to gain true knowl-edge. Unfortunately, it is very often the case that even people who practice diligently and for a long time do not understand martial arts principles. As a result, they never fully experience the feelings and power that martial arts skills can generate. Many people have "walked on the wrong path and never known." Many have quit their practice frustrated and unfulfilled.

Today, times are different and some of the traditional notions and concerns are no longer relevant. Many people now believe that martial arts skill and knowledge belong to everyone and that the historically conservative viewpoint no longer applies. Many masters believe instead that "the door to the house should be opened" so that these great skills and the many benefits they can bring should be shared with all who want to learn. It is for this reason that my Grandmaster Wang Peisheng encouraged me to write this book.

I have always liked martial arts very much. At the age of ten, I began my study of Chinese wrestling with the well-known master, Mr. Han Ying. Later, I studied Baiyuan (White Ape) Tongbei Quan with another famous master, Mr. Li Shusen, and then I became an indoor disciple of the renowned master, Mr. Luo Shuhuan, under whose guidance I studied Taiji Quan, Bagua Zhang, Xingyi Quan. At this point in my training, Master Luo sent me to my grandmas-ter, Mr. Wang Peisheng, for more intensive training at his home.

I am deeply indebted to Grandmaster Wang Peisheng for the

great kindness he extended to me by offering me his devoted and meticulous instruction. His deep, detailed, subtle, and invaluable teaching advanced my knowledge of martial arts greatly and allowed me to improve my skills significantly in just a few years. My fighting techniques were especially enhanced during this time. Grandmaster Wang's teachings led me to a true understanding of the principles of traditional Chinese martial arts and have continued to guide my development as a martial artist.

For more than thirty years, I have practiced and researched the martial arts with my *gongfu* brothers Zhang Deshan, Zhao Zeren, Zhang Yun, Gu Yun, and others. They, too, have helped me improve my knowledge and skills and have brought great benefit to my practice. I am very grateful to them for this assistance.

If one wants to study internal martial arts, he or she should first know the principles upon which they are based, the relationship between practice and principle, and the skills involved. It is also important to understand the differences between internal and external martial arts skills. Only with this knowledge and diligent practice can one have the opportunity to reach a high level of skill.

Although I have studied internal martial arts for many years, it is only in the last ten years that I have come to understand these principles and finally have been able to achieve high-level skill. The reason for this is that I thought that technique should be the most important focus of training during my early years of study. I liked carefully researching how techniques differed from each other, but I did not think enough about underlying principles, especially as they applied to fighting skills. As a result, my progress was slow despite years of intensive training. I wasted much precious time and took an unnecessarily long path to my goal.

My purpose in writing this book is to help others find an easier and more direct path to the development of high-level skills. I hope to accomplish this goal by describing my experiences and the knowledge I have gained. I have written this book both for beginners

who want to find a correct way to gain martial arts skills quickly and for experienced practitioners who wish to move from intermediate to high skill levels. I hope that this book will bring readers the benefit not only of my experience but also that of the many generations before me. I will be very happy if each reader can learn something from this book, but please be careful. Just reading is not enough. One has to practice hard.

Combat Techniques of Taiji, Xingyi, and Bagua is the distillation of many years of study and practice. The main part of the book is the sixteen-posture form. The principles and skills of the internal martial arts are the form's basic elements. Most of the techniques are derived from Taiji Quan, Bagua Zhang, and Xingyi Quan. Other techniques come from Tongbei Quan, Baji Quan, and Shaolin Quan. My goal was to combine techniques from each of these styles in order to offer a training method that is more efficient than that used in any one style alone.

The features of Taiji Quan that are represented in the sixteen-posture form are: *zhan* (stick), *zou* (go), *hua* (dissolve), and *jie* (borrow). The changing and footwork features come from Bagua Zhang; the powerful and stable internal force, from Xingyi Quan; and the quickness of movement, from external *gongfu*. The sixteen-posture form is designed to combine these features and to use each in the best way possible to facilitate the training of internal martial arts skills. When studying this form, focus your attention primarily on the *kong jin* (empty force) skill of Taiji, the *bian jin* (changing force) skill of Bagua, and the *zhi jin* (straight force) skill of Xingyi.

The sixteen-posture form includes more than thirty single techniques. All of these techniques are simple and easy to use, but all are also based on deep principles, which must be understood if high-level practice is ever to be achieved. The form charts a correct course for almost any practitioner. It is easy to master by beginners, and it can be greatly beneficial for middle-level practitioners as well. It is a very effective tool for understanding and mastering internal fight-

ing principles and skills, and it can guide not only outside movements but also internal practice. With time and assiduous training, practitioners will increase the internal feelings that follow from the correct execution of external techniques. Eventually, it will be possible to forget specific techniques and to experience the internally mastered skills as natural.

I believe that by practicing this form, one can better understand the basic principles underlying all internal martial arts skills. Such understanding, in my view, is the first step to proficiency in the martial arts. It is the key that opens the door to high-level skill. Deep thinking and diligent practice must be combined to produce complete mastery. As expressed in a traditional Chinese saying: "If you really want it, work hard and you will get it in the end," or "God rewards hard work."

It is also said, "If one has been your master even for only one day, you should treat him like your father for the rest of your life." Thus, I express my appreciation to all my masters and to my grandmaster. I also thank my *gongfu* brothers. Without the help of all of them, I would not have been successful.

I especially want to thank my *gongfu* brother Zhang Yun and his students. Master Zhang worked hard to translate this book into English. He also wrote some sections and did a significant amount of editing. His student, Ms. Susan Darley, also helped edit the book. His senior student, Mr. Strider Clark, came to Beijing to help me demonstrate the applications. My student Wang Guibin was my partner in the basic training photographs. I also want to thank my other gongfu brother Zhao Zeren, who took most of the photographs in this book.

Finally, I thank my wife Pan Guilan. Without her support, I would have accomplished nothing.

—*Lu Shengli*
Beijing, China, 2002

CHAPTER ONE

The Basic Principles of Internal Martial Arts

"Neijia Quan" is commonly translated to mean "internal martial arts." Neijia Quan and its unique skills have developed as an integral part of traditional Chinese culture. Today Neijia Quan has become very popular. In the original tradition, only Xingyi Quan, Bagua Quan, and Taiji Quan are considered to be part of the internal martial arts family because they all follow the same principles. Other martial arts, however, like Baji Quan, Tongbei Quan, and Sanhuang Paochui Quan have developed with internal influence as well. They draw on similar principles and as a result, the skills they include may be very close to those of the three primary styles. Over time, this expanding influence of the internal styles has caused some scholars to include other systems in the "internal family."

nèi   jiâ   quán
内 家 拳

In this chapter, we will review the history of the internal martial arts and the principles of this "family" as they apply to training. Knowledge of the history and principles of the internal martial arts can be of great benefit in helping students deepen their understanding and mastery.

Because the Neijia Quan family has become popular and widespread, it is impossible to describe its full history and all its lineages in detail. Instead, this chapter presents only the highlights of internal martial arts history, with attention to those most well-known and influential masters. In addition to this caution, it should be noted that any depiction of the martial arts in China is limited

by the fact that the original history was transmitted largely in oral form. As a result, many historical details have been lost and many facts have been modified over time. In general, clarity has given way to ambiguity.

We do know from oral history that the internal martial arts represent an excellent style of *gongfu,* and that they have provided training for many great masters. Recognizing that there are multiple versions of each story, we do not make any claims here for which ones are the most factual. Rather, we present the most popular version. We believe that knowledge of the history of the martial arts will improve your practice.

✪ The Development of Chinese Martial Arts

Chinese martial arts emerged several thousand years ago and evolved from the simple to the complex and from low level to high level. Through generations of martial artists, many principles and skills were developed and some, unfortunately, were lost. Lacking a continuous written record, we know only that many of these skills were high level, and that many great masters won widespread recognition and renown, but the details of the techniques they used are no longer known.

From the historical records that can be verified, we know that most of the styles and training methods we inherit today date from the Song Dynasty (960–1297). They showed rapid advancement during the Ming Dynasty (1368–1644) and were completely systematized by the Qing Dynasty (1644–1911). During the Ming and the Qing Dynasties, Chinese martial arts became highly developed and gradually separated into two main groups: Waijia Quan or the external martial arts, and Neijia Quan or the internal martial arts.

From External Martial Arts to Internal Martial Arts

In Chinese martial arts, the development of high-level internal martial arts comprises a special advance. The origin of these Neijia martial arts is unknown, but it is likely that they were created by generations of great masters who dedicated their lives to diligent and thoughtful practice. Gradually the accrual of their personal experiences and acquired wisdom resulted in the development of the internal martial arts.

The earliest records of Waijia and Neijia concepts come from three articles written within fifteen years of each other and in nearby locations. They are: "The Tombstone Inscription of Mr. Wang Zhengnan" by Huang Lizhou (1669); "Neijia Quan" ("Internal Fist") by Huang Baijia (1676); and "The Biography of Zhang Songxi" in the 1683 version of "The Government Records and Annals of Ningbo City."

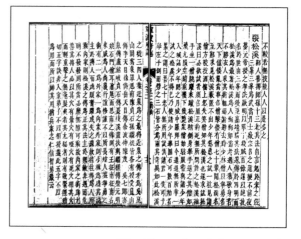

"The Biography of Zhang Songxi"

These articles provide valuable information regarding the time period during which the Neijia concept emerged and the facts surrounding the development of Neijia and its differentiation from Waijia. The articles also provide details about the Neijia's defining characteristics.

From these three articles we know that the new martial arts style of Neijia Quan was developed to a high degree and widely disseminated from the Ming to the Qing Dynasties. It advanced its own principles and had a clear lineage, although its origins remained unclear. Many people believe that Zhang Sanfeng, a famous Daoist priest of Wudang Mountain, was the founder of the internal martial arts.

Many people consider the Ming and Qing Dynasties to be the golden era of Chinese martial arts. During the Song Dynasty martial

"Ji Xiao Xin Shu"

arts spread quickly despite a lack of encouragement from the government and despite more than four hundred years of war and turmoil throughout the country. The Neijia style, as a new and unique style, did not emerge until the Ming Dynasty, during which time many different styles were developed and their skills elaborated in great detail. Published in 1584, General Qi Jiguang's book *Ji Xiao Xin Shu*—known in English as *The New Book on Effective Military Training Methods*—is our primary source of information about this period of high development in the Chinese martial arts. From it, we know that many high-level skills and concepts were developed at a rapid pace. Neijia, however, is not mentioned in General Qi Jiguang's book. From this fact, we believe that Neijia was not a popular style at the time the book was written.

The Neijia Quan style was taught in the north, middle, and southeast of China, but it was not popular and disappeared within about a hundred years of its emergence. Although some masters claim they still practice the original Neijia Quan style today, there is no independent proof that their skills are the original ones. As the original Neijia Quan skills were developed and practiced by different masters and groups in different areas, the name and principles of the style became diversified into three great styles, Xingyi Quan, Taiji Quan, and Bagua Quan. These styles arose at different times and embodied the concepts of the original Neijia Quan in different ways.

In about 1892 in Beijing, a group of great masters representing each of these styles convened under the leadership of Bagua Master Cheng Tinghua. They decided to unite the three styles under the renewed name Neijia or Neijia Quan. After some initial resistance to this grouping of Neijia martial arts into one family, people accepted the idea and it became popular. Today, this group of styles has become widely recognized. Because the original Neijia style was lost, the term "Neijia family" today usually includes its three offspring: Taiji, Bagua, and Xingyi.

Taiji Quan   **Bagua Zhang**   **Xingyi Quan**

Based on the three seminal articles, it is generally thought that the new martial arts style of Neijia Quan was practiced in the Ningbo and Wenzhou areas of southeast China from about 1500 to 1700; and that Zhang Sanfeng, the Daoist monk from Wudang Mountain, invented this style. Subsequently, Wang Zong of Shanxi became famous for his Neijia skill, and he transmitted his knowledge to Chen Zhoutong who, in turn, brought the style to his hometown of Wenzhou in Zhejiang Province. After Chen Zhoutong, there were several generations of famous Neijia Quan masters.

Except for the identity of the originator of the style, the Neijia lineage described in the three articles is widely accepted as true for several reasons. The author of the first, Huang Lizhou, was a very famous scholar; the author of the second, Huang Baijia, was a direct student in the Neijia group; and government records from the period are considered to be highly trustworthy. Only the assertion that Zhang Sanfeng was the originator of the Neijia style is held in some doubt.

Most new ideas derive explicitly or implicitly from ideas that have preceded them. When the Neijia style first appeared, Waijia was the only other martial arts style in existence. It seems clear, then, that Neijia evolved from Waijia. Over time, the variations that developed were sufficient to render Neijia a distinctive and independent style. The highest level of Waijia practice was Shaolin, and Zhang Sanfeng is known to have been an innovative student of Shaolin. He may well have made the changes in Waijia practice and concepts that provided the basis for the new style of Neijia. Although the truth of this assumption may never be known, the story strongly suggests that Neijia did, in fact, evolve from Waijia and eventually became differentiated from it.

There is no historical evidence of a name for any martial arts style before the Neijia style emerged. The term "Waijia" was coined to differentiate the new Neijia style from the previously existing Shaolin styles. The appearance of the two names marks the point at which the new style had become sufficiently distinct in concept and practice to warrant separate mention.

The Main Differences between Waijia and Neijia

shào lin

少林

wǔ dōng

武当

Because Neijia developed from Waijia, the two styles have many similarities, and some practitioners believe it is a mistake to differentiate them. If we look deeply at their principles and skills, however, we find significant differences that provide a reasonable basis for the distinction. Identifying the differences between Neijia and Waijia reveals the overall process of development in the martial arts and will clarify and improve your practice. It can also help practitioners understand Chinese martial arts more deeply, especially Neijia training. The intricate relationship between Waijia and Neijia is the focus of the remaining sections of this chapter.

Philosophy: Buddhism or Taoism

Waijia is generally considered to be a Shaolin style because most Waijia-style martial artists believe that their skills derive from those practiced at the Shaolin Temple. Accordingly, these practitioners hold the Shaolin style in great respect and seek to emulate it. The foundational philosophy for Waijia is Buddhism.

Neijia is generally considered to be a Wudang style because it is thought to derive from the teachings of the Daoist monk Zhang Sanfeng, who lived and practiced for many years on Wudang Mountain, the most famous Daoist holy place. While Buddhism provides the philosophical underpinnings of Waijia, Daoism is the philosophy that underlies Neijia concepts and training.

Shaolin Temple

Although Waijia and Neijia follow different philosophies, there are many similarities between the two families of martial arts. In China, Zen Buddhism is the most popular form of Buddhist practice, and Chinese Zen practice has its origins at the Shaolin Temple. The form of Zen Buddhism practiced at the Shaolin Temple, however, combines original Buddhist concepts with concepts derived from Daoist philosophy. Thus, the foundation of Waijia practice includes Daoist as well as Buddhist elements.

Zhang Sanfeng belonged to one of the most famous Daoist styles, known as Quan Zhan or "Complete Truth." A central notion of Quan Zhan is that the three main philosophies of Daoism, Buddhism, and Confucian-

Wudang Mountain

ism are based on similar principles, and so should be united in practice. Neijia principles include elements of Buddhism and Confucianism as well as Daoism. Such admixtures of philosophical concepts produced many of the similarities between Waijia and Neijia. It is important to note that in this context, Buddhism and Daoism are viewed as conceptual rather than religious systems. Although philosophy and religions are closely intermingled in China, they can be clearly separated in practice. Daoist principles, of course, form the basis of the Daoist religion, but one can apply Daoist concepts without subscribing to the religion itself.

Some styles have characteristics of both Waijia and Neijia, and these styles call into question a sharp distinction between the two groupings. Tongbei, for example, is usually considered a Waijia style, but it is based on Daoist concepts. Xingyi, on the other hand, was considered by some Xingyi masters from Shanxi to be an outside branch of the Shaolin style because its originator Ji Jike studied at the Shaolin Temple for about ten years before creating Xingyi.

Basic Principles:
To Increase or To Change Natural Ability

The goal of Waijia practice is to increase natural human ability, the most basic elements of which are speed, force, and the natural or normal responses we all have to incoming stimuli. All fighting skills combine these abilities. Waijia practice is designed to increase the speed and force of movement and to enhance natural reactions. In this style, the criteria for improvement in skill level are relatively clear and direct.

In Neijia practice, the more important goal is to change rather than to increase natural abilities. Neijia practitioners want to be quick and powerful but they seek to achieve these qualities by modifying their usual patterns of response. Although some Neijia training methods focus on increasing natural abilities, this goal is always secondary in importance and desirability to the goal of changing

one's normal reactions. The Neijia criteria for improvement are complex and subtle and often too difficult to understand purely by logical analysis.

Again, though, the two approaches can be combined. In high-level Waijia training, for example, emphasis is placed on changing the natural responses; and in Neijia practice, improvement in speed, force, and effectiveness occur through training. At the top level, Waijia and Neijia are interrelated, as expressed in the injunction to "practice internal and external together." Perhaps this counsel provided the impetus for the development of the Neijia Quan arts in that they incorporate internal training from the outset rather than reserve it until students have attained considerable skill. In a sense, Waijia and Neijia can be seen as selecting different training methods to reach the same end.

Because Waijia focuses first on simply increasing natural responses, it is easier to learn than Neijia at the beginning of one's training. The fact that Neijia training includes internal practice from the outset, however, gives Neijia students an advantage in progressing from intermediate to high levels of skill. As a result, many Waijia practitioners succeed in achieving middle-level skills, but few advance to a high level. Many Neijia students, on the other hand, fail to reach middle-level skill, but those who achieve middle-level skills do have a good chance to reach a higher level. This may explain why famous masters from Neijia groups are more numerous than those from Waijia groups, despite the greater number of Waijia practitioners during the past one hundred years of Chinese martial arts history.

In Waijia practice, being in good physical condition provides beginners with more obvious advantage than it does in Neijia practice because Waijia training uses natural abilities. In Neijia practice, natural ability can be a disadvantage, especially for beginners who are used to relying on superior physical strength and agility. Such reliance tends to make students reluctant to forego their habitual

physical responses in order to change these reactions so that they become more internally generated.

When students want to progress from middle-level to high-level skill, the most important aspect of their practice is internal training. This is true for Waijia as well as Neijia practitioners. Most people who have trained for a long time in Waijia will find internal training difficult because it requires an approach that is in many ways counter to the direct use of natural ability. For most middle-level Neijia students, the transition will not be as difficult because internal training, having been taught from the outset, will already be a familiar aspect of their practice.

Many Waijia practitioners who want to progress to high-level skills learn Neijia when they get older. They know how such progress should feel and realize that Waijia training alone may limit their advancement, so they incorporate Neijia practices into their training. Many Neijia practitioners decide to include some Waijia skills even at the beginning of their training because they realize that Neijia skills cannot initially be effectively used for fighting.

The different training methods of Waijia and Neijia may be seen as two different roads leading to the top of a mountain. One road is easier in the beginning but more difficult later on. The other is more difficult at the beginning but easier later on. If you reach the top of the mountain, the road you chose will not matter, but before you set out on the road, it is very important to choose the path that is more suitable for you. There are, of course, many factors that will influence your decision, but no matter what your choice, there are two things you should remember. You must work hard, and you must find a good teacher so that you will not get lost on the way. Without diligent practice and expert guidance, you will have no chance to reach the mountaintop.

Training Methods: From Outside to Inside or from Inside to Outside

It is a mistake to think that Waijia students practice only external skills and Neijia students, only internal. All Waijia and Neijia practitioners must develop both. The only difference between the two groups of practitioners is in the training methods they use. It is said that Waijia is practiced from the outside *(wai)* to the inside *(nei)*, and Neijia from the inside to outside.

In Waijia practice the physical responses of the body are trained first, and no emphasis is placed on internal or "inside" training. The initial goal is to improve the speed, agility, and force of the student's physical abilities. Only gradually is training for the internal components of *shen*, *yi*, and *qi* introduced and practiced.

In Neijia practice, the basic training is similar to that in Waijia, but an emphasis on inside training is introduced from the very beginning. As in Waijia, Neijia training improves physical abilities but it does so more gradually. Neijia practitioners hold to the view that increases in external ability without improvement in the internal components cannot result in high-level mastery. This difference in the Waijia and Neijia approaches creates clear and detailed differences in the two kinds of training methods. Understanding these differences will yield a deeper appreciation of each style.

A common misunderstanding is that only Neijia practitioners train *qi*. Perhaps this perception develops from the observation that Waijia students engage in more overt physical activity in their practice while Neijia students engage in more internal practice. This perception leads many observers to the mistaken belief that Neijia is a higher-level training than Waijia.

Basic Skills: Using External *Jin* or Internal *Jin*

Jin (or *jing*), often translated as "internal force," is more accurately translated as "trained force." It is the most important training com-

ponent in Chinese martial arts. *Jin* is not the natural kind of force used in ordinary circumstances by people untrained in the martial arts—say, in lifting a bucket or opening a door. Instead, *jin* describes the use of force developed through specialized training. There are many different *jin* in Neijia Quan. Some practitioners even believe that the core of internal martial arts skills is the practice and development of different *jin*. Basically all of the kinds of trained force can be separated into two groups. One is the external *jin* called "*wai jin*," and the other is the internal *jin* called "*nei jin*." Each is acquired through a distinctive method of training, and each has its own applications. When *jin* is applied, there are two phases. One is called "*xu jin*"—store energy. The process of *xu jin* prepares all of the related muscles to generate or accumulate power. The other phase is called "*fa jin*"—release force—which means all related muscles start to work to release the energy. The subject of *jin*—store and release—is actually quite complex since there are many possibilities in the manner in which force may be stored and then released according to particular situations that can arise in combat. Understanding this complexity is the substance of training *jin*. For the sake of simplicity, we refer only to "*jin*," with the understanding that "*jin*" always comprises both "store" and "release." In discussing *jin*, therefore, usually we refer to *jin* as simply meaning "to store and release energy in different ways."

External *jin* is conspicuous when released and is exemplified by a hard punch. Even though an external or *wai jin* punch is hard, it must also be relaxed and integrated so that it can be quick and powerful. These qualities typify all *wai jin* applications and make them highly effective for sudden, vigorous attacks. Their effectiveness, however, can be compromised for several reasons. First, *wai jin* attacks are clearly telegraphed to the opponent. They are also of short duration and difficult to change once begun, and their release and restore phases occur separately rather than in combination.

Unlike external *jin*, internal *jin* is inconspicuous when released.

wài   jìn

外 劲

nèi   jìn

内 劲

xù   jìn

蓄 劲

fā   jìn

发 劲

Peng jin, the ward-off application of *nei jin* in Taiji Quan, provides a good example of this characteristic. *Nei jin* applications are typically concealed, long in duration and changeable even in midcourse. In *nei jin* attacks, the release and restore phases are combined. While these qualities make *nei jin* especially useful for control skills, they are not as effective for intense attacks. Because *wai jin* and *nei jin* have different advantages and disadvantages, they should be used in different ways and for different purposes.

In Waijia, external *jin* is practiced from the outset of training and remains the primary focus throughout. Internal *jin* is only an ancillary part of *wai jin* practice. In Neijia, internal *jin* is a primary focus from the beginning of training, and external *jin* is ancillary. Because *wai jin* is easier to understand and learn than *nei jin*, Waijia practitioners may master *wai jin* skills and still be unable to execute *nei jin* skills well. For Neijia practitioners, familiar with *nei jin* skills from the start of their practice, *wai jin* skills are relatively easy to understand and acquire.

Fighting Strategies: To Initiate an Attack or To Defend Using Quietness

Waijia's central fighting principle is that you are the master of the fight. Your goal is to take control by making the initial attack and to maintain control throughout. The design and execution of all your moves and countermoves are determined and practiced as part of your training. The design of your attack and defense skills is defined by what you imagine your opponent will do. You follow your designed sequence of skills until you have thoroughly mastered it. Then during the fight, you have only to execute the much-practiced sequence in order to gain control and maintain the advantage. This strategy is called "fighting by initiating the attack."

The central Neijia fighting principle holds that you should remain alertly quiet as the fight begins and let your opponent take initial control. Your goal is to follow your opponent, and as soon as you

sense an opportunity, you take control. You do not design or repetitively practice a sequence of moves but rather learn about your opponent through actual contact with him. You keep changing your responses in order to follow whatever your opponent does at each moment. This strategy is called "using quietness to defend" or "yielding yourself to follow your opponent."

The Waijia fighting principle is direct and clear-cut: you must control the fight from the outset and never yield control to your opponent. This strategy is thought to offer the best chance to prevail.

The Neijia fighting principle, by contrast, is indirect and less obvious in practice. It holds that because it is not possible to maintain total control at all times, you should seek to control your opponent by understanding his movements and intentions. You can accomplish this goal by remaining relaxed and following his attack with sensitivity and patience. Do not worry if your opponent is in control. In asserting control, he is also giving you a chance to know and eventually to control him. According to the Neijia fighting principle, this is the safest and most efficient way to win a fight.

Origin of the Terms "Waijia" and "Neijia"

When a person becomes a Buddhist monk in China, it is said that he goes "outside" his family. Because the Shaolin-style martial arts originated in a Buddhist temple, follow Buddhist philosophy, and are practiced by Buddhist monks, they are referred to as outside *(wai)* the family *(jia)*. Taiji, Xingyi, and Bagua, on the other hand, were taught to family members of the Emperors in the palace in Beijing and were disseminated from that point of origin. Because the Emperors' palace was known as Da Nei or "the great inside," these styles are referred to as inside *(nei)* the family *(jia)*.

Although the distinctions between Waijia and Neijia are important and, if appreciated, can increase your understanding of martial arts practice, these two great groupings have always been bound together by countless ties. They did not develop in total geograph-

ical isolation, and they shared mutual influences as each gained in reputation and adherents. The practitioners of both groups exchanged their knowledge and experience on a regular basis. Although the two are clearly different in terms of the underlying principles from which they derive, they are not so clearly different in terms of how they are practiced. Some styles combine elements of both Waijia and Neijia, and even within one style many features may overlap. It is always said that Waijia and Neijia are both different and similar.

✪ Xingyi Quan

Xingyi Quan, also known by the older names of Yi Quan, Xinyi Quan, and Xinyi Luhe Quan, is a traditional Chinese martial art and the oldest "brother" in the internal martial arts family. "*Xing*" means "shape," "movement," or "posture;" "*yi*" means "mind," "idea," or "spirit." The basic skills of Xingyi Quan are often separated into two parts. One is called Xing Quan, which focuses on physical movement, the external component; and the other is called Yi Quan, which focuses on internal components like *yi*. In Xing Quan, fighting skills are developed by simulating the fighting techniques of twelve animals. The basic concept of Yi Quan is "*wuxing*" or the Five Elements. Wuxing Quan or the Five-element Fist derives from this concept. The term "Xingyi" means that internal and external components must be developed together in this *gongfu* style.

History and Lineage

Before Li Luoneng, the history and lineage of Xingyi Quan are not very clear. There are several different versions of this history from several different Xingyi groups. The following description comes from the most commonly held traditional version.

General Yue Fei

From Yue Fei to Ji Jike

The identity of the originator of Xingyi Quan is the subject of much debate. According to the traditional story, General Yue Fei (1103–1141), one of China's greatest heroes, was the founder of Xingyi Quan.

When Yue was young, Jin Dynasty warriors from the north of China invaded central China's Song Dynasty. Yue joined the Song army to fight against the Jin invaders. Because of his great skill in spear, arrow, and in military strategy and tactics, he rose through the ranks quickly to become a general. Always outnumbered, his forces fought about hundred and twenty battles and never lost. His enemies said of him, "It is easier to shake a mountain than to shake Yue's army."

During this period there was widespread governmental corruption, and Yue was disliked by the Emperor. After one of Yue's greatest victories on the battlefield, the Emperor had him killed, an act that was widely recognized as a great injustice. The Emperor's view notwithstanding, Yue's deeds and talents have always been held in high esteem, and his name is invoked in many martial arts skills.

About five hundred years after Yue's death, a young martial artist named Ji Jike visited the Xongju Cave on Zhongnen Mountain, where he claimed to have met an eccentric person who gave him a martial arts book written by General Yue Fei. Ji said that he followed the teachings described in the book and ascribed the source of Xingyi Quan to Yue.

Despite Ji's assertion, most people did not believe his story and considered Ji himself to be the originator of Xingyi Quan. (Many believe that it was called Xinyi Quan at that time.) This view was later promoted by the writings of Dai Longbang, who was Ji's grandstudent. Today there is still doubt about this question, but it is generally agreed that Ji Jike was the first person to teach Xingyi Quan. For this reason, he is considered the first person in the Xingyi generation.

Master Ji, whose official first name is Jike and whose private first name is Longfeng, was born in 1642 in Zun Village, Pudong County, Shanxi Province. He liked martial arts and is said to have studied at the Shaolin Temple for about ten years when he was young. He became very famous as an adult for his spear skills, and Xingyi Quan is thought by many people to have developed from Ji's spear skills.

During Ji's lifetime, China was controlled by the Qing Dynasty, which was originally composed of a small group of Manchurians from northern China who waged war for many years against Chinese forces. In many ways, the military situation faced by Ji was similar to that faced by General Yue. In both historical episodes, the Chinese people fought against invading forces; and like Yue before him, Ji became a leader of the resistance. Many people believe that because of Yue's place in history as a renowned general, Ji invoked Yue's name as founder of Xingyi Quan when, in fact, it was Ji who created this fighting style.

Not much is known about Ji's life and teachings. His most famous disciple was Cao Jiwu, about whom we know only three things. He was a disciple of Master Ji; he became a general in Shanxi Province after winning first place at the county, provincial, and national martial arts examinations in 1693; and he had two famous disciples, Ma Xueli and Dai Longbang.

Ma Xueli and Henan Style

Ma Xueli was born in Nanyang County, Henan Province. His place in the Xingyi lineage is somewhat obscure. Most people believe that he was Cao Jiwu's disciple because Dai Longbang mentioned in his seminal article that he and Ma Xueli were *gongfu* brothers. Others believe that Ma was Ji Jike's disciple because according to a traditional story he had studied Xingyi Quan with Ji. If this story is true, Ji must have been very old when Ma studied with him. The most probable case, which accords with Chinese tradition, is that

Ji taught Ma but listed Ma's name under Cao's generation. Ma, then, was officially Cao's disciple although he studied with Master Ji.

Ma Xueli liked martial arts so much that when he heard about Master Ji's excellent *gongfu*, he went to Ji's home hoping to become a student. He knew, though, that Ji preferred to keep his techniques secret, so Ma did not say he wanted to study martial arts when he went to Ji's home. He asked only to be hired as an employee of Ji's family.

For about three years, Ma stole glances as Ji practiced, and then he went off by himself to practice what he had seen. When Ma thought it was time to leave the employ of Ji's family, he bid Ji good-bye and told him that he had been secretly studying Ji's techniques for the three years he had been in the household. Ji was so impressed with Ma's commitment that he said: "If you can stay more time, I will teach you all I know."

Ma stayed with Ji for more than three additional years and studied diligently. Ji explained everything in complete detail. When Ma understood all that Ji had to teach, he returned home to Henan Province, where he taught Xingyi Quan and soon became famous for his excellent *gongfu*.

Ma continued to use the old name of Xinyi Luhe Quan instead of Xingyi Quan, and his style became known as Henan style, or southern style. In the tradition of Chinese martial practice, challenges were often given in order to test the effectiveness of a particular method, style, or system. Most often in these challenges, the fighting was hard, but it was typically expected that participants would emerge from these challenges perhaps injured but alive. With this particular style, hard, powerful strikes were emphasized, and the masters in some of the Xinyi Luhe Quan groups felt it necessary to provide the ultimate illustration of their power, often killing their opponents. Not surprisingly, these masters would not often have the opportunity to teach their high-level skills, so their *gongfu*

never became popularized. It was not until 1928 when Jiang Rongjiao from the northern Xingyi group met Bao Xianting, a famous master from the Henan Xingyi group, that masters in the north even became aware of the southern style.

Ma Xueli had only two excellent disciples: Ma Sanyuan and Zhang Zhicheng. Ma Sanyuan executed all Xingyi applications very vigorously. He beat and killed several masters in fights and, as might be expected, he died young, leaving no good students to carry on his teachings. Zhang Zhicheng was good but more conservative than Ma Sanyuan in his fighting style. The only student to whom Zhang taught high-level skills was his nephew Li Zheng, who was also very conservative. Li Zheng agreed to teach only his friend Zhang Ju and began instructing Zhang only after making him wait ten years.

Zhang, in turn, taught his son Laoge, who became highly skilled and at fifteen had already injured and killed several masters. Like Ma Sanyuan, Laoge died young. Zhang's nephew, Mai Zhuangtu, who studied with his uncle, was able to pass on Zhang's techniques. Mai had many students but only An Daqing excelled. Of An's many good students, Bao Xianting was the best. Bao taught many martial artists, some of whom are still alive today. He also published several books that popularized the Henan style.

Dai Longbang and Old Shanxi Style

It is said that Dai Longbang was born in approximately 1732 in Qi County, Shanxi Province. When he was young, he accompanied his father to Anhui Province on a business trip. During that sojourn, he began his study of Xingyi Quan with Master Cao Jiwu and eventually became Cao's disciple in Qiupu County.

Dai practiced very hard and thought deeply about Xingyi Quan. It is said that when Dai was studying with Cao, Xingyi Quan included only ten animal skills. Through careful observation, Dai invented two new animal skills: *tuo* or alligator, and *tai*, which has been

variously interpreted as a large fish, a large bird like an ostrich, or a wild horse. Since Dai's time, Xingyi Quan has included twelve animal skills.

Dai's *gongfu* was exceptional and he became famous. His two sons, Dai Wenzun and Dai Wenxiong, also developed high-level *gongfu* as a result of studying with their father.

Dai eventually opened a very successful security company, but after he retired and went back to his hometown, a group of thieves who had tried to rob Dai's business many years earlier and had been caught and beaten by Dai's security forces attacked Dai's family again. They sought revenge against Dai's family because several members of their gang had been killed by Dai's security guards in the earlier robbery attempt. Dai's oldest son was murdered by the thieves in the revenge attack. After this loss, Dai's physical and emotional health deteriorated and he soon passed away. During his last days, Dai told his second son Dai Wenxiong that their family had suffered great troubles because of martial arts, and that if Dai Wenxiong taught at all, he should teach martial arts only to family members.

After his father's death, Dai Wenxiong moved to Xiaohan Village outside Qi County and became a hermit. He taught Xingyi Quan only to his son Dai Wuchang, his daughter Dai Huanu, his nephew Dai Liangdong, and his cousin Guo Weihan. Because only a few people learned and practiced Dai Longbang's Shanxi-style Xingyi, it is often referred to as Dai family Xingyi Quan.

Li Luoneng, the Greatest Xingyi Quan Master

Li Luoneng was born in 1802 in Douwang Zhuang Village, Yangwo Xiang, Shen County, Hebei Province. His official first name was Feiyu, and his private first name was Nengran. His nickname was Luoneng, the original meaning of which was "old farmer." He is known popularly by his nickname rather than by his real name.

Li Luoneng, as the nickname indicates, was a farmer. He liked

martial arts and studied hard-style martial arts in his hometown. When he heard about Master Dai Longbang's excellent Xingyi technique, he traveled to Shanxi Province in the hope of studying with the Master. The year was 1839, and Li was thirty-seven years old.

By the time Li arrived in Qi County, Master Dai Longbang had passed away. Li asked to study with Dai's son Dai Wenxiong but Dai Wenxiong, following his father's last wish, was no longer teaching, certainly not anyone outside his family. Although Dai rejected Li's request, Dai's cousin Guo Weihan liked Li, and he agreed to teach Li the family style.

Some people believe that it was Guo who changed the name of the style from Xinyi Quan to Xingyi Quan during the time he taught Li. In the old meaning of "Xinyi," "*xin*" means "heart," and "*yi*" means "mind." Both the heart and the mind are considered to be internal. With the new name, however, "*xing*" means "shape" or "movement" (and "*yi*" still means "mind"). Shape and movement are considered to be external. So the new term, "Xingyi," is thought to include both internal and external aspects. People believe that the new name conveys a more accurate sense of the system. Li practiced very hard and after some time, Guo suggested that Li visit Dai Wenxiong again. This time Dai was moved by Li's sincere desire to study with him and accepted Li as a disciple. Li studied in Dai's home for about ten years.

For a long time it was thought that Li studied directly with Dai Longbang, but by checking dates, we find that this is almost impossible. More likely, Dai Wenxiong put Li under his father's name because, according to Chinese tradition, he had to obey his father's injunction not to teach and so would not want to be officially listed as Li's teacher. This is, of course, only conjecture; the truth of what really happened will probably never be known.

After studying Xingyi Quan from Dai's family for more than ten years, Li went to Taigu County of Shanxi Province in 1849 and became a security guard for a very rich, famous family headed by

Meng Beru. Li began teaching Xingyi Quan during this time and accepted his first disciple, Che Yizhai, in 1856. In 1867, Li returned to his hometown and became a professional martial arts master. He did a lot of research and systematized Xingyi Quan principles clearly and completely. He also developed an excellent training system and had many famous disciples. Through his efforts and those of his disciples, Xingyi Quan became popular and very highly regarded. Because he taught in both Shanxi and Hebei Provinces and because the two groups of disciples practiced in slightly different ways, a distinction was made between Shanxi and Hebei styles. Eventually, Hebei style became more widespread and popular than all other styles of Xingyi Quan.

Although there are not many stories about Master Li, he is regarded as the greatest master in Xingyi Quan history. One day in 1890, he sat down on a chair, smiled, and passed away.

Che Yizhai, Song Shirong, and the New Shanxi Style

Che Yizhai, whose private first name was Yonghong, was born in 1833 in Taoyuan Bao, Shanxi Province. When he was young, he was a wagon driver in Meng Beru's home and studied Xingyi Quan with Master Li Luoneng. In time, he became Master Li's first disciple.

Che Yizhai

Che practiced very hard and so impressed Li with his dedication and skill that in 1863 Li introduced Che to Dai Wenxiong for advanced study. Dai came to like Che, too, and gave him Dai Longbang's Xingyi Quan book, "The Edited Version of the Xinyi Quan Guide." This book, never published, existed only in hand-written form.

By the time Che returned to his village, his *gongfu* was very good and he quite quickly gained renown. His disciples included Li Fuzhen, Lu Xielong, Wang Fenggao, Meng Xide, Fan Yongqing, Guo Yushen, Bu Xiekuan, and Liu Jian, all of whom also became

famous. Che and his students created many new forms, and today his group practices more forms than any other group. Che died in 1914.

Song Shirong, whose private first name was Yiezhai, was born in Beijing in 1849. When he was young, he moved to Taiguo County of Shanxi Province and became a craftsman who repaired clocks and watches. He and his brother, Song Shide, studied together with Master Li and both became very good martial artists. They were known as "double Song" until Song Shide became a monk and ended his study of Xingyi Quan. Song Shirong went on to become master to many famous disciples, including Ran Erqi, Jia Wanguo, and Song Hucan and Song Tielin, who became known as "young double Song." Song Shirong did a lot of research on both Xingyi Quan and internal Qigong practice and left a wealth of valuable knowledge to subsequent generations. He died in 1927.

After Master Li returned to Hebei Province, Che Yizhai and Song Shirong continued teaching Xingyi Quan in Shanxi Province. The style they taught became known as the new Shanxi style to distinguish it from the Dai family's old Shanxi style. The new Shanxi style became the more popular of the two because of the Dai family's small size and their reluctance to train new students. Today when people speak of the Shanxi style, they are usually referring to the new Shanxi style.

Later Li Luoneng's students in Hebei developed Xingyi Quan Hebei style. The new Shanxi style and the Hebei style are closely related because both derived from Li Luoneng's teaching. Masters in both groups frequently exchanged experiences. The most important difference between the two styles before 1900 was that the Hebei style included only ten animal skills. In 1900, Li Cunyi went from Hebei to Taiguo to visit his *gongfu* uncle Che Yizhai. During that visit, Che taught Li the two additional animal skills that Dai Longbang had originated. Currently, martial artists from both styles practice all twelve animal skills.

Song Shirong

Xingyi Quan is sometimes said to include two styles, northern and southern. The northern style is made up of the old and new Shanxi styles and the Hebei style. The southern style refers to the Henan style. (See "Ma Xueli and Henan Style," above.)

Guo Yunshen, Liu Qilan, and Hebei Style

On his return to Hebei Province, Master Li Luoneng taught Xingyi Quan to numerous students, some of whom became very famous. These included Guo Yunshen, Liu Qilan, Liu Xiaolan, Li Jingzhai, Liu Yuanheng, Zhang Shude, Bai Xiyuan, He Yongheng, Li Guangheng, Li Taihe, and Liu Zhihe. The skills of this group of students further enhanced the reputation of Hebei-style Xingyi Quan. Guo Yunshen and Liu Qilan were the best of Master Li's Hebei disciples, and most Hebei-style Xingyi Quan practitioners today are under their lineage.

Guo and Liu were close friends who studied and traveled together to demonstrate their *gongfu* and test their skills against many competitors. Guo won great renown for his fighting skill. It was said that no one in the world could defeat his half-step *beng quan*, a straight powerful center punch, commonly translated to "smashing, erupting, or explosive fist." Liu, also a great Xingyi Quan Master, was highly educated and used his knowledge to develop a notably efficient training method. He was highly regarded as a teacher and trained many famous disciples. Guo and Liu brought Xingyi Quan to Beijing, Tianjin, and other big cities and greatly increased its popularity and fame.

Guo Yunshen and Liu Qilan won all their fights until they met Master Dong Haichuan, the founder of Bagua Zhang. When Guo and Liu visited Dong, Guo and Dong experimented with their respective techniques, and finally Guo concluded that Dong's skill was greater than his. The three masters discussed the principles underlying their techniques and discovered that Xingyi and Bagua were very similar in principle but different in their training methods. Guo,

Liu, and Dong became close friends and then blood brothers. They combined their styles, and soon Xingyi and Bagua came to be thought of as members of the same family.

Guo Yunshen had relatively few students, of whom only Li Kueyuan, Xu Zhanao, Qian Yantang, and Wang Xiangyuan became well known. Liu Qilan, on the other hand, had many famous students, including Li Cunyi, Zhang Zhaodong, Wang Fuyuan, Liu Wenhua, Liu Dekuan, Zhou Mingtai, Gang Chengxin, Tian Jingjie, and Liu Fengchuan. Because of this disparity, Liu's influence in the history of Xingyi Quan is considered greater than Guo's.

Later Generations and My Personal Xingyi Quan Lineage

Through the teachings of Li Luoneng and his students, Xingyi Quan became very famous in Hebei and Shanxi Provinces and then spread to northern China. By the third and fourth generations, masters under Li's name made Xingyi Quan famous throughout China and overseas.

In the Shanxi style, the most famous teachers were Che Yizhai's students Li Fuzhen and Bu Xuekuan, and Song Shirong's student Song Tielin. These masters devoted their lives to teaching Xingyi Quan.

Li Fuzhen

Bu Xuekuan

Song Tielin

Li Cunyi

Zhang Zhaodong

Han Muxia

In the Hebei style, the most famous masters were Li Cunyi and Zhang Zhaodong. Li and Zhang were very close friends, and each had studied Xingyi Quan with Liu Qilan. Li's *gongfu* was excellent and his reputation great. It was Li who expanded the Hebei style from ten to twelve animal forms after three trips to Shanxi Province to visit his *gongfu* uncle Che Yizhai, from whom he learned *tuo* and *tai* and other skills like *za shi chui*. Through his efforts, the Hebei style became a complete system, and he is duly credited with making a great contribution to the development of this style. Li later became President of the Chinese Martial Artists Association, one of the most famous martial arts organizations at the beginning of the twentieth century.

Zhang Zhaodong, also known by the name Zhang Zhankui, lived next door to Liu Qilan. When he was ten years old, he started training with Liu. By fourteen, he was accompanying Liu on travels to compete with other martial artists. Zhang's fighting skill became great and widely respected. He was known especially for the quickness of his movements, which earned him the nickname Shan Dian Shou or Lightning Hands. He became a policeman in Tianjin and was famous for subduing armed gang members with his bare hands.

In the fourth generation under Li Luoneng's name, the most famous Xingyi Quan masters were Han Muxia, Shang Yunxiang, and Sun Lutang.

Han Muxia was the most outstanding Xingyi Quan master in his generation. He had already gained fame by the time he was fifteen. He studied a variety of martial art styles with nine different masters, one of whom was Zhang Zhaodong, who taught him Xingyi Quan and Bagua Zhang. Of Han's many fights, one of the most famous was against a powerful Russian opponent in 1918 in Beijing. Han won eleven gold medals for his performance in this fight. For many years, Han directed The Professional Martial Arts Academy, a very famous martial arts school in Tianjin.

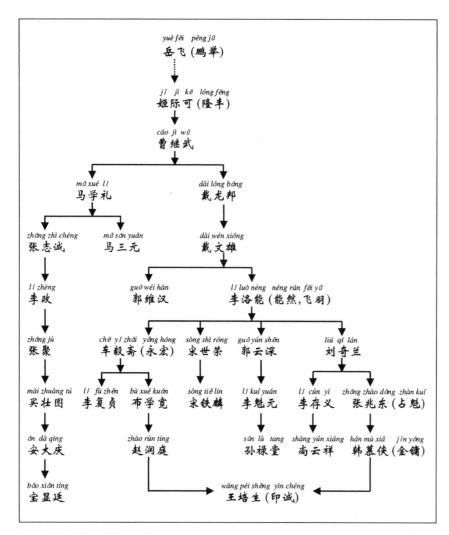

Shang Yunxiang

Sun Lutang

Part of the Xingyi Quan Lineage

Shang Yunxiang, born in 1863, studied with Li Cunyi and became one of Xingyi Quan's greatest masters. He earned a good reputation even as a youngster due to his hard practice. When Shang's grandmaster Master Guo Yunshen heard about Shang's talent, Guo went to visit Shang to test his skill. Guo was impressed enough to take the young man on as a direct student. Shang developed into a highly skilled fighter and is famous, among other accomplishments, for helping the government arrest a notorious robber.

Sun Lutang was another very famous Xingyi Quan master. He learned the art from Li Kuiyuan and also received instruction from his grandmaster Guo Yunshen. He studied Bagua Zhang with Cheng Tinghua, and Taiji Quan with Hao He. Later, he created Sun-style Taiji Quan. He taught widely and wrote several martial arts books.

I began my study of Xingyi Quan in the early 1980s under the tutelage of my grandmaster Wang Peisheng. Master Wang learned both Shanxi- and Hebei-style Xingyi Quan. When he was young, he learned Shanxi style with Master Zhao Runting, who was an early disciple of Bu Xuekuan's, and Bu was Che Yizhai's disciple. In the mid 1940s, Master Wang and the famous Xingyi and Bagua master Ma Yilin became blood brothers, and Ma introduced Master Wang to Hebei-style Xingyi Quan through Ma's master and father-in-law Han Muxia.

Basic Principles and Features of Xingyi Quan

Although the original principles of Xingyi Quan are not clearly known, it is certain that mind or *yi* training was involved in Xingyi Quan practice from the very beginning. Like we mentioned before, most people believe that it was Li Luoneng who developed Xingyi Quan principles to a high degree and made the training system complete. The name Xingyi Quan is considered by many to date from Li's time.

xíng quán

形 拳

yì quán

意 拳

As the name implies, Xingyi Quan is separated into two parts: Xing Quan and Yi Quan. Yi Quan, which derives from the *wuxing*-five elements concept in traditional Chinese philosophy, is the foundation or root of the system; while Xing Quan, which derives from twelve animals' fighting skills, concerns the applications of the system.

The *wuxing* concept is thought to have originated five thousand years ago. The earliest written record dates from three thousand

years ago and comes from the book *Shang Shu*. Later, the concept was elaborated and incorporated into many traditional philosophical systems, including Daoism and Confucianism.

In ancient Chinese thought, the universe was made up of five basic elements: metal, wood, water, fire, and earth. These elements are not related to the elements of modern chemistry but rather are conceptual attributes assumed to provide the foundation of all things. From these elements, all aspects of the universe are generated, changed, and ultimately destroyed.

The five elements are grouped into two basic circles, which express the mutual influences between the elements and the rules for the development and change of elements. One circle is called *sheng*, which means to create, produce, generate, or initiate. The other circle is called *ke*, which means to subdue, destroy, restrain, control, overcome, or surmount.

In the *sheng* circle, it is said that metal can produce water, water can produce wood, wood can produce fire, fire can produce earth, and earth can produce metal. In the *ke* circle, it is said that metal can subdue wood, wood can subdue earth, earth can subdue water, water can subdue fire, and fire can subdue metal. An understanding of the *wuxing* principle allows one to understand the rules by which all things in the universe are changed. It has been applied to social systems, politics, science, philosophy, medicine, and religion.

The Yi Quan or mind training part of Xingyi Quan resulted from an extension of the *wuxing* principle to the martial arts. Five basic Yi Quan postures were designed using the *wuxing* concept.

wŭ   xíng   xiāng   shēng

五 行 相 生

wŭ   xíng   xiāng   kè

五 行 相 克

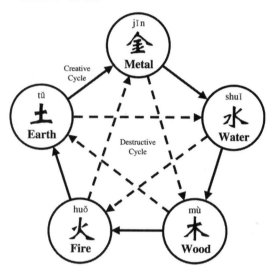

Sheng and Ke Circles of Wuxing

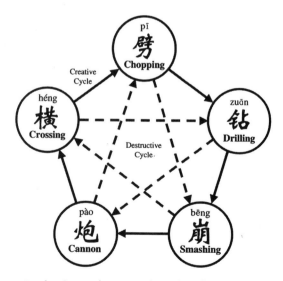

Production and Destruction, Five-Element Fist

Pi Quan

Application of Pi Quan

They are: *pi quan,* which means chopping or splitting fist and derives from the element metal; *beng quan* or smashing fist, which derives from the element wood; *zuan quan* or drilling fist, which derives from the element water; *pao quan,* which means pounding or cannon fist and derives from the element fire; and *heng quan,* which means side-striking or crossing fist and derives from the element earth. According to the *sheng* cycle, *pi* can produce *zuan, zuan* can produce *beng, beng* can produce *pao, pao* can produce *heng,* and *heng* can produce *pi.* According to the *ke* cycle, *pi* can destroy *beng, beng* can destroy *heng, heng* can destroy *zuan, zuan* can destroy *pao,* and *pao* can destroy *pi.*

The practice of these five postures can develop basic internal power, *qi,* and special fighting abilities. It can also adjust the body internally to promote good health. The postures provide the foundation of Xingyi Quan and are the basis for all Xingyi fighting skills.

It is said that when Ji Longfeng observed an eagle and a bear on Zhongnan Mountain, he intuited the classic martial arts notion that one should attack like an eagle and defend like a bear. An

Eagle and Bear

attack should be quick, accurate, and hard like an eagle hunting its prey; a defense should be stable and powerful like the carriage of a bear. Ji's notion was the starting point for the Xing Quan component of Xingyi Quan. Later, postures derived from the characteristics of other animals were developed: ten in the Henan style and twelve in the Shanxi and Hebei styles.

In Xingyi Quan, animal simulation skills are very different from most other animal simulation styles. In Xingyi Quan animal skills, it is more important to express the animal's inner character and spirit rather than to mimic its physical movement. The dragon's attribute, for example, is to shrink, twist, and quickly spring upward as though flying from a small space toward the heavens. When performing the dragon skill, one must feel and express the magic, awe, and power of the moment when the dragon springs free with quickness, agility, flexibility, and grace.

In the classic work *Xingyi Quan Pu* that describes Hebei- and Shanxi-style Xingyi Quan, twelve sentences portray the twelve animal attributes. They are as follows:

龙有搜骨之法勇
虎有扑食之能
猴有纵山蹄之功灵
马有疾蹄水之性
鼍有浮争斗之势巧
鸡有钻天水之精形
鹞有抄水草之技
燕有拨草撞之力
蛇有崩拿顶之
䏝有捉拿顶之
鹰有竖顶之

Twelve Animal Attributes Poem

1. **Dragon:** "*Long you sou gu zhi fa*" or "The Dragon Possesses a Brisk Technique"

   Long or dragon is a mythical animal idealized by the ancient Chinese and thought to have miraculous abilities that reflect all of nature's wondrous powers. Its attribute is to shrink, twist, and quickly spring upward as though flying from a small space toward the heavens.

2. **Tiger:** "*Hu you pu shi zhi yong*" or "The Tiger Is Fearless as It Pounces"

   Hu or tiger, the "king of all beasts," is considered the most powerful and ferocious of all animals. It symbolizes power, control, and the ability to do whatever one wants. Its attribute is movement so powerful and quick that nothing can stop it.

3. **Monkey:** "*Hou you zhong shang zhi neng*" or "Monkey Has the Nimbleness to Scale Mountains"

   Hou or monkey is thought to be the smartest and most nimble animal. It can go anywhere it wants in its mountain environment. Its attribute is movement that is quick, nimble, and skillful.

4. **Horse:** "*Ma you ji ti zhi gong*" or "The Horse Has Churning Footwork"

   Ma or horse is a strong animal full of vitality. Its attribute is quick, powerful, and continuous strikes that mimic the quality of a galloping horse's churning legs.

5. **Alligator:** "*Tuo you fu shui zhi ling*" or "The Alligator Can Float and Swim Well"

   Tuo or alligator can swim quickly and smoothly and also remain very still in the water when readying an attack. Especially powerful when it rotates, the alligator's attribute is a combination

of quietness, nimbleness, and a sudden, smooth, and quickly twisting force.

6. **Rooster:** *"Ji you zheng dou zhi xing"* or *"The Rooster Is Born with a Competitive Nature for Fighting"*

   Ji or rooster is an animal whose nature, according to ancient stories, is to fight. In competition, it fights bravely and hard and does not quit easily. Its attribute is the courage and perseverance to fight valiantly.

7. **Sparrow Hawk:** *"Yao you zuan tian zhi shi"* or *"The Sparrow Hawk Can Pierce the Heavens"*

   Yao or sparrow hawk is a quick, agile bird of prey. In *zuan tian* or upward flight, its strength is displayed; when it flies downward, its agility is apparent. When it flies through the forest, it shows how accurate it is, and when it turns over in flight, it shows how nimble it is. Its attribute is a piercing movement that is quick, hard, and straight but also very nimble.

8. **Swallow:** *"Yan you chao shui zhi qiao"* or *"The Swallow Has the Agility to Skim Over the Water"*

   Yan or swallow can fly very quickly with accurate movements. Its attribute is light, quick movement, the effectiveness of which derives from its accuracy.

9. **Snake:** *"She you bo cao zhi jing"* or *"The Snake Has the Refined Skill to Move the Grass Aside Neatly"*

   She or snake is considered a vicious animal that can hide well, move quietly, and attack suddenly. When it prepares for an attack, it moves from side to side, so it is difficult to predict where the attack will come from. The snake attribute is a light, quick, sudden, and accurate strike that comes from an unpredictable direction.

10. **Ostrich:** "*Tai you beng zhuang zhi zing*" or "Tai Are Skilled at Collision and Ramming Forward"

Tai is variously interpreted as a mythical bird resembling an ostrich in Hebei-style Xingyi groups or a large fish or wild horse in other groups. Conceptualized as a bird, this animal is thought to be able to flap its wings so powerfully that they can knock over anything in their path. Its attribute is movement that is strong, quick, and able to destroy anything that tries to block it.

11. **Eagle:** "*Ying you zhou na zhi ji*" or "The Eagle Is Skilled at Capture"

Ying or eagle circles the skies and dives suddenly and swiftly down on its prey. Its dive must be powerful and accurate. In Xingyi Quan, every attack skill should be as accurate, quick, and powerful as the grip of an eagle's talons. The opponent should have no chance to fight back or run away. The eagle attribute is sudden, powerful, and accurate movement that is carefully controlled from start to finish.

12. **Bear:** "*Xiong you shu ding zhi li*" or "The Bear Shows Its Power When It Stands Up"

Xiong or bear is a very powerful animal whose force is shown clearly when it rears up on its hind legs and squares its shoulders and arms. Its stance is so strong and stable that nothing can unsettle it, even during an attack. In Xingyi Quan, it is said that when you defend, you should be like a bear standing up. The bear's attribute expresses strength and stability.

Through the generations, many Xingyi Quan fighting techniques have been derived from these principles and skills. The primary aspects of Xingyi Quan involve combinations of hard and soft, quick and slow, internal and external, powerful and relaxed, and straight and slanted. *Yin* and *yang* are fully integrated and mutually

Tiger

Hawk

aided. *Qi* flows smoothly and becomes stronger. There is also continuous mutual influence of the *sheng* and *ke* circles. Today, the theory of Xingyi Quan is complete and the training system has been perfected, making Xingyi Quan one of the most famous and widely practiced Chinese martial arts.

Analysis of the Xingyi Quan Training Method

The training system of Xingyi Quan is unique and includes three stages. Because of this tripartite division, Xingyi Quan is popularly described as containing three practice methods that use three kinds of breathing to improve three-step *gongfu* trainings and to follow three levels of principle.

The three Xingyi Quan practice methods are *ming jin*, the use of evident trained force; *an jin*, the use of hidden trained force; and *hua jin*, the changing or turning of trained force. Here *jin* is translated as "trained force" instead of the more commonly used "internal force" because we think it is more accurate and it avoids confusion between the two kinds of trained force, *wai jin* or exter-

nal trained force and *nei jin* or internal trained force. The three kinds of breath are outside breath, inside breath, and *tai xi* or the breath of a child in utero. The three *gongfu* training steps are *yi gu* or changing bones; *yi jin* or changing tendons; and *xi sui* or washing marrow. The three levels of principle are "transforming *jing* to *qi*"; "turning *qi* to *shen*"; and "returning *shen* to *xu*."

The First Stage

ming jìn

明 劲

The practice method *ming jin*, or evident trained force, is described in the classics as being "in the hands," which means that all positions and movements are visible and should be executed clearly and correctly. They must be precise and harmoniously coordinated. The application of each must be accurate, and every aspect of the positions and movements must accord with specified standards.

According to this method, all forces can be moved and changed to follow movement. Gradually, the forces sink down throughout the body and become stable, strong, and integrated. These effects can be obvious to the eyes. All postures should appear ample and majestic. To achieve these qualities, all movements should be performed slowly and smoothly so that all parts of the body work together in a coordinated way. With patience and enough practice, you will gradually feel your body being infused with power. You should follow this feeling by intensifying your practice. Little by little, you will feel your body increasing in strength as your *qi* flow increases. This, in turn, will create the very powerful force called *jin* or trained force. *Jin* is sometimes referred to as "internal force" because it is generated deep within the body.

wài xī

外 息

The kind of breath used in the first stage is called *wai xi*, or outside breath. Air should pass only through the nose and mouth and then be drawn deeply down into the middle and lower body. The top of the tongue should touch the roof of the mouth behind the teeth, and the mouth should appear to open and close. Breathing should be natural. Do not think about it. Just let it adjust naturally to your

movements. This kind of breathing is external and occurs high up in the body.

The *gongfu* training step in the first stage is *yi gu,* which means "to change bones" or to build basic skills by improving one's strength. The goal is to increase power and stability using a wide variety of hard physical practices that build up the body and strengthen the bones.

yì   gǔ
易 骨

The principle of "transforming *jing* to *qi*" can be understood in terms of both the martial arts and *qigong.* In martial arts terms, it means that natural force is changed or transformed into *jin* or trained force. Here *jing* means "energy," and it exists in every part of the body. Without martial arts training, it is not efficient because the movements of the body are not coordinated. In the first stage of Xingyi Quan training, the main focus is on integrating *jing* from all parts of the body. The natural force that was originally expressed by the tensing of external muscles is transformed *jin* that is led and moved by *qi. Jin* gradually replaces natural force in leading the body's movements.

liàn jīng huà qì
练 精 化 气

In *qigong* terms, the principle of the first stage refers to *xiao zhoutian,* "the microcosmic orbit" that means *qi,* with practice, becomes stronger and more integrated and can rise up or sink down naturally along the two centerline meridians—*Dunmai* on the back and *Renmai* on the front of the body. The free, smooth flow of *qi* through the two meridians creates a connection between them, and this improves the efficiency of *qi.* The source of *qi* is *jing. Jing* energy comes from two sources: one's genetic inheritance and one's environment, including most importantly air, water, and food. The *jing* that exists from the moment of conception is called *yuan jing* or original *jing.* The *jing* that derives from the environment is called *hou tian jing* or post-natal *jing.* If *jing* is strong, the whole body will be strong, but many circumstances, such as becoming over-tired, can consume or weaken *jing.* The first basic skill in *qigong* practice is *gu jing,* which means to set or fix *jing.* With practice,

xiǎo zhōu tiān
小 周 天

jing is transformed into *qi,* and as *qi* becomes stronger, so does your body.

The fighting principles of the first stage emphasize quickness and power. The classics advise that you move like an arrow shot from a bow. You should always strive to move more quickly. When you attack, the movements of your body should be integrated so that your power can overcome all obstacles. You should feel as though you have so much more power than your opponent that fighting is easy, like taking a walk. Your opponent should be like a blade of grass that gives way as you stride by. No matter how strong your opponent may actually be, you should feel as though you can destroy him at will.

The Second Stage

àn   jìn
暗 劲

The practice method in the second stage is *an jin* or hidden trained force. The classics locate *an jin* "in the elbows," the implication of which is that the movements and expression of trained force have been practiced to the point that they are no longer visible to an outside observer. A movement may appear to be straight, for example, but the internal trained force associated with it can be diagonal, or the movement may appear to be diagonal while the internal trained force is actually applied in a straight line. Sideways internal trained force, called *heng,* cannot be seen from the outside but is experienced only internally. In general, second-stage applications are concealed and complex.

Using the *an jin* method, trained force becomes nimble, light, smooth, and varied. External movements have great stability but inside, there is a pervasive quality of nimbleness. *Shen,* the internal component akin to attention or spirit, becomes strong while outwardly all is calm and peaceful.

nèi   xî
内 息

The breath characteristic of the second stage is called *nei xi,* or inside breath. It is accomplished by letting *qi* sink down to *Dantian.* This kind of breathing is not related to movement. There

should be an awareness of *Dantian* but no highly focused attention on the act of breathing. The *Dantian* is a special point in *qigong* and martial arts practice. In Chinese *dan* means a special pill that is good for health and long life, and *tian* means field. So *Dantian* means the place to create this "pill." Usually people think it is in the center of the lower abdomen just below the navel, but different styles may have slightly different definitions of where *Dantian* should be.

The *gongfu* training step in the second stage is *yi jin*, which means "to change tendons." In this instance *jin* means "tendons." It is different from the word "*jin*" used previously to describe "trained force." This involves increasing the nimbleness and continuity of movement, thus allowing internal trained force to reach every part of the body smoothly and efficiently. With practice, internal trained force becomes much stronger and more nimble, resulting in a rapid advance in one's *gongfu*.

yi   jîn
易 筋

The principle of "turning *qi* to *shen*" in the second stage involves developing *qi* so that it can follow and become more integrated with *shen*. As a martial arts principle, the focus is on how to move, change, and apply internal trained force, and this goal can be realized by training the internal harmonies or integrations. According to the internal harmonies, *shen* leads *yi* or mind; *yi*, in turn, leads *qi*; and *qi* leads *jin*. Wherever and whenever *shen* and *yi* lead, *qi* and *jin* must follow.

liàn   qì   huà shén
练 气 化 神

Although this description implies that *jin* exists only in specific places at specific times, it is actually being used throughout the body at all times. Because its expression is related to the movements of *shen* and *yi* rather than to the movements of the body, internal trained force can become very nimble.

From a *qigong* point of view, the second stage involves "*da zhoutian*," "the macrocosmic orbit." The goal of this practice is to strengthen the flow of *qi* throughout the body so that it cannot be broken or stopped under any circumstances. All meridians through-

dà   zhôu tiân
大 周 天

out the body become joined together by the *qi* flow, and the flow itself becomes more spontaneous and unimpeded.

The fighting principles in the second stage emphasize relaxation, agility, softness, changeability, and subtlety. The classics assert that whenever you attack or defend, your movements should be relaxed, soft, and small. You should not let your opponent sense what you want to do. You should be agile and able to change skills easily and unobtrusively, so that you never move directly against your opponent but find instead an easy way to beat him. Your plan for attack or defense should never be apparent to your opponent. Attack and defense skills should be combined so that each includes the other. You should use your power only after finding a weakness in your opponent, and you should use the internal components to lead external skills. Everything should start from your heart and be accomplished by skills founded on the integration of internal components and movement.

The Third Stage

huà   jìn

化 劲

The practice method in the third stage is *hua jin*, which means to dissolve trained force in your body. According to the classics, *hua jin* is "in the body," meaning that in this stage, trained force is merged with the body so that it functions in a completely natural manner. Although the internal components of *shen, yi, qi,* and *jin* and the external components of position and movement are the same in all three stages, they become fully coordinated only in the third stage.

In this stage, the *yin* and *yang* aspects of *jin* can be changed smoothly and naturally. Practicing martial arts at this stage has been variously described as: *quan wu quan,* practicing as though you were doing nothing; *yi wu yi,* practicing as though you were using your mind without having to think; and *wu yi zhi zhong shi zhan yi,* practicing without mental effort so that the true meaning of the skills emerges naturally. Each of these expressions conveys

the same truth: that everything you do must be accomplished in a wholly natural way.

The goal of this method is to integrate *shen, yi, qi, jin,* and movements so fully that the coordination among them seems to occur spontaneously. Every aspect of your practice should come to feel as natural as a reflex. The correct applications should happen without conscious thought as though it had always been your nature to do them in just that way, as though you never had to practice them at all.

Third-stage breathing is called *tai xi,* which refers to the breathing of a baby in its mother's womb. This means that if you are quiet, empty of intent, and natural in whatever you do, things will go smoothly. It is not necessary to exert conscious effort or to follow a rule. Responses that originally had to be acquired through training have now become second nature. Your training has brought you to the point at which you can trust these new natural responses.

tāi xǐ

胎息

The *gongfu* training step in the third stage is *xi sui* or washing the marrow. In this step, the focus is on practicing an inner sense of stillness and emptiness and an outer quality of natural relaxation. *Jin* and outside movements spontaneously follow *qi, yi,* and *shen,* and all applications are naturally coordinated.

xǐ sui

洗髓

The principle of "returning *shen* to *xu*" in this stage is based on the premise that all movement and forces must return to nature. In a martial arts context, this means that *shen* must return to *xu,* the empty and quiet state of being. There is nothing one wants or needs to do. Everything that has been practiced so diligently and for so long is now part of you and has led to the creation of new natural capabilities. There are no images, methods, or conscious efforts that need to be constructed or followed. The whole body is in immediate touch with its own nature and the nature around it. All action is natural and spontaneous.

liàn shén huán xū

练神还虚

In *qigong* terms, *xi sui* is the highest level of *gongfu.* At this stage, there is no need to practice nor to think before taking action.

xìng mìng shuāng xiū

性命双修

Everything happens according to nature. When you reach this level, called *xing ming shuang xiu*, the classics say that your temperament will be balanced in understanding the meaning of your life as well as in obtaining good health and a long life. At this level, you have achieved an understanding of the Dao.

The fighting principle in this stage is that you can do whatever feels natural because by this time, all specially trained internal components and physical movements or skills have become part of your nature. The classics declare that there is no skill or particular mindset needed in order to fight successfully. The only true thing is nothing. If you need to show your skill, you are not good enough. Any part of your body can be used at any time to do anything. Everything happens naturally.

In the three stages of Xingyi Quan practice, the physical movements are the same but the internal practices are different. If you follow the traditional Xingyi sequence of methods, breathing, *gongfus*, and principles, you will have a chance to understand the true meaning of the internal martial arts.

tài   jí quán

太极拳

⭐ Taiji Quan

The principle of *taiji* is one of paramount importance in traditional Chinese philosophy. In Chinese *tai* means "very very big" or "great," and *ji* means "extreme" or "limit." As a philosophical premise, "*taiji*" refers to the basic natural laws of the universe and is thought to be all-encompassing. The *taiji* principle examines the relationship between *yin* and *yang* and expresses the rules by which all changes occur. It describes ancient Chinese notions about the fundamental nature of the universe. Developed over the course of thousands of years, the *taiji* principle has influenced every aspect of traditional Chinese culture, and when applied to the martial arts, it generated the unique, complex, and high-level style known as Taiji Quan. Today Taiji Quan is the most popular Chinese martial

art. As the foundation of the principle of Taiji Quan, the *taiji* concept is intended to be applied in every aspect of Taiji Quan. Because of the many years of effort and the contributions of dedicated and ingenious masters, Taiji Quan theory has become a complete whole—a true reflection of the principles of the *taiji* concept in its application to martial art. The techniques of Taiji Quan have been refined to their highest potential.

Taiji Diagram

History, Lineage, and Styles

The Old Legends

The identity of the founder of Taiji Quan has puzzled people for two hundred years. According to legend, there were originally five different kinds of Taiji Quan. All were based on Daoist philosophy but each had its own distinctive set of movements.

The oldest style of Taiji Quan originated with Han Gongyue, who lived about 1,600 years ago during the Liang Dynasty. It is not known whether he invented this style or learned it from someone else. Cheng Lingxi, who lived in Xiouning County of Hui Zhou and was one of Han's students, became famous for his mastery of this style. Having distinguished himself in battle, Cheng was rewarded by the government with an appointment as governor of a Jun, an administrative body responsible for overseeing five counties.

The next practitioner who gained renown for this style was Cheng Bi, a high-level officer in the Song Dynasty. He wrote several articles describing the principles on which the style was based and changed the name from Taiji Quan to "Xiao Jiu Tian" or "Small Nine-Level Heavens."

Xu Xuanping, a hermit who lived on Chengyang Mountain during the Tang Dynasty, practiced a form of Taiji Quan called "San Shi Qi" or "Thirty-Seven Postures." He was tall, had long hair and a

xiǎo jiǔ tiān

小九天

hán gòng yuè

韩拱月

sān shí qī shì

三十七式

xǔ xuān píng

许宣平

long beard, and could run as fast as a horse. Every day he carried wood down the mountain to town to barter it for alcohol. Then he disappeared back up the mountain. Li Bai, a very famous poet of the period, wanted to meet the elusive Xu but could never find him.

The movements of Xu's Thirty-Seven Postures form, known as Chang Quan or the Long Form, are very close to what we practice today. Originally, each position was studied separately and could be freely combined with the others in any order. The resulting form could be long or short, but the postures had to flow in a smooth sequence. A famous poem portraying Taiji principles has been attributed to Xu Xuanping.

Several hundred years later, Song Yuanqiao became famous for his Long Form technique. Sometime between 1910 and 1929, Song Shuming—who claimed that he was Song Yuanqiao's lineage descendant—brought this style to Beijing. He espoused the old classics, and several well-known masters like Ji Zixiu, Wu Jianquan, and Liu Dekuan studied with him, but many people doubted his credentials.

xiān tiān quán

先天拳

lǐ dào zǐ

李道子

Li Daozhi was a Daoist priest who lived in the Nanyan Temple on Wudang Mountain during the Tang Dynasty. The style he practiced was known as "Xiantian Quan," which can be translated as "Pre-birth Skills." Li wrote a poem called *Shoumi Ge* or "Teach a Secret Song" in which he described the high-level relationships among Dao, *qigong,* and the martial arts.

The Xiantian Quan style then passed to the Yu family of Jing County in Ningguo Fu. Some Yu family members, including Yu Qinghui, Yu Yicheng, and Yu Lianzhou, gained fame for their mastery of Xiantian Quan skills.

hòu tiān fǎ

后天法

hú jìng zǐ

胡镜子

Also during the Tang Dynasty, a martial artist named Hu Jingzhi from Yangzhou developed a style called "Houtian Fa," which means "the training method that allows one to go back to nature." This style contains sixteen elbow techniques, all of which are very use-

ful for fighting. Hu's most well-known student was Song Zhongshu. In a later generation, Yin Liheng became famous for his skill in this style.

Zhang Sanfeng's Taiji Quan is called *Shi San Shi* or "The Thirteen-Posture Form." It has become very popular and is the form most commonly practiced today. When people say Taiji Quan, they are usually referring to Zhang Sanfeng's form. The main variants of this style are Chen style, Yang style, Wu (tone 2) style, Wu (tone 3) style, and Sun style.*

Today, with the exception of Zhang Sanfeng's form, the old styles of Taiji Quan are almost lost. Only a few old masters know anything about them. Some people even doubt the existence of these old styles, believing instead that the forms were devised within the last one hundred years.

shi sān shì

十 三 式

zhāng sān fēng

张 三 丰

Zhang Sanfeng and the Martial Arts

Facts about the life of Zhang Sanfeng are scarce. The common view is that he was a Daoist priest who lived during the Ming Dynasty, although there are also claims that he lived during the Song or Yuan Dynasty about one hundred years earlier. There is even conjecture that there were two historically important Daoist priests with the name of Zhang Sanfeng.

---

*This word "Wu" appears frequently but is denoted by a different pronunciation. Chinese is a tonal language. In all languages we find the use of tone or pitch to express emphasis, emotion, and other nuances in speech. In Chinese, tone is also used to distinguish meaning. There are four tones in the standard Chinese spoken language. Following are examples of each. First tone: When we pronounce the "woo" in "wooden" we are using the first, or flat, intonation. Second tone: When we pronounce the "Woo" in "Wooster Street" we're using the second, or rising, tone. In Taiji Quan, Wu Jianquan's family name is pounced like "Woo" in "Wooster." Third tone: When someone asks the question "would you do me a favor?" the "wou" in "would" is an example of the third tone, which is a down-and-up pitch. In Taiji Quan, Wu Yuxiang's family name is pronounced using the third tone. Fourth tone: When you answer the above question "Yes, I would," you use a downward, or falling, pitch when pronouncing the "wou" in the word "would."

Zhang Sanfeng's first name was Junbao, and his other first name was Quanyi. He was also given the special name of Tongwei Xianhua Zhenran by the Emperor because of his great Daoist expertise. The name Tongwei indicated that he was thought capable of making accurate and detailed prophesies; Xianhua meant that he could appear immediately wherever he was needed; and Zhenran denoted a person who understood Dao as deeply and thoroughly as an immortal being. Popularly, Zhang Sangfeng was known as Zhang Zhenran.

Zhang Sanfeng was born in Yizhou, Liaodong Province, and is said to have had large round eyes, big ears, and a wiry beard. His body was strong, with a back like a turtle's and legs like a crane's. When young, he studied a wide variety of subjects. He was smart and had very good memory. After passing the national examination, he became a government officer, but several years of Daoist practice led him to relinquish his government post and enter the priesthood.

Zhang did not care about the usual comforts nor did he follow social conventions. From summer to winter, he wore only a Daoist robe and a straw hat. Because he never changed his clothes, shaved or cut his hair, he acquired the nickname of Zhang Lata or slovenly Zhang.

After becoming a priest, Zhang traveled long distances to counsel people and promulgate the Daoist principles he had learned. He visited many famous priests and temples where he studied with famous masters. When he reached Zhongnan Mountain, he met a Daoist priest named Huolong Zhanran, who taught him many profound aspects of Daoism that were not commonly known. These teachings opened Zhang Sanfeng's mind and greatly deepened his understanding of Dao.

There are many legends about Zhang's life, practice, and martial arts knowledge. The most famous story relates the events that led him to create Taiji Quan. According to this account, Zhang Sanfeng journeyed to Wudang Mountain. At that time, all the Daoist

temples had been destroyed by war, and all the priests had fled. Zhang proclaimed that the monastery on Wudang Mountain must be rebuilt and began the mountain's renewal by constructing a small thatched cottage where he lived for more than nine years practicing meditation and martial arts daily.

One day, Zhang noticed a crane and a snake fighting in the grass. Although he had already achieved a high level of Shaolin *gongfu*, this fight inspired a sudden insight that helped Zhang understand how Daoist concepts provided the foundation for his martial arts practice. The principle for Taiji Quan arose from this insight. Zhang continued to practice and develop his ideas, and gradually a new martial art emerged. It consisted of eight basic hand skills or *bamen* associated with the eight-trigrams principle of *bagua,* and five basic step skills or *wubu* associated with the five-elements principle of *wuxing.* Given the sum of these elements, Zhang's style is always referred to as Thirteen-Posture Taiji Quan.

Zhang Sanfeng

Questions have been raised about whether Zhang Sanfeng created Taiji Quan or Neijia Quan, as is mentioned in some historical records. The debate has led to two points of view. One is that Zhang created a martial art style that was called Neijia Quan when it was taught in southern China, and Taiji Quan when it was taught in northern China. The other view is that Zhang had nothing to do with the creation of Taiji Quan and that all the stories about him and Taiji Quan were concocted in the nineteenth century. The arguments continue to this day.

Different Lineage Versions before Chen Changxing

Although it is not clear who invented Taiji Quan nor when it first appeared, it is agreed that Chen Changxing—a member of the

fourteenth generation of the Chen family in Chen Village of Henan Province—was a great Taiji Quan master who taught in the nineteenth century. He occupies a central place in the different explications of Taiji Quan's origins. Three main lineage versions, each of which is popular and widespread, have been advanced.

The first version is the traditional view that Zhang Sanfeng invented Taiji Quan and then passed it on to Wang Zong. After several generations, the skill passed to Wang Zongyue and then to Jiang Fa. Later, Jiang passed his knowledge of Taiji Quan to Chen Changxing.

A variation of the first version holds that Jiang passed Taiji Quan to Chen Wangting, a ninth-generation family member of Chen Village, from whom it was then passed down through generations of family members in Chen Village. In this version, Chen Changxing would have learned Taiji Quan from his father. This view seems reasonable, is supported by considerable evidence, and is accepted by most traditional Taiji Quan groups.

The second version of Taiji Quan's lineage history was first put forth in the 1930s and proposed that Chen Wangting personally invented Taiji Quan. This version was promoted by the Chinese government and has become increasingly popular since the 1950s but is not supported by sufficient evidence.

In a third version, Jiang Fa is thought to have learned Taiji Quan from Wang Linzhen in Shanxi Province. He then passed it to Xing Huaixi in Zhaobao Village of Henan Province. There, Taiji Quan was passed down from generation to generation until at some point it reached Chen Village and Chen Jixia, an eleventh-generation member of the Chen family. Evidence in support of this view is mounting.

Despite much argument about who invented Taiji Quan, there is no doubt that Wang Zongyue was the greatest Taiji Quan master. He lived before Chen Changxing was born, and so it can be assumed that Taiji Quan was already highly developed by the time of Chen

Changxing's birth. The only thing clearly known about the life of Wang Zongyue is that he wrote the most famous Taiji Quan classic—*Taiji Quan Lun* or "Discussion of Taiji Quan Theory." Because of his excellent scholarship, it is possible to understand what Taiji Quan should be.

It is also justly claimed that Chen Changxing, born in 1771 in Chen Jia Go or Chen Village in Wen County, Henan Province, was a great Taiji Quan master. He practiced very hard and earned great renown. His nickname was "Paiwei Xiansheng" or "Mr. Tablet." Paiwei (meaning "tablet") refers to a piece of wood, typically narrow and tall. Usually a person's name is written on this tablet, which is placed standing upright on a special table. It is intended to express respect for a person from an older generation in a group or family, somewhat like a stone grave marker. Thus Paiwei's nickname—because he always kept his body straight and was so quiet and unassuming. Chen taught Taiji Quan most of his life and was a tutor in Chen Dehu's family for many years.

The clear and detailed history of Taiji Quan dates from Chen Changxing's teaching. He had many students who were Chen family members, but the best student he had was a slave in Chen Dehu's household named Yang Luchan. Many years after Chen Changxing's death in 1853, Yang Luchan brought Taiji Quan to Beijing, the capital city of China. Yang won a great reputation and increased the popularity and eminence of Taiji Quan.

The Great Master Yang Luchan

The most significant growth in the popularity and renown of Taiji Quan occurred as a result of Yang Luchan's teachings. Yang's private first name was Fukui, and his *hou* or special literature name was Luchan. He was born to a poor family in Yongnian County, Hebei Province, in 1799. When he was about ten years old, he and another young boy, Li Bokui, were sold to Chen Dehu's family as slaves.

Although Chen Dehu was a resident of Chen Village, he owned a drug store in Yongnian County, and after purchasing Yang and Li, he took them to Henan Province to live in Chen Village.

Chen Dehu was a devotee of the martial arts and had invited Chen Changxing to teach Taiji Quan in his home. Many students came to Chen's house each evening to practice. During the lessons, Yang Luchan was expected to make tea and perform other tasks for Chen Changxing. While performing these duties, he was able to watch and listen to Chen Changxing's instruction. During the daytime Taiji Quan classes for Chen Dehu's children, Chen Changxing always used Yang to demonstrate various skills. Although Yang endured many hard strikes in these demonstrations, he had a chance to experience Chen Changxing's skill directly. Yang used his free time every day to review and practice what he had learned. Eventually, Yang gained a thorough understanding of Taiji Quan, along with the admiration and respect of Chen Changxing.

In time, both Yang and Li were accepted by Chen Changxing as disciples. Yang was very smart and practiced with great dedication. He became the best of Chen Changxing's disciples and lived in Chen Village for about thirty years until Chen Dehu died, at which point Chen's widow gave Yang his freedom and allowed him to return to his hometown.

Back home, Yang could not find a job so he started teaching Taiji Quan. The local people called his style Mian Quan or Soft Fist. He quickly became famous and won many fights, thus earning the nickname Yang Wudi, which means "invincible." It is said that one day he injured a person so badly in a fight that the opponent was taken for dead, and his family immediately began plotting revenge. Wisdom being the better part of valor, Yang departed hastily for Beijing.

Beijing is not far from Yongnian County but because Yang was a stranger there, he had difficulty finding work. He was eventually hired as a tutor to the two sons of a man named Mr. Zhang Fengqi,

Yang Luchan

who owned a soy sauce factory that produced the salty vegetables sold to the Emperor's court and other wealthy households. Yang had become educated while living in Chen Dehu's household and was well equipped to teach Zhang's sons to read and write. He did not mention his martial arts proficiency to his employer, however, and worried constantly about the revenge plans of the family in Yongnian.

(Note: Mr. Zhang's home and factory were in a suburb northwest of Beijing where some of the current residents knew Yang and tell stories about him to this day. Several of Zhang's factory buildings still exist, and I had the good fortune to tour them with my Grandmaster Wang Peisheng when he visited the site in 1981 to conduct personal martial arts research.)

Initially, Yang led a quiet life in Zhang's home. The days passed uneventfully until one evening when Yang heard a commotion and the clash of weapons in the factory yard. Taking his long pipe with him as usual, he left his room to investigate and soon discovered that forty of Zhang's factory workers and guards had been overwhelmed and tied up by twenty brigands from a nearby factory after a heated dispute. The captured guards warned Yang to leave right away because of the danger, but Yang ignored their warnings and without hesitation beat up the brigands while serenely puffing on his pipe throughout the melee. He untied Zhang's workers and guards and bound up the brigands instead. This triumph established Yang's reputation as a martial arts master, and with Mr. Zhang's permission, Yang started teaching martial arts classes for the guards and for the many friends and students who visited the Zhang home.

One day a very polite young man appeared at the Zhangs' gate to visit "Uncle" Yang. When Yang drew near, the young man suddenly attacked him but Yang responded quickly and easily defeated the stranger. The assailant fled, but Yang suspected that the attack was an attempt at revenge for the man he had injured in Yongnian. He

realized that more attempts might be imminent and decided once again to leave town. When he told Mr. Zhang about his past exploits and explained that he did not want to create any trouble, Mr. Zhang counseled Yang that running away might not be a good idea. He suggested instead that because of Yang's high-level *gongfu* he would make an ideal teacher for the Emperor's family. Mr. Zhang offered to introduce Yang to King Duan, the Emperor's brother, who was (like many members of the royal family) an avid admirer of the martial arts.

When King Duan met Yang, he immediately recognized the excellence of Yang's technique and offered him very good living conditions in return for lessons. At that time in Beijing, nobody knew about Taiji Quan so people were amazed by Yang's skill. His movements looked soft and slow but had extraordinary results. Many people challenged Yang and he beat them all. As a result, he and Taiji Quan attained quick and far-reaching distinction. Yang's position was expanded to include instruction of the Emperor's security guards, and Taiji Quan became ever more popular as it gained adherents and students. Yang Luchan taught Taiji Quan in Beijing for about twenty years and died in 1872.

The Different Schools of Taiji Quan

Wu Style, Hao Style, and Sun Style

Wu (tone 3)-style Taiji Quan began with Wu Yuxiang, whose private first name was Heqing. Wu was born into a rich family in 1812 in Yongnian County, Hebei Province. Many members of his family were government officials; all of them, starting with his great-grandfather, liked martial arts. He and his two brothers, Wu Chengqing and Wu Ruqing, were well educated and had studied Taiji Quan with Yang Luchan after Yang returned home from Chen Village.

In 1852, Wu Yuxiang set out to visit Chen Changxing. On the

way, he lived for a while in Zhaopao Village, where he met a Taiji Quan master named Chen Qingping. This man had a deep knowledge of Taiji Quan and could expertly guide Wu's study. Wu stayed in the village and studied with Chen Qingping until he truly understood Taiji Quan principles. Then he went on to Wuyang County where his brother, Wu Chengqing, was the governor. While there, he acquired Wang Zongyue's Taiji Quan classic, "Discussion of Taiji Quan Theory," from Yandian, a small town in Wuyang County. This was the first opportunity people had to read the famous article. Wu Yuxiang's thinking was greatly stimulated by the article, and he wrote several subsequent articles about Taiji Quan principles. These articles made important contributions to the elucidation of Taiji Quan's essential nature. Because Wu studied with both Yang Luchan and Chen Qingping, he drew from the two sets of teachings to develop a new Taiji Quan style that came to be called Wu (tone 3) style. Wu died in 1880.

Wu Yuxiang

Wu Yuxiang practiced hard and his *gongfu* became very good, but he did not particularly like teaching. He had a few students but only his nephew Li Yiyu (1832–1892) inherited Wu's technique. Li, whose other first name was Jinglun, wrote several good Taiji Quan classics, as his uncle had, and also shared with his uncle a dislike for teaching. Of his few students, only Hao He was good.

Li Yiyu

Hao He (1849–1920), whose private first name was Weizhan, was a powerfully built person who practiced diligently and became famous. He and his son Hao Yueru (1877–1935) were responsible for popularizing Wu style to such an extent that the style was occasionally referred to as Hao style.

In 1911, Hao He embarked on a journey to Beijing to visit a friend but fell sick along the way. When Sun Lutang (1861–1932), a famous martial arts master, heard about Hao's misfortune, he went to meet Hao and provide aid. In return for Sun's help, Hao taught him Taiji Quan. Sun had also studied Bagua Quan with Cheng Tinghua and Xingyi Quan with Li Kuiyuan, so he combined

Hao He

Sun-style Taiji Quan

Taiji, Bagua, and Xingyi concepts to create a new Taiji Quan style called Sun style.

Yang Style

Yang Luchan had three sons. The oldest, Yang Qi, was a farmer and never studied martial arts. The second, Yang Yu, whose private first name was Banhou, studied and then taught Taiji Quan, as did the third, Yang Jian, whose private first name was Jianhou. Both younger sons became famous. In the next generation of the Yang family, Yang Jianhou's sons, Yang Shaohou and Yang Chengfu, became well-known and through their teaching brought Taiji Quan into even greater favor.

Yang Banhou (1837–1892) received his education and learned basic *gongfu* in Wu Yuxiang's home when he was young and then practiced intensively with his father Yang Luchan. When his *gongfu* became good, he was made an instructor in the camp of the Emperor's security guard. He became famous for his fighting techniques and beat many famous masters, some of whom died in the process. His favorite punching technique was *banlan chui*.

Because of his mean and jealous disposition, however, Yang Banhou was not well liked. Even when he taught, he beat people very hard. Not surprisingly, he did not attract many students and for the most part, his skills were not passed down. He was wary by nature and did not like to show his skill. Fortunately, he was not successful in his many attempts to dissuade his father from teaching high-level techniques to numerous dedicated students for many years.

Yang Jianhou (1839–1917), also called Jinghu, was a much kinder man than his brother. As a youngster, he did not especially like martial arts but his father urged him very strongly to study Taiji Quan and eventually he complied. His *gongfu* became good, though not better than Yang Banhou's. He was, however, happy to help his father teach Taiji Quan, and he went on to teach many of his

own students, who benefited from his goodness as well as his knowledge. Some of his students became famous Taiji Quan masters, as did his sons Yang Zhaoxong and Yang Zhaoqing.

Yang Zhaoxong, also called Mengxiang and well known as Shaohou, was famous for his fighting skill. Because his favorite technique was *Lu* or rolling back, he got the nickname "Fei-Lu Yang Shaohou" which means that he could beat people with his *Lu* technique as if they were flies. His fractious personality, much like his uncle Yang Banhou's, led him to do just that. He beat even his students, of whom he soon had only a few. Yang Shaohou, impoverished in old age, committed suicide.

Yang Zhaoqing (1883–1936), whose private first name was Chengfu, was the most famous Yang-style Taiji Quan master. When he was young, he did not like martial arts and studied Taiji Quan only out of loyalty to family tradition. After his father died, he began to appreciate the importance of Taiji Quan to his family and practiced very hard, eventually becoming highly skilled. His internal force was especially notable. He was a nice person and traveled all over the country to teach many eager Taiji Quan students. His *gongfu* became the most popular style, and today when people talk of Yang-style Taiji Quan, they are usually referring to Yang Chengfu's style. In the 1950s, the Chinese government put forth a

Yang Banhou   **Yang Jianhou**   **Yang Shaohou**

Yang Chengfu

standard Taiji Quan short form with twenty-four postures based on Yang Chengfu's style.

Li Style—Taiji Wuxing Chui

Wang Lanting was a housekeeper in King Duan's household. When Yang Luchan taught King Duan, Wang joined in the lessons and by diligent practice became very skilled. One day he met a famous martial arts master named Li Ruidong. Li had excellent *gongfu* in Cuojiao and Fanzi, Chinese wrestling, and Longchan *gongfu*. He was also the successor of Jinchan Pei, the Golden Toad style. His nickname was "Bizi Li" or "Nose Li" because his nose was deformed. He was a longstanding supervisor of the Forbidden City Security Guard.

When Li and Wang met, they talked about their respective martial arts. Li thought he was very good but when Wang beat him, Li was shocked because he had always assumed that Taiji Quan was ineffective. Li decided to study Taiji Quan with Wang, and the two men became close friends and practice partners. Later, Wang introduced Li to Yang Luchan and listed Li's name under Yang's. Li understood Taiji Quan very well and advanced quickly. Soon other friends, like Li Binpu and Si Xingsan, joined Wang and Li and they all became blood brothers.

When Yang Luchan died, tradition dictated that his body be sent back to his hometown for burial. Wang Lanting wanted to help and so accompanied Yang's family on the trip. One night during the journey, Yang Banhou tackled Wang in his hotel room. He said: "My father always said that you practiced hard and had good *gongfu*. I would like to push hands with you right now." Wang thought Yang's attitude was friendly so he agreed.

When the push hands started, Yang felt that Wang was, indeed, very good and he became immediately jealous. Yang used a very hard technique to attack Wang. Recognizing Yang's ill will, Wang

became angry and said, "I know your personality, and I know you are jealous. If you don't approve of my practicing your father's *gongfu*, I will quit right now and promise never to practice your family style again."

Wang returned to Beijing at once and told Li Ruidong and his other friends what had happened. Li told Wang that Yang Luchan had trusted him and taught him very well and that he should not quit his style. He urged Wang to ignore Yang Banhou's jealousy and to keep practicing. Wang agreed that Li was right but felt that he had to stand by his vow, so Li suggested that they invent a new style. They worked together for years and succeeded in establishing a new style called Taiji Wuxing Chui.

Li Ruidong

This style combined Taiji concepts with the Jinchan style that Li Ruidong had learned from his master, the Buddhist monk Longchan who, some believe, had studied with Zhang Songxi. Because the primary techniques of the new style were the five fist punches of Taiji Quan, the new style was called Wuxing Chui or Five-Star Fist. It included four empty-hand forms and a variety of weapons forms. Most of the movements of this style require a very low stance so strong legs are necessary. It is probably for this reason that the style is not very popular today. Many people contributed to the development of the new style but Wang Lanting and Li Ruidong were the most important. Wang always remembered his promise and never did much teaching. Li taught this style to many students and made it famous. Today, it is generally known as Li-style Taiji Quan.

Chen Style

In October 1928, a middle-aged farmer came to Beijing. He was a simple man who did not like to talk and who dressed without adornment, but when he showed his martial art technique, he surprised all onlookers with the speed and power of his movements. His name was Chen Fake and he came from Chen Village. Using Chen-style Taiji Quan, he won competitions with many famous masters.

Chen Fake

Chen Fusheng (1887–1957), Chen Changxing's great-grandson, was well known as Chen Fake. He studied Chen-style Taiji Quan from a young age, practiced the form more than thirty times every day, and developed very good *gongfu*.

When Taiji Quan gained popularity and admiration in Beijing, people became curious about its origins and invited Chen to come to the city. Chen's Taiji Quan, especially the second form, was so different from other styles that a great debate was initiated and continues to the present. The first issue in the debate concerned the lineage of Taiji Quan—that is, who invented it. The second issue concerned the question of whether Chen-style Taiji Quan really belongs within the Taiji Quan family. Even the great master Chen Fake could not resolve these issues, but his indisputably excellent *gongfu* won many adherents and greatly increased the popularity of Chen-style Taiji Quan.

Today when people practice and research Chen-style Taiji Quan, they always mention the name of Chen Xin. He was the only person in the Chen family who kept a written record of Chen-style Taiji Quan principles. Chen Xin's (1849–1929) private first name was Pinsan, and he was born and raised in Chen Village. Although both his father and brother had good *gongfu*, his own was not outstanding. He noticed, though, that despite the fact that Taiji Quan had been practiced in Chen Village for many years, there were no good articles describing fundamental Chen-style Taiji Quan principles. He chose to devote twelve years to the writing of a now famous book called *The Book of Taiji Quan Illustrative Teaching Materials*. This book is highly revered in the Chen-style group and has become one of the most important Taiji Quan classics.

Wu Style

When Yang Luchan taught Taiji Quan in "Shenji Ying," the Emperor's security guard camp, only three people thoroughly mastered his techniques. They were Wan Chuan, Ling Shan, and Quan You.

Wan Chuan developed powerful internal force; Ling Shan had especially effective throwing skills; and Quan You was known for mastering all the details of every technique, especially the most important Taiji Quan skill *rou hua,* the use of softness to defend against hard attacks. Little is known today about Wan Chuan and Ling Shan because they did not teach very much and had no outstanding students who could inherit their techniques. Quan You's group, however, was large and gave rise to a new style.

Quan You was born in 1834 to a Manchurian family in Beijing. He liked martial arts and as a young man joined the Emperor's security guard, where he studied with Yang Luchan. He practiced very hard but like most people, he had trouble understanding Taiji Quan. One reason for this difficulty was that Yang did not like to reveal the details of his skills. After several years, Yang got sick and Quan You nursed him faithfully back to health. Recognizing the compassionate and loyal nature of Quan's character, Yang began to teach him Taiji Quan skills in complete detail. Quan You thought deeply about Taiji Quan principles and practiced hard so he advanced quickly and soon became very famous.

Because Quan You was Manchurian and at that time Yang Luchan was King Duan's Taiji Quan master, Yang could not accept Quan You as a disciple. According to Manchurian custom, Quan was considered a slave of the King and had to refer to King Duan as his master. If Yang accepted him as a disciple, he would then become the King's *gongfu* brother, an unthinkable breach of convention. Instead Quan You, Wan Chuan, and Ling Shan became Yang Banhou's disciples, according to Yang Luchan's order. Quan You died in 1902.

After the Republican Revolution, Quan You's family adopted Wu (tone 2) as its family name, and the style of Taiji Quan developed by his group became known as Wu style. Quan You was the first-generation master of Wu style.

Ei Shen, born in Beijing in 1870, was Quan You's son. He stud-

Wu Jianquan

ied Taiji Quan with his father from an early age, practiced hard, and grew into a fine man. After the Revolution, he adopted the Chinese name of Wu (tone 2) Jianquan and dedicated his life to teaching Taiji Quan. Until 1928, he taught in Beijing where Wu and other masters—including Wang Maozhai, Guo Fen, Liu Dekuan, Ji Zixiu, Xia Guixun, and Heng Tai—practiced together and did careful research into the principles and techniques of Taiji Quan. They developed many new skills and forms, especially weapons forms. In 1928, Wu went to southern China to teach Taiji Quan, and in 1935 he established the Jianquan Taiji Quan School in Shanghai. He died in Shanghai in 1942.

After Wu Jianquan passed away, his sons, daughter, and students continued to teach Wu style in Shanghai and abroad. In 1948, one of his sons taught in Hong Kong, and Wu style soon became famous in Southeast Asia and then in North America. Today, the three major groups of Wu-style practitioners are in Beijing, Shanghai, and Hong Kong.

My Taiji Quan Lineage

Wang Youlin, better known as Wang Maozhai, was Quan You's best student. He was born in Ye County, Shandong Province, in 1868. When he was young, he went to Beijing to study business administration but also liked martial arts and practiced several hard styles for many years. He often delivered building materials to the camp of the Emperor's security guard, where a variety of famous masters demonstrated and taught their skills. Whenever he was there, he watched the students practicing and found himself particularly drawn to Quan You's Taiji Quan style.

He asked Quan You to be his teacher, but Quan You reserved his answer until he had tested the strength of Wang's desire. He taught Wang only one position, called Golden Cock Standing On One Leg, and required Wang to study and practice only this one position for seven months. Wang complied with great dedication and without complaint, and Quan was duly impressed by Wang's patience and commitment to practice. Quan recognized that Wang was deserving of detailed and intensive Taiji Quan instruction. Wang was thirty-two years old when Quan accepted him as a student.

Wang Maozhai

Wang Maozhai's business was successful and he was able to open his own building materials company. Although he practiced hard and achieved good *gongfu*, he did not really understand Taiji Quan so his progress stalled. He needed one more step to advance. One day, on a visit to his hometown, he saw stonemasons working beside the road outside his village. He stopped and watched.

At first he thought only that it was interesting to see how they worked, but then he had a sudden insight and realized the deep relationship between the qualities of hard and soft. The stonemasons' hammers, for example, were heavy and force was needed to wield them, but he also noted that the stonemasons were relaxed as they made their hammer strikes. At last he began to grasp the essence of Taiji Quan. While home, he kept thinking and practicing and made great leaps in his understanding of Taiji Quan. When he returned to Beijing a few days later, he surprised his friends with his newfound skill. At the age of fifty-two, he was beating all challengers and had achieved the highest level of Taiji Quan mastery.

Wang did not have much time to teach because of the pressures of running his burgeoning business. He did establish the Beijing Taimiao Temple Taiji Quan Institute, which soon became the biggest Taiji Quan school in Beijing. Wang managed to visit the school every day but only as a spectator. Every evening at home, he gave private lessons to his indoor disciples. He transmitted all his knowl-

Yang Yuting

edge to his senior disciple Yang Yuting, who then taught the many students at the school.

In 1928, Mr. Wang Xiaolai, the president of the Shanghai Business Association, invited Wang Maozhai to teach Taiji Quan in Shanghai, but Wang did not want to leave Beijing. He recommended his *gongfu* brother Wu Jianquan for the post, so Wu set out for Shanghai and once there quickly became very famous throughout southern China.

The frequently heard expression "south Wu and north Wang" reflected the widespread view that the two most famous Taiji Quan masters of the time were teaching simultaneously—Wu in the south and Wang in the north. Wang Maozhai died in 1940 in a melancholy frame of mind because his second son had been killed in an accident.

Of all the styles practiced in Beijing at that time, Quan You's Wu-style Taiji Quan, practiced under the leadership of Wang Maozhai, was the most popular and well known. After Wang's death, Yang Yuting (1887–1982) became the leader of the group, and during the more than seventy years that he taught Taiji Quan, thousands of people studied with him. In the next generation, Wang Peisheng succeeded Yang as the group's leader.

Wang Peisheng was born in Wuqing County, Hebei Province. His official first name is Liquan, and his special literary name is Yin Cheng. From the age of twelve, he studied Yin-style Bagua Quan with Ma Gui, and when he was thirteen, he began his study of Taiji Quan with Yang Yuting.

Later, because of his exceptional talent in martial arts, Wang had the opportunity to study directly with his grandmaster Wang Maozhai, who showed his regard for the new student by training him intensively. For many years, Wang Peisheng was received in Wang Maozhai's home every evening for private lessons. His *gongfu* advanced quickly, and when he was eighteen he started to teach. Besides Taiji Quan, Wang developed superior skill in Bagua Zhang,

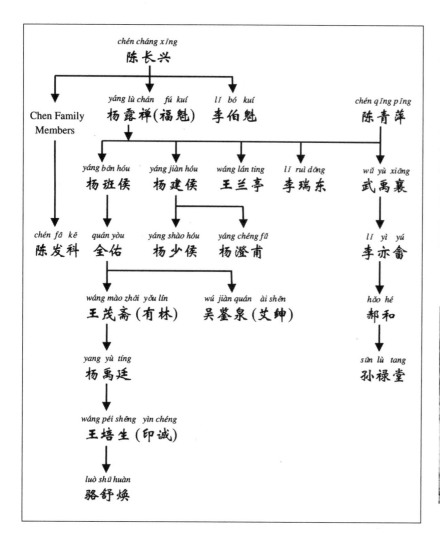

Wang Peisheng

Luo Shuhuan

Part of the Taiji Quan lineage

Xingyi Quan, Tantui (Spring Leg), Baji Quan, Shaolin Quan, Tongbei Quan, Chinese wrestling, Qinna, *qigong,* and Chinese medicine. He also gained thorough knowledge of traditional Chinese philosophy, art, and religion.

In 1953, Wang Peisheng developed a new Taiji Quan form known as the Thirty-Seven Posture Form. Derived from traditional Wu-style Taiji Quan, it was not invented simply by omitting postures from the traditional form. Rather, it included the basic character-

istics of the traditional form while also summarizing Wang Peisheng's personal experiences and research. It is a very efficient form to practice and was the first Chinese Taiji Quan short form ever developed. It was followed in 1990 by the Sixteen-Posture Form, another Taiji Quan short form designed by Wang Peisheng.

Wang Peisheng has many students in China and in foreign countries. Luo Shuhuan, who started studying Taiji Quan with Wang when he was thirteen years old, is Wang's senior disciple. In 1968, I started my Taiji Quan studies with Luo. In 1976, Master Luo sent me and some of his other students to the home of his master, Wang Peisheng, for intensive training. Starting that year, I studied directly with my Grandmaster Wang. In 1984, Master Luo accepted me and some of his other students as indoor disciples.

Basic Principles and Features of Taiji Quan

The central principle of Taiji Quan derives from one of the most fundamental concepts in traditional Chinese culture. The concept first appeared in *Yi Jing* (*I Ching*), the book written about 1000 BC that delineates the laws of universal change; the *yi* in the title means "changing." A famous line in *Yi Jing* asserts, "There is *taiji* in *yi,* the laws of change, and *liangyi* is generated from it. *Liangyi,* in turn, generates *sixiang* and *sixiang* generates *bagua.*" Also stated is the principle that "one *yin* and one *yang* united comprise Dao." Here, the term Dao is synonymous with *taiji.*

Yi Jing played a central role in the development of Chinese philosophy. Its profound ideas were seized upon by such renowned thinkers as Kongzi (Confucius) who formulated Confucianism, and Laozi, who originated the tenets of Daoism. The influence of *Yi Jing* has permeated every aspect of traditional Chinese culture.

Laozi, for example, said that *wuji,* meaning the "state of nothingness or non-being," is the beginning state of the universe; and that *you* or *taiji,* which means "having" or "being," is the mother

of all things. He posited that everything in the universe is generated from *you*, and that *you* is generated from *wu*. "I do not know the name for the mother of all things," he said, "so I just call it Dao." "All things," he declared, "convey *yin* and hold *yang*."

In the millennium that followed the founding of Daoism by Laozi, the Taiji principle was further refined, eventually reaching maturity with the contributions of Chen Tuan and successive generations of his students. Chen Tuan (?–989), a famous scholar and Daoist priest, devoted his life to the study and research of *Yi Jing*, the philosophies of Laozi, and the health practices of *qigong*. His thinking may also have prefigured the martial arts, and the followers of some styles claim him as their founder. The diagram of *Taiji* has been purported either to have been invented by him or to have been passed down by him. Many of his writings had a profound influence on Chinese culture. His article "Xian Tian Tu" or "The Pre-birth Diagram" included a depiction of the basic *qigong* practice principle.

In accordance with Chen's central ideas, the famous scholar Zhou Dunyi, Chen's third-generation disciple, wrote a famous article called "Taiji Tu Shuo" or "The Explanation of the *Taiji* Diagram," in which the *taiji* principle as we know it today is described systematically and completely. This work includes the *Taiji* diagram first presented by Chen Tuan but explicates the illustration differently. Later, the famous Song Dynasty philosopher Zhu Xi provided annotations and explanations for Zhou's article. Together these writings elucidated the standard definition of the *taiji* principle and formed the foundation of the Daoist worldview.

Taiji Quan is based on the *taiji* principle that expresses the traditional Chinese view of the origin of the universe. *Tai* means "immense" or "great"; *ji* means "extreme" or "limit." The term "*taiji*" thus describes a great principle that applies to everything. In

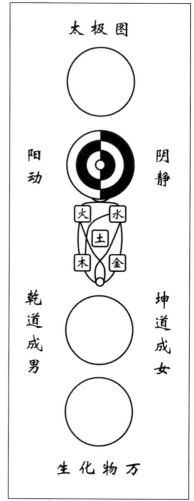

The Diagram of Taiji

traditional Chinese culture, Taiji is the same as Dao; both refer to the basic, all-encompassing natural law of the universe. All things must be in harmony with Dao in order to prosper or function well. The *taiji* principle is expressed in all aspects of traditional Chinese culture.

According to the *taiji* concept, the world started from *wuji*, a state of nothingness or non-being, or a homogeneous mixture of all things sometimes likened to a cloud. *Wuji* describes the universe in its most primal form, before there was any differentiation of matter. When the universe began to emerge from the *wuji* state, *yin qi* (*yin* energy) and *yang qi* (*yang* energy) were created and became differentiated. The *yang qi*, which was light in weight, rose up to form the sky; and the *yin qi*, which was heavy, sank down to form the earth. With the differentiation of *yin* and *yang*, the life of the universe started from this new state called *taiji*. *Taiji* state is the source of all things, so sometimes people like to say *taiji* is mother of all things. The *taiji* principle became the most important concept in ancient Chinese cosmology.

In the *taiji* state, *yin* and *yang* do not exist as separate entities. Although they can be conceptually distinguished, each contains the other and cannot be considered alone. In the next emergent state called *liangyi* or the "two appearances," *yin* and *yang* become distinct and separate entities. Each can be independently considered in terms of its unique qualities. *Liangyi* gives rise to the state of *sixiang* or the "four shapes"; and *sixiang*, in turn, generates *bagua* or the "eight trigrams." The eight trigrams can be combined to form sixty-four *gua* or hexagrams, and in this manner the universe evolves from the simplest beginning to a complex of myriad forms. Everything is created from the emergence and changing energies of *yin* and *yang*. This is the key principle of *taiji*.

In traditional Chinese philosophy, *yin* and *yang* describe opposing qualities or concepts, but these qualities also support each other. Each exists because the other exists; the existence of one necessar-

ily implies the existence of the other. *Yin* and *yang* complement each other, and each is capable of changing its state and emerging as the other. Although used as abstract concepts, *yin* and *yang* can also be applied to the description of concrete objects.

The usual attributes of *yin* include soft, quiet, passive, obedient, receptive, restorative, substantial, internal, and beneath. In the physical world, *yin* is associated with the earth, moon, darkness, cold, and femaleness. The usual attributes of *yang* include hard, moving, initiating, guiding, giving, releasing, insubstantial, external, and above. In the physical world, *yang* is associated with the sky, sun, heat, light, and maleness.

In Taiji Quan practice, the concepts of *yin* and *yang* are used ubiquitously in the description of techniques. The back of the body, for example, is *yin* and the front is *yang*; the lower part of the body is *yin* and the upper part is *yang*. When a palm faces the body, it is called a *yin* palm; when it faces away from the body, it is called a *yang* palm. The leg that supports the weight of the body is called *yin*; the unweighted leg is called *yang*. Soft movement is *yin* and hard movement is *yang*. Defense is *yin* and offense is *yang*. It is commonly said that Taiji Quan is about *yin* and *yang*.

Taiji Quan was clearly derived from the *taiji* principle in traditional philosophy. In the most famous and important Taiji Quan classic, the first sentences state: "*Taiji*, born of *wuji*, is the potential for either *dong* (movement) or *jing* (stillness), the potential for a state of being that is either dynamic or static. It is the mother or the source of *yin* and *yang*." This passage describes the basic concept of *taiji* and signals that a martial art bearing its name must follow its principles. It also defines the principle of Taiji Quan. It is very important to keep the *taiji* principle in mind at all times while training and to apply it devotedly in practice. If an action does not obey the *taiji* principle, then it is not a Taiji Quan skill.

The main ideas encompassed by the *taiji* principle and explained in Zhou Dunyi's article, "The Explanation of the *Taiji* Diagram," are:

dòng   jìng

动 静

1. *Wuji* becomes *taiji*. This is called Dao, the fundamental, universal law of nature. Dao is invisible and controls every aspect of the universe.

2. The two basic attributes in Dao are *dong* (movement) and *jing* (stillness). *Dong's* attribute is *yang* and *jing's* attribute is *yin*. *Yin* and *yang*, as carriers of Dao called *qi*, make Dao manifest. This is expressed in the classics as "one *yin* and one *yang* together are Dao." *Yin* and *yang* must be attached to *qi* before Dao can be made visible and applied.

   In *liangyi*, *yin* and *yang* separate. Movement generates *yang*; but when movement reaches its limit, stillness arises. Stillness generates *yin*. When stillness reaches its limit, movement is reborn. Movement, thus, is the root of stillness and stillness the root of movement. This does not mean, however, that movement and stillness are the beginning or end of each other. There is no beginning and end. The life of the universe proceeds in never-ending cycles.

3. In *taiji*, *yin* exists because *yang* exists, and *yang* exists because *yin* exists. *Yin* and *yang* support each other and can transmute into each other. *Yang qi* generates maleness, and *yin qi* generates femaleness. These two basic *qi* are expressions of the law of nature and create all things.

4. *Yang* contains some *yin*, and *yin* contains some *yang*.

5. Everything is generated from *yin* and *yang*. They give birth to endless change and development. All change follows the basic principle of Dao or Taiji.

6. Taiji or Dao is the fundamental principle. It encompasses the whole universe yet is small enough to reside in the tiniest fragments of matter. It dwells in everything and extends everywhere. The starting point for this principle is the concept of "*wu zhong sheng you*," which holds that "being" or "having" comes from "non-being" or "not having."

As *taiji* is born from *wuji* and is the source of *yin* and *yang*, there should be no intention or movement as you begin your Taiji Quan practice. This condition reflects the original *wuji* state. When an attack comes and you start to react, you enter the *taiji* state in which *yin* and *yang* are generated according to your opponent's movements. Because all skills follow the *yin-yang* principle, it is sometimes said that Taiji Quan is the practice of *yin* and *yang* skills. Because everything in Taiji Quan derives from the change, conversion, and development of *yin* and *yang*, an understanding of the principle and practice of *yin* and *yang* is clearly vital to your training.

The most important thing to understand in your training is the relationship between dynamic and static states, between movement and stillness. Change is a permanent state, but stillness must always be maintained internally. Stillness is a temporary state, but the tendency for change must always be kept alive within. The existence of each state always implies the existence of the other. This is a very difficult point to understand and distinguishes Taiji Quan from all other martial art styles. Other styles apply *yin* and *yang* as separate concepts and express the *liangyi* state. It is intuitively easier to understand dynamic and static states as separate and distinct than it is to conceive of them together as a single potential for both movement and stillness.

The integration of *yin* and *yang* is often called "keeping the center." The usual term for this in Taiji Quan is *zhong ji* or central limit. It is also referred to as *xuan*, which means "mystery" or "darkness." *Xuan* is described in a famous passage as "the mystery that can be either *yin* or *yang* or neither *yin* nor *yang*. Mystery upon mystery, it is the doorway leading to the refined understanding of all concepts."

Since Taiji Quan is founded on the principle of *taiji*, this principle must infuse your practice at all times. All discussions and expressions of *taiji* should include an understanding of *yin* and *yang*. In Taiji Quan practice, *yin* is expressed in responses that are soft, sub-

stantial, still, passive, and that yield to the movements of the opponent; *yang* is expressed in responses that are hard, insubstantial, moving, active, and that lead or direct the opponent. Defense skills are usually characterized as *yin* because they are receptive or passive; offensive skills are usually characterized as *yang* because they initiate action. It is important to remember that in Taiji Quan all action and reaction must be consistent with the *yin-yang* principle as expressed in the *Taiji* circle. Inside this circle, *yin* and *yang* are in a state of continuous change and mutual support.

You must always be aware of the opportunity or potential for either movement or stillness. This requires that you avoid all preconceived notions or plans for what to do next. Every action must be based solely on your feeling at the moment. In push hands, for example, when you touch your opponent you should maintain *wuji* by not planning your response. When you receive information from touching your opponent, you enter *taiji* by either attacking (which expresses movement) or defending (which expresses stillness). Your choice should depend only on your feeling. Keep in mind that your attack also encompasses your defense; and your defense contains within it your next attack.

In most martial arts, whether simple or complex, the techniques used in practice and fighting are the same. The purpose of practice is to be able to apply these techniques directly in fighting. Taiji Quan practice is different in that it focuses on the expression of the *taiji* principle. The skills practiced are designed to illustrate this principle and to help students develop responses that apply the principle correctly. There is no training of preset sequences of movement that can be repeated directly in fighting situations. Rather, the skills are applied solely in response to the student's immediate feelings during a fight. This is a specialized ability developed only in Taiji Quan training, which is said to have no techniques; movement itself is the method.

Another distinction between Taiji Quan and the other martial

arts is that in the latter, offensive and defensive skills are practiced and applied separately. Even if they are performed simultaneously, they are experienced internally as separate. This method expresses the *liangyi* state, and the skills developed are *liangyi* skills. In Taiji Quan skills, *yin* and *yang* are inextricably bound together, with each one generating the other.

In Taiji Quan practice, internal training is emphasized much more than external training. All physical movement should occur naturally without conscious intent or a sense of restriction. It should start from a state of nothingness or insubstantiality that nevertheless has limitless potential. This method proceeds from *wuji* to *taiji*. In Taiji Quan practice, the mind and heart should be quiet, reflecting stillness, but this stillness is not synonymous with an absence of movement. There is movement inside stillness and it can be initiated by the slightest touch.

Although Taiji Quan practice involves constant change expressed as movement, this movement does not imply the absence of stillness. There is stillness inside movement so that an inner sense of calm and quiet can be maintained even during the most vigorous activity. This is referred to as *bao yuan shou yi* or maintaining the original *shen, yi,* and *qi* and keeping the focus on Dao. The key to Taiji Quan is the interacting potential of movement and stillness.

Given that *yin* and *yang* skills contain each other and can be transformed seamlessly from one to the other, it is always the case that during an attack, whenever the defense component becomes greater than the offense component, the movement is changed from an attack to a defense. A defensive movement can be changed to an attack in a similar manner. This gradual exchange of attack and defense is called *zhuan hua,* and it should occur as a smooth and slow dissolution of one into the other. *Zhuan hua* also occurs when *yin* converts to *yang* and *yang* converts to *yin*.

zhuăn huà

转化

In *taiji, yin* and *yang* are always in balance. It is not possible to shift abruptly from one to the other like a digital switch. Such a

chā yì

差异

dichotomous change is called *cha yi,* and it illustrates the way *yin* and *yang* are usually understood and applied in martial arts other than Taiji Quan. When *yin* and *yang* are applied in Taiji Quan, *zhuan hua* is the more descriptive concept and one of most important to understand. The contrast between *zhuan hua* and *cha yi* is another key difference between Taiji Quan and other martial arts.

When the *taiji* principle and its related concepts are applied to fighting situations, the basic fighting principle of Taiji Quan emerges. This principle holds that one must use the most efficient way to win a fight. It shapes the training method of Taiji Quan and differentiates Taiji Quan from other martial arts.

Although the physical movements of Taiji Quan are similar to those used in other martial arts, they arise from internal events rather than from observable events. In most martial arts, the goal is to increase power; in Taiji Quan you should constantly be asking yourself how to reduce your force and still win. The goal is to achieve maximum efficiency and the appearance of "small force." If the goal is reached, a less physically powerful person can defeat a more powerful opponent. To attain this result, a specific method of practice is needed.

Taiji Quan strategies for achieving the highest efficiency in fighting include: borrowing force from your opponent and turning the force back against him; luring your opponent to move in for an attack and then pulling back into emptiness; and using four ounces to defend against a thousand pounds. The basic skills used are: *zhan* which means "to stick to and bounce up"; *nian* which means "to adhere to"; *lian* which means "to link"; and *sui* which means "to follow." All the techniques of Taiji Quan are based on these four skills, and sensitivity is a prerequisite for developing each of them. Sensitivity allows you to apprehend your opponent's plans and capacities as well as to understand your own.

zhān   *nián*   *lián*   *suí*

沾　黏　连　随

The highest level of achievement in Taiji Quan training is the ability to "use four ounces to beat a thousand pounds." As this adage suggests, if you are exerting 100 units of force to beat 200 units, you are already in the right mode of practice, and further practice will improve your skill. To become more efficient, you must borrow force from your opponent. This, in turn, requires that you induce him to commit himself to an attack and then follow his movement until you sense a vulnerability in his offense. You must, in other words, "lure him into emptiness" by yielding and following. To do this, you need a well-developed sense of timing and direction. This in turn depends on your ability to identify and locate *yin* and *yang* and to understand *jin* or internal force. All of this is possible only if you develop your sensitivity so that you are able to know yourself and your opponent.

Analysis of the Taiji Quan Training Method

Because of its principle and special features, the training method of Taiji Quan is very different from that of other martial art styles. For empty-hand skill training, there are four steps: basic *gongfu* training; form training; push hands training; and fight training. These training practices allow you to reach the three levels of *gongfu* skill: *zhao shu, dong jin,* and *shen ming.* The Taiji Quan classics specify that *zhao shu,* which is a familiarity with techniques, gradually leads to *dong jin,* which is an understanding of the use of trained force. This knowledge leads step by step to *shen ming,* which is the highest level of skill and signals a complete understanding of the *taiji* principle.

In the term *zhao shu, zhao* means "technique" and *shu* can be understood as being familiar with or knowing a subject very well, being perfect, being proficient, or being skilled. Literally though, *shu* means "ripe" and when used with *zhao* indicates that it takes time to master techniques. It is necessary at the outset of your train-

zhāo shú
着熟

dǒng jìn
懂劲

shén míng
神明

ing to practice every technique repeatedly until you can do it very well. It may take a long time for the movements and techniques you practice to become the natural responses of your body and to be fully synchronized with the changing mental focus that accompanies all your movements.

Dong jin is the second level of Taiji Quan practice, marking the achievement of true Taiji Quan skill. *Dong* means "understanding" and *jin*, commonly translated as "internal force" or "internal strength," is a trained force that is very different from the simple kind of muscle strength most people normally use. Trained force can be developed only through extended practice. After you have practiced Taiji Quan techniques correctly for a long time, training both your mind and body, you will notice that the quality of your internal awareness changes. You will have new feelings and sensations that will deepen your understanding of the *taiji* principle and allow your training to proceed at a more advanced level.

As your understanding of Taiji Quan gradually deepens from *zhao shu*, you will be able to learn how to apply the principle of *taiji* to the use of *jin*. If you reach the level of *dong jin*, you will have understood the true meaning of Taiji Quan, and you will be using true trained force when you apply Taiji Quan techniques rather than external muscle power. Because the correct use of *jin*, like everything else in Taiji Quan, requires an understanding of *yin* and *yang*, reaching the level of *dong jin* indicates that the *taiji* principle has been incorporated into your use of *jin*.

In the term *shen ming, shen* means "spirit" or "god" and *ming* means "bright," "clear," or "illuminated." *Shen ming* denotes enlightenment and refers to the achievement of the highest possible level of Taiji Quan skill. It can be attained only through a complete understanding of the *taiji* principle. *Shen* in Chinese also means "incredible effect," something that only gods or immortals can accomplish. In Taiji Quan, it refers to skills that surpass normal human abilities.

The *dong jin* level signifies a correct understanding of Taiji Quan, and from this point on, correct progress is virtually guaranteed. You will know what to do in every circumstance and will be approaching the highest level of skill. There is only one path to this level of understanding and it requires practice that is diligent and unwavering.

Because the principles and techniques of most martial arts other than Taiji Quan are based on natural instincts and abilities, most students can understand them relatively quickly and easily. Hard practice will usually bring visible progress. With Taiji Quan, however, the guiding principle is difficult to understand and the skills, which are not based on natural abilities and instincts, may at first seem entirely confounding.

However difficult it is to describe Taiji Quan principles and techniques clearly, using them correctly in practice is far more difficult. Beginning students may easily become discouraged. For a long time, progress is usually very slow, if discernible at all. During this time, do not be surprised if you can perform a technique well occasionally but be unable to reproduce the correct response when you try to repeat it. You should also expect that longer and harder practice will not always translate into more rapid progress. Sometimes intense practice may even lead you farther astray. Once you have gained a deeper insight into the true meaning of the *taiji* principle, your practice cannot go wrong, but before you have achieved such knowledge, it is quite easy to make mistakes that can become hardened into habits by repeated incorrect practice.

Once you reach the *dong jin* level, harder practice will translate directly into faster progress. You are on the right path and cannot make mistakes as long as your practice adheres to the *taiji* principle. At this stage,

Taiji Quan Form Practice, Single Whip

Taiji Quan Form Practice, Brush Knee and Twist Step

you have achieved an understanding of Taiji Quan concepts and have incorporated the *taiji* principle into your practice. With enough time and persistent effort and dedication, you will be able to reach the highest level of practice.

Form practice is the most important training practice for building a sound foundation in Taiji Quan. It develops the external physical components of strength and relaxation, stability and nimbleness, and the coordination, flow, and vigor of movements. It can also increase your internal power and develop the internal components. It increases the focus of *shen* or spirit, the concentration of *yi* or mind, and the gathering of *qi*. Finally, form practice enhances the integration of the internal and external components.

To practice form, you first need to make sure that all your movements are correct. Correct movements promote the feelings and insights that will help you advance more quickly. The many benefits of form training come only from slow yet internally animated and relaxed practice done on a daily basis.

You should also practice the applications of each movement and be very careful to follow the *taiji* principle rather than the hard-style approach espoused in the external martial arts. The most important goal of form training is the integration of internal and external components. This and all the other aspects of form practice should be guided by *yi* or mind. The ability to use your mind rather than force is considered a foremost accomplishment in Taiji Quan.

Push hands practice is essential to your training regimen because it, too, promotes understanding of Taiji Quan skills. It will help

you concentrate on the details of every skill and increase your balance, control, and ability to change skills effortlessly. Push hands practice can refine your skills more effectively than any other kind of training.

To practice push hands, you should first focus on *zhan, nian, lian,* and *sui.* These comprise the foundation for all skills, and each relies on sensitivity, which encompasses many features. Sensitivity refers to the ability to sense precisely the balance, force, and intent of your opponent. Regarding balance, sensitivity means that you can tell when your opponent's balance is stable or unstable and, if it is unstable, when and in which direction you can most easily gain control of him. With respect to force, sensitivity means that you can tell when your opponent wants to use force and how much force he will release in any direction. You can also anticipate both the point of impact of the force and how to defend against it in the most efficient way. Finally, sensitivity allows you to know what is in your opponent's mind—not only what he is doing and to what end, but also what he plans to do.

Push hands practice, like form practice, yields its benefits only after long training. You must be patient. Fixed routines should be practiced for a long time before freestyle training is undertaken. Always keep in mind that push hands training will lead you to a more complete understanding of Taiji Quan. Push hands is not meant to be a competition or fighting match with your training partner. When you practice push hands, you should pay great attention to the correct use of the *taiji* principle and no attention to whether you win or lose. If you always want to win in push hands training, it will be difficult if not impossible to understand real Taiji Quan skill. There are spe-

Taiji Push Hands Solo Practice

Taiji Push Hands Practice

cialized Taiji Quan training methods for learning to fight; push hands provides the foundation for all of them.

While push hands training can help you understand the true nature of Taiji Quan, fight training can help you learn how to apply this understanding to combat situations. The skills and principles of push hands do not differ fundamentally from those of fighting; only the speed and intensity of the skills differentiate the two situations. In push hands training, skills are usually executed more slowly and less intensely than in fight training, but with repeated practice these same skills can be swiftly and effectively used in a real fight.

Fight training includes freestyle (no rules) and moving-step push hands training, both of which are extremely helpful for developing fighting ability. The controlling skills often emphasized in push hands training also help develop fighting technique. In most combat situations, if you can control your opponent, the fight will quickly be over and you will prevail. You will also have the option of throwing your opponent once you gain control.

Taiji Quan Fighting Practice

In addition to controlling and throwing skills, you also need to learn how to deliver hard, injurious strikes. All such strikes must conform to the Taiji Quan principle, which dictates that the timing, location, and direction of each strike should be maximally efficient. In Taiji Quan, striking is usually most efficient once your opponent has lost control and balance, at which point he will be in a difficult position to defend himself, and your strike can easily hurt him. Because of the risk of serious injury in this kind of training, it is often

ignored, leaving the mistaken impression that Taiji Quan cannot be used for combat.

In Taiji Quan fight training, the most important skill is *jie shou*. *Jie* means "to connect," "link," or "be in contact with"; *shou* means "hand" and in this context refers to your opponent's attack movement. *Jie shou* describes ways to make contact with your opponent, and it will be a new element in your training because push hands—the focus of the preceding training step—usually starts with the two opponents touching each other. Only in fight training is it important to know how to make initial contact with your opponent.

The basic principle of *jie shou* skill is never to resist the pressure of your opponent's touch. You should instead always make contact by following his movement. This is difficult for beginners because it is not a natural reaction, but there are some training methods that can help students develop the response of following the opponent's force. Practice should proceed step by step from contact that occurs slowly to contact that is initiated very quickly.

Form and push hands are the core aspects of all Taiji Quan training. Form provides the foundation for all other training, and push hands develops an understanding of Taiji Quan skills. With this understanding, fight training will be relatively easy and fighting skills can be mastered. Without such understanding, your fighting skills will not express the *taiji* principle and no matter how victorious you may be, you will not be using true Taiji Quan skills.

✪ Bagua Zhang

bā guà zhǎng

八卦掌

The philosophical doctrine of *bagua* originated from Chinese cosmology in deep antiquity. Generally attributed to the sage Fu Xi six to seven thousand years ago, the system conceptualized eight *(ba)* trigrams *(gua)* that were thought to express natural phenomena and explicate the laws by which changes occur in nature. These trigrams were also considered useful for foretelling events.

About three thousand years ago during the Zhou Dynasty, the laws of change were further elaborated by the king Zhou Wenwang while he was imprisoned by a rival king. Zhou Wenwang's great work, known as the *Yi Jing*, was edited about five hundred years later by Kongzi, more commonly known as Confucius, one of the greatest Chinese thinkers. Confucius definitively elucidated the philosophy of *bagua*, and his opus became a cornerstone of traditional Chinese culture and later, an important component of Daoism.

Bagua Zhang, also called Bagua Quan or simply Bagua, is a Chinese martial art based on the idea of *bagua*. The term *zhang* means "palm" and indicates that Bagua Zhang includes many palm techniques. In fewer than two hundred years, many famous masters have been trained in Bagua Zhang and in the process have extended its techniques. Today Bagua Zhang—the youngest brother in the traditional internal martial arts family—is popular and well known, but many of its essential features are gradually disappearing.

History, Lineage, and Styles

Dong Haichuan and Bagua Zhang

No one knows with certainty who created Bagua Zhang, but Dong Haichuan was the first person to teach it publicly and is usually regarded as the inventor of this art. He is respected as the first-generation master of Bagua Zhang.

Dong Haichuan was born on October 13, 1797, in Zhu-Jia-Wu, the Zhu family village of Wen-An County, Hebei Province. When he was young he studied Shaolin Shiba Luohan (Eighteen Buddha) Quan and practiced it with great dedication. As his *gongfu* improved, he traveled through the country searching for an excellent master of a high-level martial art. It is not known where he went or what happened to him during his quest, but after many years he appeared in Beijing, where he demonstrated a very special *gongfu* and related an intriguing tale.

In this story, he said that he had traveled to many places and met many masters, but nobody could satisfy his desire for a high-level martial art. Adhering to a belief commonly held at that time that if you wanted to find a wise person, you should go to high mountain, he went to the Jiuhua Mountain in Anhui Province, where he found a young boy practicing martial arts on a big rock. The boy's movements were unlike any Dong had ever seen. He watched for a long time and then asked the boy what style he was practicing. The boy replied that he didn't know what to call his movements but practiced them only according to his master's instructions. When Dong asked if his skills were good for real fighting, the boy smilingly challenged Dong to a competition. Dong sprang onto the rock, fought with the boy, and much to his surprise was soundly defeated.

Dong knew that he had found the martial art he desired and asked the boy to introduce him to his master. The boy hesitated but Dong persisted, and eventually the boy led him to a small thatched cottage on the mountainside. Bi Dengxia, the old Daoist priest who lived there, asked Dong many questions and then accepted Dong as his disciple. Dong lived in the cottage and studied with Bi for more than ten years.

Dong Haichuan

According to Dong's story, Master Bi's *gongfu* was very special. First he taught Dong to walk the circle and then he taught Dong the many changes that can be performed while circle-walking. He taught Dong the philosophical concepts of *bagua* and instructed him in the acquisition and use of internal force. Dong practiced every posture very carefully each day and thought of how to develop each one. He also studied Daoism because he knew that any high-

level study must be based on a thorough understanding of high-level principles. Through his diligent and intelligent efforts, Dong earned Bi's admiration and affection.

One day Master Bi told Dong that he had learned all that Bi could teach, all that Bi himself knew. He advised Dong to descend the mountain that day and start a new life. He assured Dong that with continued practice, he would become an outstanding master. Dong wanted to stay with Master Bi and was despondent at the thought of leaving, but the Master said that departure was necessary so Dong obediently resumed his travels. In the years that followed he visited many places, won many fights, and finally headed for Beijing.

The Manchurians who ruled the Qing Dynasty loved martial arts. The Emperor routinely invited good masters to teach his special army and security guards and often members of the royal family as well. Good masters had many opportunities to teach and develop their skills during this golden age of the martial arts.

When Dong Haichuan went to Beijing, he wanted to observe the skills of these masters before demonstrating his own skills. He was hired as a servant to the family of the Emperor's brother King Su, who was (like his brother) fond of martial arts and who had invited many famous masters to his palace. Sha Huizi, the supervisor of the king's security guards, was the best of these masters, and Sha's wife Ma Jinfeng was also a respected master.

One day King Su threw a large party. Amid the crowd of revelers, all the servants except Dong were having a difficult time passing through the throng. Dong, on the other hand, was able to walk rapidly among the guests without touching anyone. The king noticed this and was amazed. He asked Dong how he managed his job so well and guessed that Dong must practice a martial art. When Dong confirmed the king's conjecture, the king asked if Dong would give a small demonstration of his skill.

Dong went to the yard and performed his Shaolin forms, but the

king expressed doubt that this was all Dong knew and politely asked Dong to demonstrate his best skills. Accordingly, Dong performed the very special and beautiful techniques that Master Bi had taught him. The techniques were exciting to watch. The movements changed constantly and looked very useful, leaving the onlookers speechless. None of them had ever before seen a style like this.

When Dong finished, the king asked him what his style was called. It was a fair question, and although a king's questions must always be answered, Dong was silent for several awkward moments. Master Bi had never mentioned the name of his art. Quickly, Dong thought of the *bagua* principles he had learned from Master Bi and answered, "It is Bagua Zhang."

The king was delighted and asked for more information about the new art. Dong explained the basic ideas and skills of Bagua Zhang, and the king declared Dong a great master. Dong was immediately promoted from servant to member of the king's security guard and was congratulated by everyone except Sha Huizi, the angry and jealous supervisor of the security guards.

Sha Huizi resented the fact that everyone thought Dong Haichuan was great and wanted to prove that he himself was still the best fighter in the palace. He asked the king to allow him to challenge Dong. The king, of course, was eager to see such a match and asked Dong if he would accept the challenge. Dong agreed and the fight began. Sha executed all of his techniques very forcefully in an attempt to kill Dong but because of Dong's ability to remain relaxed, his internal force was very strong, stable, and quick. He defended himself but did not attack often. Everyone saw this and understood that Dong could have easily beaten Sha but was too considerate to do so. Sha also sensed this and relinquished the fight, blushing with shame. When the king replaced Sha with Dong as supervisor of the security guard, Sha's hatred of Dong grew even stronger and he vowed to seek revenge.

Knowing that Dong could not be beaten in a public challenge,

Sha and his wife Ma Jinfeng planned to assassinate him. One night after everyone had gone to bed, Sha wielded a sword and Ma carried a gun as they crept quietly into Master Dong's bedchamber. Much to their surprise, the room appeared to be empty. Suddenly Dong dropped down from the ceiling, quickly seized both weapons, and subdued Sha and Ma. The two would-be assassins knew they would die if Dong took them to the king and reported what they had done. They begged Dong to allow them to run away and promised in return that they would respect Dong always as their master. They also vowed that they would leave Beijing and never return. A compassionate man, Dong agreed, and that very night Sha and Ma fled to northeast China. They taught martial arts and became locally famous. Many years later, when Dong was old, Sha is thought to have broken his promise and, still seeking revenge, secretly returned to Beijing and murdered Ma Weiqi, one of Master Dong's most famous students.

On the day he demonstrated his *gongfu* in the king's courtyard, Dong Haichuan became instantly famous. He had a good job and made many loyal friends with whom he practiced and researched the martial arts. He was widely regarded as the greatest master of his time, and many students sought him out. Often challenged to prove his skills in combat, he was always victorious.

In addition to Dong, many other great masters lived in Beijing during this time. They included Yang Luchan, the great Taiji Quan master and the first person to bring popularity and fame to his martial art; Guo Yunshan and Liu Qilan, both great Xingyi Quan masters who traveled and won competitions throughout China and popularized Xingyi Quan; and Song Mailun, the greatest San-huang Pao-chui master, who established Hui-you Biao-ju, the most successful security company in China. All these Beijing masters and Dong were friends and regularly fought, researched, and developed their skills together. There are many stories about them, and Dong is consistently praised as the best of the group.

One interesting story relates a fight between Dong and Guo Yun-shan, the Xingyi master. The fight went on for three days, at which point Guo decided that Dong was the better fighter. After discussing their respective techniques, they decided that Xingyi and Bagua should be taught concomitantly; everyone who studied Xingyi would have to study Bagua, and vice versa. As a result, Xingyi and Bagua are said to be one family.

Dong worked for the king for more than twenty years. During that time he did not do much teaching because he resided in the king's palace and, as a result, was inaccessible to ordinary students. After he retired, however, he taught Bagua to many students and disciples, some of whom became very famous. These include Yin Fu (Shou Yin), Cheng Tinghua (Yanjing Cheng), Song Changrong, Song Yongxiang (Huayuan Song), Ma Weiqi (Mei Ma), Liu Dekuan (Daqiang Liu), Liu Fengchun (Cuihua Liu), Shi Jidong (Zei Tui), Wei Ji, Liang Zhenpu (Guyi Liang), and Wang Lide. Students who became famous from the Xingyi group include Li Cunyi (Dendou Li), Zhang Zhankui (Shandian Shou), Geng Chengxin, and Zhou Mingtai.

When Dong taught Bagua, he used a special method. He taught his students the *bagua* idea and then taught the movements of Bagua Zhang according to each student's personality and body type. He also allowed students to change the movements as long as the changes did not violate basic *bagua* principles. The great variety among the styles of Bagua practiced today and the fact that these variations date from Dong's teaching lead many to believe that he, not Bi Dengxia, was the founder of Bagua Zhang.

There is considerable doubt that Dong even studied Bagua with Bi Dengxia. Dong might well have fabricated the story out of respect for the traditional Chinese view that good things always come from a secretive source and must have a long history. There are two reasons for the belief that Dong rather than Bi Dengxia invented Bagua. One is that every Bagua practitioner's genealogy originates with

Dong; no one was known to have practiced Bagua before him. Only his story suggests otherwise, and it is possible that he proposed the tale because he thought it appropriately modest to credit his success to a skilled teacher.

A second factor that supports the view that Dong was the originator of Bagua was his willingness to allow changes in Bagua movements. This behavior does not accord with Chinese tradition, which holds that significant deviation from what your master taught you indicates a lack of respect for him. It is unlikely that Dong would have allowed changes in Bagua if this behavior signaled disrespect for an alleged master. Despite these arguments, the question of whether Dong originated Bagua is still unanswered today.

The current most common hypothesis is that Dong learned hard-style martial arts when he was young. During his travels, he had an opportunity to learn "Zhuan Tian Zuan," which is a Daoist practice method used in southern China that emphasizes circle-walking practice. It is thought that Dong drew on this experience to create the Bagua training method and that he developed most of the Bagua Zhang skills during his first ten years in Beijing. It is likely that his early disciple Yin Fu provided considerable help to Dong in this endeavor. Some researchers believe that Dong presented only the basic ideas of Bagua Zhang and that the system was actually completed in the second generation. Different masters of this generation elaborated the system and developed a variety of styles.

Dong Haichuan died on October 25, 1882. Waking that day with a premonition that it would be his last, he called his disciples together and urged them to look after each other and to work hard so that their group would prosper and grow. He expressed the hope that the essence of Bagua Zhang would be promulgated and preserved for all time. Then, sitting in his chair and with a smile on his face, he passed away. Hundreds of people mourned him at his funeral. Dur-

ing a lifetime of legendary deeds and accomplishments, he made a unique contribution to the Chinese martial arts. Although he never married, his family was large indeed.

Master Dong Haichuan had great disciples and almost every one of them developed his own style. Some studied other styles of *gongfu* before studying Bagua and mixed these styles with their Bagua Zhang skills. They kept the main idea of *Bagua* and developed many different movements and techniques. Of the four most famous Bagua Zhang styles—Yin, Cheng, Song, and Liu—the first two became the largest and most popular.

Yin-Style Bagua

Yin Fu, the number-one disciple of Dong Haichuan, was also known as Dean, whose special literary name was Shoupeng and whose nickname was Shou Yin or "Thin Yin." He was born in 1840 in Ji County, Hebei Province. When he was young, he settled in Beijing with his family and because the family was poor, he started working at an early age. He worked in a small restaurant and sold pancakes every day on the street.

Yin liked martial arts and had learned some external styles in the countryside before moving to Beijing. In Beijing he heard about the great master Dong and made a point of selling his pancakes just outside the king's palace in hopes of meeting Dong. After a long time, Dong did notice the young boy and one day called Yin over and asked what he wanted. Yin said that he wanted to study martial arts with Dong. Yin sounded sincere and Dong thought he might have talent, so Dong allowed him to practice in the palace.

Yin came every day after work and practiced very hard. First Dong taught him Shaolin Eighteen-Luohan Quan, and then Bagua. Yin's *gongfu* advanced very quickly during the next several years. The king took a liking to him and permitted him to join the palace security guard. Yin's favorite weapon was the *pan-guan bi,* which means "the pen of a ghost judge"; this is actually a pair of iron

Yin Fu

Niushe zhang of Yin-style Bagua

Chinese pens. When Dong retired, Yin took over as supervisor of the king's security guards.

Later Yin worked for the Emperor in the Forbidden City. The Empress Dowager admired his skill and wanted to study with him. Despite his wealth and fame, Yin never became arrogant or unkind. He always helped other people and never injured anyone who challenged him.

Yin Fu's style of Bagua Zhang has always been known as *dong cheng zhang* or "eastern city palm" because Yin lived and taught on the east side of Beijing. Yin-style Bagua is also called *niushe zhang* or "bull tongue palm" because the palm shape in this style resembles a bull's tongue. Yin adopted this palm shape in his Bagua because it was used in Shaolin Eighteen-Luohan Quan, the martial art style that he had originally studied.

Yin-Style Bagua, Pierce Palm

Yin-Style Bagua, Hold Up and Push Down Palm

Master Yin taught many students Shaolin Eighteen-Luohan Quan followed by Bagua Zhang. His style of Bagua includes eight sections, and each section includes eight positions. Of his great disciples including Ma Gui (Mu Ma), Men Baozhen, Gong Baotian, and Cui Zhendong, Ma Gui was the most outstanding. Yin Fu's son, Yin Yuzhang, was also very skilled. Master Yin Fu died quietly on June 28, 1909.

Cheng Tinghua

Cheng-Style Bagua

Cheng Tinghua, also known as Yingfang, was born in 1848 in Cheng-Jia-Cuen, the Cheng family village in Shen County of Hebei Province. When he went to Beijing, he opened an eyeglass shop on Huashi Street, and his nickname became Yan-jing Cheng or "Glasses Cheng."

When he was young, Cheng Tinghua practiced Chinese wrestling and Shaolin Quan for many years and became quite good. When he was twenty-eight, he studied Bagua Zhang with Dong Haichuan. He practiced hard, won an excellent reputation for his fighting skill, and had many students. Today, Cheng style is studied by more people than any other style of Bagua. Cheng style is also known as *nan cheng zhang* or "southern city palm" because Cheng lived and taught on the south side of Beijing. The other common name for this style is *longzhao zhang* or "dragon's claw palm" because of the palm shape that typifies the style. In the second generation of Bagua Zhang, Yin Fu and Cheng Tinghua were the most famous masters, and Cheng's school was the largest.

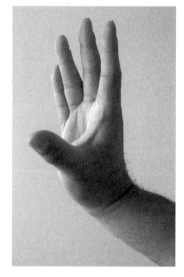

Longzhao zhang **of Cheng-style Bagua**

Cheng style consists of eight basic postures, usually called eight mother palms, and eight main postures, usually called eight big palm changes. Cheng wanted his students to practice the

**Cheng-Style Bagua, Black Dragon
Turns Back Its Head**

**Cheng-Style Bagua, Big Boa
Turns Over Its Body**

eight basic palms first and then the eight main postures. After this training the applications of changing were taught. With this method students develop internal components first and then fighting skills. Cheng's great disciples include Feng Zunyi, Sun Lutang, Zhang Yukui, Han Qiying, Zhou Xiang, Li Wenbiao, Kan Lingfeng, and his sons Cheng Youlong and Cheng Youxin. Cheng Tinghua's brother Cheng Dianhua and his nephew Cheng Yougong were also famous. After Master Dong's death, some of his students—Cheng's *gongfu* brothers—continued their studies with Cheng.

In 1900, the Eight-Country Union Army warred with China and occupied Beijing. During this period, twenty German soldiers attempted to rob Cheng one day as he was walking along East He-be-chang Street. Angrily, he resisted and beat them so badly in hand-to-hand combat that they resorted to shooting him. Cheng died of these gunshot wounds.

Liu-Style Bagua

Liu Dekuan, also known as Jingyuan, was born in Cang-Zhou County of Hebei Province. When he was young, he studied Shaolin

Liuhe Quan with Tian Chunkui and then the Yue-style link form Yue-Shi Lian-Quan and Ying-Zhua Quan or Eagle Claw with Liu Shizun. Liu Shizun, whose nickname was Xiong-Xian Liu or "Xiong County Liu," was a martial arts coach for the Emperor's security guard team.

Liu Dekuan practiced hard, and his superior spear technique earned him the nickname Da-Qiang Liu or "Big Spear Liu." When he worked as a security guard for the famous Changxin Security Company in Mao County, people there nicknamed him Mao-Zhou Liu to honor his excellent work.

Liu had already achieved renown by the time he arrived in Beijing. Once there, he challenged Dong Haichuan and having lost, he wisely decided to study Bagua Zhang with Dong. He practiced hard and was able to understand deeply the essence of Bagua Zhang. Through his studies of Bagua, Liu realized that if students paid attention to developing internal components when they walked the circle, they tended to overlook the development of fighting skills, and vice versa. Only gifted students could do both well.

Liu-Style Bagua, Four Dragons Draw Water

Liu-Style Bagua, Elbow Strike

To circumvent this problem, Liu devised a new form that included sixty-four fighting skills practiced in a straight line, similar to Yue-Shi Lian-Quan. Each skill was derived from traditional Bagua, but none of them were practiced by walking the circle. Liu suggested that students of Bagua first practice basic skills to develop internal components by walking the circle and then practice fighting skills using his straight-line form. This separation in training made it easier for students to understand and master the Bagua Zhang principle and Bagua skills. Liu's form was called Liu-style Bagua or Straight Bagua. The majority of Bagua masters accepted Liu's concept, and today most Bagua groups use his straight style but practice it in conjunction with a circle style. Liu's form only included fighting skills, so it is not a complete training system of Bagua; today it is included in many groups of different styles. Because of this, Liu-style Bagua is sometimes not considered an independent style in its own right.

My Bagua Zhang Lineage

In the third generation of Bagua Zhang, Ma Gui, also well known as Ma Shiqing, was the most famous Bagua master. Born in Beijing in 1853, he had many nicknames: Mu Ma or "Wood Ma" because he owned a wood factory; Ma Cuo-zi or "Short Ma" because he was small; and Pang-xie Ma or "Crab Ma" because he liked to draw crabs. He was also called Tie-ge-bei Ma or "Iron Arm Ma" because his arm was extremely hard and because he always used it in his famous fighting technique *zhi-bi wan-da*, a wrist punch with a straightened arm. He was widely celebrated for this skill and many others.

As a youngster, Ma Gui studied Bagua Quan with Yin Fu and advanced very quickly, especially in fighting skills. Yin liked Ma Gui so much that he brought him to study directly with Dong Haichuan, who was impressed by the eager young student. Later, when Dong retired from his job at the king's palace, he lived in

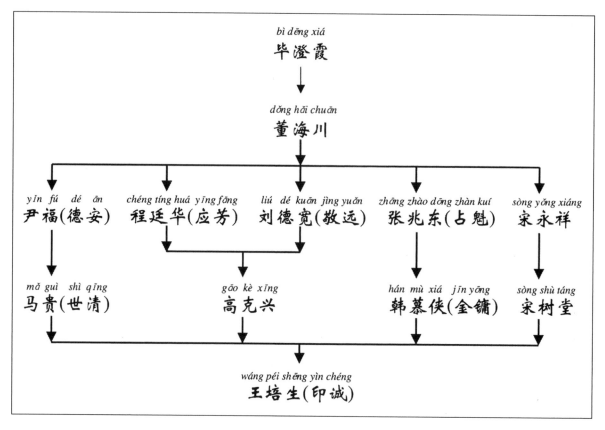

Part of Bagua Zhang Lineage

Ma's home and taught him for several years. Ma regularly practiced with iron rings weighing about ten pounds on each wrist.

By the time he was twenty years old, Ma was already highly respected. He liked fighting and beat many masters. He worked for King Duan and Duke Lan for many years and then became teacher to King Duan's son. Because the Emperor had no son at that time, the King's son was the first in line to succeed the Emperor. As teacher to a future emperor, Ma's reputation was greatly enhanced by this job. After the Republican Revolution, he worked in the President's Office and eight years later became a martial arts coach at the National Police School.

As well as being famous for his *gongfu* skill, Ma was also known for the conservative way in which he chose students. He did not

accept many students because he worried that if they did not apply themselves and perform well, his own reputation would be tarnished. In his old age, however, Ma met a young boy named Wang Peisheng and admired his abilities so much that he accepted Wang as an indoor disciple and trained him intensively for many years. Ma Gui was Master Wang Peisheng's first martial arts master.

Wang learned Taiji Quan from Yang Yuting, whose good friend Gao Kexing was a famous Bagua Zhang master. Yang had taught Gao Taiji Quan, and Gao had taught Yang Bagua Zhang. Later, Yang sent Wang to Gao's class where Wang learned both Cheng- and Liu-style Bagua. Wang also received private training in Bagua Zhang with Master Han Muxia (who was Zhang Zhaodong's disciple); and Zhang learned Bagua Zhang with Dong Haichuan.

From the early 1980s, I learned Yin-, Cheng-, and Liu-style Bagua from my Grandmaster Wang Peisheng.

The Basic Principles and Features of Bagua Zhang

Bagua Zhang is based on the traditional *bagua* concept, one of the most important principles in Chinese culture. As previously mentioned, it is generally believed that the idea of *bagua* was first formulated by Fu Xi about six to seven thousand years ago. At that time, the main occupations in China were hunting, fishing, and simple farming. Because the success of all these activities is directly and critically related to nature, natural phenomena were closely observed, recorded, and analyzed. Inferences about and explanations of natural events abounded as people attempted to understand and perhaps even predict the natural occurrences on which their survival depended.

Based on careful observations of the sky and earth, Fu Xi is reputed to have summarized the rules of natural changes and then created eight symbols to express the eight most important compo-

nents of nature. The eight symbols are: the sky and the earth, comprising the universe; wind and thunder, the two magic powers originating from the sky; mountain and marsh, the two basic shapes of the land; and water and fire, the most necessary elements for maintaining life. Later, these symbols were used to refer more abstractly to the basic attributes of nature.

The term *bagua* is composed of two characters: *ba*, which means "eight," and *gua*, which means "trigram." Each of the eight symbols in the *bagua* system is a trigram composed of three line positions. Each line position is either *yin*, designated by two short lines, or *yang*, designated by one long line. The trigrams describe the changes of *yin* and *yang* attributes. In the martial arts, *yin* and *yang* refer respectively to attributes such as soft and hard, still and moving, insubstantial and substantial, closing and opening, and defense and attack.

Because *bagua* is composed of *yin* and *yang*, all *yin* and *yang* principles are embedded in the *bagua* principle and the result is a complete system. The *bagua* principle holds that the universe started from "*wuji*" and that *wuji* generated "*taiji*." Then *yin* and *yang*—which emerge within *taiji*—separate to generate "*liangyi*" or "the two appearances." *Yin* and *yang* change in *liangyi* to generate "*sixiang*," "the four shapes"; and subsequent changes of *yin* and *yang* in *sixiang* generate "*bagua*."

Because eight trigrams are not enough to express the more complex changes that occur in nature, two trigrams are combined, one above the other, to form a hexagram. All possible permutations of trigrams result in sixty-four hexagrams. The hexagrams, like the trigrams of which they are composed, are also called *gua*. *Yi Jing* explains the complex changes represented by each of the sixty-four hexagrams, each of the eight trigrams, and each line or *yao* in the hexagrams. The relationships between *yao*, trigrams, and hexagrams are also described in *Yi Jing*, which gradually evolved from a fortune-telling tool to a philosophy book. As a philosophical system,

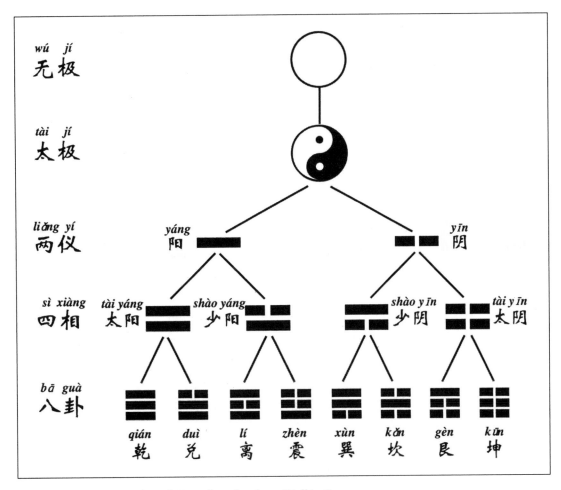

Yin and Yang Changing from Wuji to Bagua

bagua not only describes the changing and emerging laws of nature but applies these laws to every aspect of life.

Bagua Zhang is the traditional internal martial art based on the Bagua principle. Because *bagua* is about change, the main idea of Bagua Zhang is *bian* or changing. It is said that wherever there is movement, there is change that never ceases. Change in this context refers to the changes of *yin* and *yang*. Physically, all change is said to come from and return to the crossing of arms or the walking of the circle.

From a technical point of view, Bagua Zhang includes eight main

skills reflecting each trigram of the *bagua* system and sixty-four skills representing the concepts of *Yi Jing*. The eight main skills are the foundation of Bagua Zhang, and the sixty-four skills are the applications. In Bagua Zhang, most skills use the palm and so are called *zhang* which means "palm," or *huan zhang* which means "palm change." Deriving from the different *yin* and *yang* representations in the various line positions, each Bagua Zhang skill focuses on a different way to practice and coordinate the internal components of *shen*, *yi*, *qi,* and *jin* and the external component of movement. Each skill follows the law of change specified by the patterning of *yin* and *yang* lines.

The fighting concepts of Bagua Zhang are: never stop walking and never stop changing; always combine the qualities of soft and hard and those of internal and external; appear suddenly and disappear suddenly; move close quickly and leave quickly; and never struggle directly with an opponent. If a movement seems difficult, change it so that it becomes easier; if a movement begins as direct, change it so that it comes from the side and vice versa.

The changes required in Bagua Zhang have been traditionally described by a series of lyrical metaphors. All changes, for example, are likened to a fish touching a net; whenever there is touching, there must also be changing. *Bagua* changes are portrayed as using the shadow rather than the body, which means that the qualities of substantial and insubstantial must always be changing. The observation that a flower hides under the leaves refers to the necessity in Bagua Zhang to hide one's intent; and reference to a running horse turning its head back urges a quick and sudden change of direction.

Analysis of the Bagua Zhang Training Method

Despite its current popularity, the essential foundation of Bagua Zhang is gradually being lost. There are three main reasons for this

Circle-Walking of Cheng-Style Bagua Zhang

unfortunate circumstance. First, Bagua Zhang is too difficult for most practitioners to master. Anyone who wants to study Bagua must work extremely hard and concentrate upon every moment. Second, the fundamental concepts of Bagua Zhang are very difficult to understand, and there are not enough good classics to describe sufficiently its principles and training methods. Finally, there are only a few good masters who really understand Bagua. Most masters know the movements of Bagua Zhang but do not understand the underlying concepts on which the movements are based. This makes it almost impossible for their students to advance to high-level mastery.

The feature that most distinguishes Bagua Zhang training is circle-walking. Every skill of Bagua Zhang starts from circle-walking, and in almost all Bagua Zhang styles circle-walking is the first phase of training. Because the main idea of all Bagua Zhang skills is to keep moving, footwork is strongly emphasized, and circle-walking is the most important and basic training. It is said that if there is no circle-walking, there can be no Bagua Zhang skill. All basic *gongfu* skills and applications derive from circle-walking.

For historical reasons, there are many styles of Bagua Zhang and many different training methods, but all of them must follow the same principles. All are founded on the recognition of continual change, the fundamental laws of change as delineated in the *Yi Jing*, and the correct application of these changes. With an understanding of these fundamentals, the skills of Bagua Zhang will be relatively easy to master. Without such understanding the true meaning of Bagua Zhang will elude you, and your skills will be flawed no matter how long you practice.

Using Cheng style as an illustrative example, Bagua Zhang train-

ing can be divided into three steps. The first step is designed to build up practitioners' basic skills. This is most commonly accomplished by *ba mu zhang* or "eight mother palms" training, which involves walking in circles and serves a function similar to post standing in other martial arts schools. In accord with the *xiantian* or the pre-birth *bagua* concept, this training adjusts both internal and external components so that they become coordinated and integrated. *Qi* flow becomes smoother, and internal and external trained power increases, as does the body's ability to maintain relaxation. Movement becomes more nimble and more stable.

The second training step focuses on developing practitioners' basic changing abilities, and the most common method for achieving this goal is *ba da zhang* or "eight big palm changes" training. This step develops the foundation for the changes involved in Bagua applications. It is designed according to the *houtian* or post-birth *bagua* concept and involves basic Bagua Zhang methods for promoting smooth and integrated changes in the internal and external components.

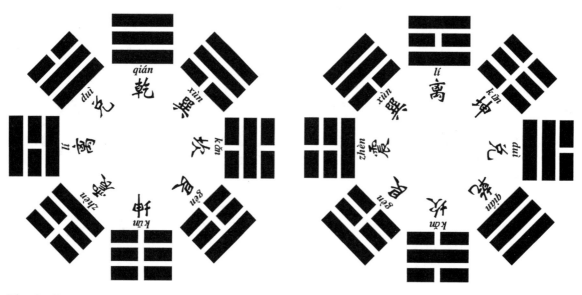

Xiantian Bagua   **Houtian Bagua**

The goal of the third step is to build up practitioners' fighting skills, and the common training method for this phase is *liushisi zhang* or "sixty-four palms" training. This basic application training is designed according to the sixty-four hexagrams of *Yi Jing*, and it helps practitioners not only to learn many useful skills but to understand the laws of skill-changing in its many manifestations. Finally, practitioners learn how to acquire and augment changing skills. It is said that if you master the sixty-four skills, your ability to change becomes limitless and your skills become countless.

There are many application skills in Bagua Zhang, and as with the changing skills, it is usually necessary to progress through three stages to learn and master these application skills. The three stages are "fixed posture," "alive posture," and "changing posture." In the fixed-posture stage, practitioners learn and practice each skill according to technical criteria. All movements must be performed clearly and correctly and must follow the standard specifications for each posture. Movements that are well executed will naturally create correct internal feelings, and these feelings will gradually become stronger and enhance all the internal components of *shen*, *yi*, *qi*, and *jin*.

Black Dragon Turns Back Its Body

Back Inserting Down Palm

In this stage, practitioners develop a clear understanding of every movement of each skill. They also learn how to determine the direction, angle, and timing of each movement and how to use force efficiently. It is also important to coordinate the details of movement with the internal components. Everything should be practiced slowly to make sure that it is done properly. Because this stage measures all skills against fixed standards, it may be frustrating to beginners and seem ineffective, but it is critical for developing a firm foundation. The skills

Bagua Zhang Fight Practice

of this stage must be mastered before practitioners can advance to the next stage.

In alive posture each skill can be practiced in different ways without adhering to an external standard. Internal feelings as well as physical movements must be varied and spontaneous. In this stage, practice should be conducted like real fighting, which means that students have to consider all the possible problems that might confront them and how to respond effectively to each one. It is not enough to practice only ideal responses or situations. Rather than performing every skill in the standard way, it is necessary to change skills according to the actions of the opponent. When students can do this well, their fighting skills will almost always be successful.

Practitioners in the changing-posture stage have acquired the ability to change skills naturally. This stage differs from the alive-posture stage in the degree to which the movements are designed ahead of time. In alive posture, the first task is to research every possible circumstance that might arise in a fight and to discover how to change skills so that each circumstance can be responded to successfully. Then, variations of these responses are rehearsed in situations similar to actual fights.

In the changing-posture stage, nothing is pre-designed. Every skill becomes a spontaneous expression of the student's true nature. Practiced or pre-planned movement means nothing. There is no need to perform skills clearly; every movement becomes a skill. No effort is needed to integrate internal and external components; this occurs naturally. At this stage there is no skill and no mind focus. Everything is natural and effortless.

✪ Other Styles of Internal Martial Arts

It is said that there are about five hundred martial arts styles practiced in China today. Of these, approximately one hundred and forty styles have clearly defined principles and lineages. Most of them belong to the external martial arts family. Because these styles predate the internal martial arts styles and, in part, gave rise to them, external martial arts practitioners were well placed to assimilate the emerging principles of the internal styles into their training. Historically, famous masters from the external styles were often friends with internal martial arts masters and as a result, experiences on both sides were easily and readily exchanged. Some of the external martial arts groups were strongly and obviously influenced by the development of the internal styles. Among the styles that appeared from this cross-fertilization are Tongbei Quan, Baji Quan, and Sanhuang Paochui Quan. The principles of Tongbei Quan and Baji Quan are presented in this section because several useful skills from these styles are included in the "sixteen-posture form" that we describe later in this book.

tōng bèi quán
通背拳

Tongbei Quan

Tongbei Quan is a traditional martial art with a long history. The earliest written reference to Tongbei appeared a thousand years ago, but neither the date of origin of the art nor its originator is known. The historical record mentions that General Han Tong,

who lived at the beginning of the Song Dynasty, knew Tongbei Quan; and a second historical document dating from four hundred years ago states, "You Shen's Tongbei skill is the best." These references prove only that Tongbei has been practiced for hundreds of years.

In most Tongbei groups, the development of the martial art is attributed to Bai Shikou, whose official first name was Yisan and whose Daoist name was Dong Lingzi. He was respected among Chinese martial arts groups and is thought to have passed his skill to Wang Dao, Li Yi, and Han Cheng.

The legend tells of an old and famous martial artist named Yuan Gong who lived during the Spring and Autumn Time around 500 BC. He had white hair and a white beard and always wore white clothes. Having challenged another master to a fight, Yuan lost and was transformed into a white ape, whereupon he fled into the forest. Known as Baiyuan Laoren, which means "old man like a white ape" or "claimed to be the white ape in human form," he was believed to be an immortal ape who always taught his skill in secret. Of course this story, not surprisingly, was viewed with widespread skepticism by most people, but it is also a familiar tale far and wide. More recent researchers believe that the true name of Baiyuan Laoren is Bai (white) Shikou or Yisan. From his name we find the Chinese characters comprising the names Shikou and Yisan, which conceal the character for "ape."

Because Tongbei Quan is a kind of ape imitation style martial art, people naturally make a connection between the style lineage and the old story of Baiyuan Laoren. Although most people preserve this legend, they do not really believe it.

Chen Tuan

bái yuán lǎo rén

白猿老人

chén tuán

陈抟

lǔ yún qīng

鲁云清

shí hóng shèng

石鸿胜

Li Zhendong

Li Shusen

Another version of Tongbei history that is more realistic (but is subscribed to by only a few groups) provides a clear lineage and a list of all the famous Tongbei masters in each generation. According to this version the original founder of the style was Chen Tuan (?–989), a Daoist master and respected scholar who lived during the Song Dynasty. He elucidated many Daoist concepts and is credited with the design of the famous *Taiji* symbol. Some of his students became distinguished scholars in their own right. It is generally thought that Chen invented Tongbei Quan and Shuigong Fa (a *qigong* method) during the time he lived and practiced Daoism on Hua Mountain. Although there is no proof that Chen is the originator of Tongbei Quan, he is regarded by some groups as the first-generation Tongbei Quan master.

Perhaps practiced a thousand years ago, Tongbei Quan did not become popular until the early nineteenth century when the Daoist Master Lu Yunqing taught this skill. Master Lu's famous disciples were Qi Xin and Shi Hongsheng, each of whom later developed his own style and further popularized Tongbei Quan. Today these styles are called Qi-style Tongbei Quan and Shi-style Tongbei Quan, and each has been elaborated into a variety of offshoots. The basic training in Qi style consists of the one hundred and eight solo techniques, sometimes called *chai quan* or "take apart skill." The basic training in Shi style is the twenty-four postures, sometimes called *lian quan* or the "connected form." Both training systems follow similar principles.

I studied Shi-style Tongbei Quan beginning in the early 1960s with the well-known Master Li Shusen, whose nickname is "Iron Arm Li." Li's master is Li Zhendong, also known as "Quick Hand Black Li." Li Zhendong learned with Zhang Wencheng, who studied directly with Shi Hongsheng. In the 1980s I received intensive Tongbei training from Master Wang Peisheng, who had learned a variation of Baiyuan Tongbei called Ruyi Tongbei from Liang Junpo.

This training clarified and deepened my understanding of Tongbei Quan principles.

Baiyuan Tongbei Quan is the full name of the original style of Tongbei Quan. In the term "Tongbei," *tong* means that things are connected or joined together in an open, unobstructed way, and *bei* translates as "arms" or "back." Taken together, the two characters mean that the arms and back are connected so fully that the arm can become elongated, and *qi* and internal force can pass smoothly all the way to the hands. The word *tongbei* is also used in other martial arts styles to describe techniques that involve stretching the arms, relaxing the shoulders, or engaging in some other back or arm practice, such as *shan tongbei* in Taiji Quan.

The term "Baiyuan" means "white ape." A paramount goal of Tongbei Quan practice is to increase the length of one's arms and through their movements to express an ape-like quality. In fact, one kind of ape found in China is known as the *tongbei yuan*—here *yuan* means "ape" because of this animal's exceptionally long arms (much longer than those of other apes).

Many Chinese martial arts styles include skills that mimic the movements or qualities of animals. One of these is Tongbei Quan and as a result, it is sometimes considered an animal imitation style. It differs from the others, however, in one important respect. In Tongbei Quan, the intent is not to imitate an ape's external movements but rather to convey its disposition. This is referred to as "studying the ideas but not the movements of the ape." Given this distinction, many Tongbei groups take strong exception to the idea that Tongbei Quan is an animal imitation style.

Since the philosophy of Tongbei Quan is based on Daoism, and many Tongbei practice methods are similar to those used in the internal martial arts styles, Tongbei

liáng jùn bō

梁俊波

bái yuán tōng bèi quán

白猿通背拳

Black Hammer

Quan is sometimes viewed as an internal style, or at least as a hybrid that draws upon internal concepts. Tongbei Quan practice has two main components: martial arts applications and *qigong*. The martial arts component focuses on a study of the attributes of apes and develops many useful, efficient, and simple techniques, all of which are used exclusively for fighting. It is the fighting skills that have made Tongbei Quan famous. Tongbei *qigong* practice follows the Daoist *qigong* style and is designed to promote good health and to improve character.

Because Tongbei's useful and efficient fighting techniques allow practitioners to progress rapidly, this martial art is often thought to be easy to master. For many beginners, it may seem as though the skills studied one day can be used in fights the next. While it is true that most people can reach mid-level skill more quickly and easily in Tongbei Quan than in many other styles, only a few students ever reach high-level mastery. The excellent fighting skills of famous Tongbei masters in different generations like Zhang Wencheng, Liang Junpao, Ma Xiaohe, Zhang Ce, Li Zhendong, and Li Shusen are rare and exceptional.

xin yuán

心猿

xin yì

心意

xin ji

心极

The key Tongbei Quan concepts are *xin yuan*, *xin yi*, and *xin ji*. These refer respectively to the qualities of the heart, mind, and movements of apes. Regarding their hearts, apes are considered to be unstable or changeable, so in Tongbei Quan fighting, practitioners should be ready to change at any moment. They should also hide their intentions from their opponents, again exhibiting a characteristic attributed to apes. Apes always react quickly and without warning, and Tongbei fighters should do likewise. Each of these characteristics reflects inherent qualities underlying ape behavior.

The features of Tongbei skill are *leng*, *tan*, *cui*, *kuai*, *ying*, *suo*, *xiao*, *mian*, *ruan*, and *qiao*. *Leng*, which means "sudden," indicates that the technique's movement should be so surprising that an opponent cannot easily defend himself. *Tan*, meaning "spring," denotes that the internal force should be like a spring so that force released

lěng	tán	cuì	kuài	yìng	suō	xiǎo	mián	ruǎn	qiǎo
冷	弹	脆	快	硬	缩	小	绵	软	巧

forward also generates force backward. *Cui*, which means "crisp" or "fragile," specifies that every technique should be done clearly and that the contact time should be short so that an opponent has no chance to respond. *Kuai* means "quick" and is a desired quality in every technique. *Ying* means "hard" and describes many Tongbei practices, like iron arms, that train the body to become harder. *Suo* means "to shrink" and suggests that the size of movements should be reduced during fights to improve efficiency. *Xiao* means "small," and the smaller the movement used in a technique, the more effective the technique will be. *Mian* means "soft" or "following" and indicates that when an opponent touches you, you should be soft and follow his movements rather than resist them. *Ruan* means "relaxed," "soft," or "smooth." Although hard attacks are usually preferred in Tongbei, they should not be used exclusively. All movements should be relaxed, soft, and smooth most of the time. *Qiao*, which means "skillful," "ingenious" or "clever," indicates that all Tongbei techniques must be useful and efficient.

Tongbei applications must be quick, aggressive, accurate, clever, and changeable. Quickness refers to your mind, eyes, and movement; it is said that "even if you can thread the needle in the instant that lightning brightens the night, that still may not be quick enough." In heart, the Tongbei Quan practitioner should feel mean-spirited. An old adage admonishes that if you are a kind person, you should not study Tongbei. Tongbei techniques must be delivered with great accuracy. It is said that if you miss the target, you waste your time. There should be no unnecessary movement, and only the best, most efficient skill for each situation should be used. A Tongbei fighter should be able to change his movement at any time; the traditional saying advises that you should be able to change from one technique to three, and from three to nine.

Except for some basic *gongfu* practices, every Tongbei skill is developed for efficiency in fighting. Some may look beautiful but any quality other than efficiency is considered irrelevant and is disdained by Tongbei Quan practitioners. While most Chinese martial arts styles include form practice, forms are considered useless and are ignored in Tongbei training. Shi-style Tongbei does include several forms, but these are not often taught. Only after a student executes every skill well is he permitted to study forms. This does not signify that form practice requires a high level of mastery but rather that forms are not seen as important and are not allowed to take up valuable time better used for more essential training.

Traditional Tongbei Quan training includes basic *gongfu* training, basic skills training, two-person help training, two-person freestyle training, weapons training, and *qigong* training. In basic *gongfu* training, there are many practices designed to increase relaxation and to stretch the body, especially the back and arms. There are also exercises to increase the basic internal force of the arms, legs, waist, and back and to improve the root. Techniques for adjusting the internal components of *shen*, *yi*, and *qi*, and practices like iron palm, iron arm, and iron body (designed to increase hardness) are also included in basic *gongfu* training.

In basic skills training, each technique is practiced repeatedly. Students may not advance to a new technique until they have demonstrated mastery of the previous one. In two-person help training, there are fixed routines for attack and defense. A Tongbei adage counsels that if you want to master Tongbei skills, you must always fight with a partner. After fixed routines training, partners engage in freestyle fighting training that closely mimics real fighting.

In Tongbei Quan, only fighting skills are considered necessary and only these skills are admitted into Tongbei training. The movements of Tongbei techniques are usually large when practiced in training, but smaller and more powerful when used in application. Detailed attention is paid in Tongbei training to combining hard

Baiyuan Tongbei Quan

and soft and to finding a balance between the two. In fighting, it is important to stay relaxed and soft until you touch your opponent. It is said, "Once the clothes of the opponent have been touched, force should be released immediately."

Great emphasis is placed on strengthening internal force. Students are first trained to relax and stretch their bodies and then to allow *qi* to move smoothly and harmoniously. Next they are taught how to release internal force quickly and without warning. The whole body must be coordinated and integrated during this release. The more relaxed the body is, the more energy is stored and the more force released. Quick and hard attacks are always considered the best way to fight. Ideally, only one attack should be needed to finish a fight. For this reason, iron arm, iron palm, and iron body practices are often combined with intensive training of Tongbei techniques.

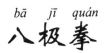

bā   jī   quán

Baji Quan

Baji Quan was mentioned in General Qi Jiguang's book *Ji Xiao Xin Shu* ("The New Book on Effective Military Training"), published in 1584, and seems to have become a well-known martial art by that time. Its history, however, is unclear. Most people believe that Baji Quan was originally known as Bazi Quan, in which *bazi* means "rake." The style acquired this name because of the shape of most of the fists used. The term *bazi* was later changed to *baji*, which means "to reach far away in all directions." This was considered a more apt and noteworthy description of the style because it suggests the ability to achieve great things. Baji Quan is thought by some historians to have originated at the Shaolin Temple; others think it originated at the Yueshan Temple.

In the most common version of the Baji Quan lineage, the first master who made Baji Quan famous was Wu Zhong (1712–1802), who lived in Meng Village of Cang Zhou, Hebei Province. He liked martial arts and had already learned some skills by the time he was eight. One night as Wu practiced sword in his yard, a Daoist master whose name is not known came to watch and then spoke with Wu about martial arts. Wu recognized that this stranger had exceptional ideas and skills and asked if the priest would be his master. The master agreed and stayed in Wu's home for about ten years teaching him Baji Quan and *liuhe daqiang,* or the six-integration big spear. The teacher remained nameless all those years, even to Wu.

wú zhōng

When the master felt that Wu's skill was sufficiently good, he prepared to leave. Just before departing, he told Wu that the first word of his name was Lai. He said that only someone who was his disciple would know this word of his name. Then he left, and no one ever discovered where he went.

Two years later, a second stranger came to see Wu and announced himself as Lai's disciple. Like Lai, he did not tell Wu his full name

but just the one word, Pi. He stayed with Wu and taught Wu many detailed spear skills. He also gave Wu a book about secret Baji principles.

After Master Pi left, Wu continued to practice hard and became famous. He made his way to Beijing, where he became master to the prince. In honor of his great spear-fighting skill, he was nick-named Shen Qiang Wu Zhong or Magic Spear Wu Zhong. As an old man, Wu returned to his home village and taught his skill to many students. Many famous masters in each generation of the Baji group trace their lineage back to Wu Zhong. They include Zhang Keming, Huang Sihai, Li Shuwen, Huo Diange, and Wu Xiufeng. I received Baji Quan training from Master Wang Peisheng and Master Bi Yuanda, both of whom are disciples of Wu Xiufeng. Wu Xiufeng was the sixth-generation family member from Wu Zhong.

The full name of Baji Quan is Kai Men Baji Quan or Open Gate Baji Quan. In Chinese martial arts, the posture that is held first and from which skills are executed is usually called a gate. The use of an effective defense skill—one that neutralizes the opponent's attack—is referred to as "closing the gate." "Opening the gate" refers to an effective offensive skill that opens the opponent to an attack. The term "Kai Men" indicates that the skills of this style can open any gate and that no defense skill can be effective against them. While this may not always be true in practice, Baji Quan has earned a deservedly high reputation.

The two main styles of Baji Quan practiced today are called "Small Form Baji Quan," also known as Old Baji or Still Baji, and "Big Form Baji Quan," alternatively known as New Baji or Alive Baji. Both styles are based on the same principle. While the small form is generally considered better for developing basic skills, the big form is preferred for practicing applications.

The movements of Baji, though not complex, are very useful and justly famous for the power they generate. Baji Quan attack skills are

zhāng kè míng
张 克 明

huáng sì hǎi
黄 四 海

lǐ shū wén
李 书 文

wú xiù fēng
吴 秀 峰

dǐng

顶

bào

抱

dǎn

掸

tí

提

kuà

胯

chán

缠

always swift, violent, and powerful. They appear to be unstoppable. Baji Quan is also known for its training of three kinds of internal power: *shizi jin*, which is a crossing trained force; *chuansi jin*, a silk-reeling trained force; and *chenzhui jin*, a sinking trained force. The six great opening-gate skills called *liudakai* and the eight main skills called *badazhao* offer very useful Baji fighting techniques.

Liudakai include six basic methods for the use of fundamental internal components. They are *ding* or "clash," *bao* or "hold," *dan* or "brush," *ti* or "take up," *kua* or "carry on," and *chan* or "reel." The eight basic application skills of *badazhao* are described lyrically as: "the king of hell waves his hand three times"; "a fierce tiger climbs a mountain"; "three undefended skills at the front door"; "the king of kings breaks the reins"; "palm faces the sun"; "a force opens the door left and right"; "a yellow bird grips with both claws"; and "a cannon in the sky." The release of trained force in Baji should be *ying* or "hard," *wan* or "stable," *tu* or "sudden," *beng*, which means to burst forth like a mountain landslide, and *han*, which means to shake like a quaking mountain.

In Baji Quan fighting, the intent is to move quickly toward the opponent and release great destructive power at close range. There are many elbow strike skills and stamping and shaking steps in Baji practice and applications. All Baji skills should be in a constant state of change, and although some skills are soft, great emphasis is placed on quick, hard, sudden strikes. Baji skills should be characterized by the kind of explosive force used to break down a door. Because most Baji skills are applied directly forward at close range, practitioners must have stable postures, powerful strikes, and hardened bodies.

Baji Quan training is characterized by several special features. It emphasizes *chuang bu* or rush-in steps that move the body quickly forward in powerful charges, and *zhen jiao* or sudden foot stamps that involve a sinking of *qi*. In these stamps, the foot should fall as though it were a heavy object being dropped to the ground. The

Baji Quan, Straight Punch

Baji Quan, Straight Elbow Strike

stamping should be accompanied by loud vocalization and should create a sensation of the ground shaking underfoot.

Baji Quan training also emphasizes *zhuang gong* or "post standing" which develops the internal components, and *cao zhuang* or "post hitting" which involves hitting a post with every part of the body in a training exercise designed to increase the practitioner's ability to emit and use power. The goal of all Baji practices is to increase power, and Baji Quan practitioners are often thought capable of releasing more power than practitioners of any other style.

The several bare-hand Baji Quan forms differ slightly from group to group. They include a long form, several short forms like *liudakai*, and some two-person application forms. Baji groups also practice many weapons skills. The weapon skill for which Baji is most famous is *liuhe daqiang* or six-integration big spear. In Baji history, Masters Wu Zhong, Zhang Keming, Li Shuwen, and others achieved great renown for their spear skills.

Although Baji Quan is primarily a hard-style martial art, it includes some internal martial arts principles. Some Baji Quan

techniques, like hard foot stamping, were modified by Baji masters to provide an increased focus on internal components and thus to take advantage of the unique features of the internal martial arts.

CHAPTER TWO

The Fundamentals of the Basic Movements Used in Applications

All martial arts applications are made up of basic movements. It is very important for beginners to understand the essential components of these basic movements. Such understanding will help the practitioner build up a strong foundation and develop a more thorough comprehension of fighting skills. Without proficiency in the fundamentals, it is not possible to reach high-level mastery. In this chapter we introduce some of the most common components of the basic movements used in practice and fighting. Each section focuses on the movements, positions, and skills associated with a particular part of the body.

✪ Hand Skills

Hand skills are very important in all martial arts movements. The final skill used in a fight will most often be a hand skill. Different hand skills require that the hand assume different shapes and functions. Understanding these shapes and functions will help you master the skills. The three main hand shapes are fist, palm, and hook.

Quan—Fist or Punching

In Chinese, *quan* means either "fist" or "punching." In internal martial arts there are several different fist shapes that can generate different power for different kinds of punching.

Fist Shapes

The basic fist shape is formed by bending the fingers to the center of the palm and then putting the thumb on the second joint of the index and middle fingers (figs. 2-1a and 2-1b). Different parts of the fist have different names. The third or lowest finger joints, which should usually be lined up so that they present a flat surface, are called *quanmian* or "the face of the fist." The back surface of the hand is called *quanbei* or "the back of the fist." The opening at the index-finger end of the fist is called *quanyan* or "the eye of the fist." The edge of the palm at the little-finger end of the fist is called *quangen* or "the root of the fist."

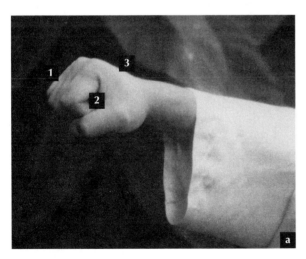
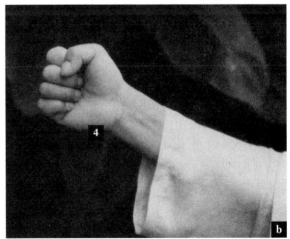

2-1: The Face (1), Eye (2), and Back (3) of a Fist   The Root (4) of a Fist

The main difference between the kind of fist used in the internal martial arts and the fist used in the external martial arts is that

the center of the internal martial arts fist is not closed. This kind of fist is called *kongxi quan* or "empty-center fist." Although there should be space inside an empty-center fist, the outside surface should be taut. The combination of firmness outside and softness inside makes it possible for your punch to be hard and strong, and your arm to remain relaxed and flexible.

Punching Skills

When throwing a punch, the fist can be used in many different ways. This section presents some of the commonly used punches.

Zhi quan—straight punch: The face of the fist is used, and the fist is thrown straight ahead (fig. 2-2).

Zuan quan—drilling punch: The face of the fist is used, and the fist is thrown upward while twisting slightly as though it were drilling a hole from the bottom up (fig. 2-3).

Zai quan—planting punch: The face of the fist is used in this punch, and the fist is thrown downward (fig. 2-4).

  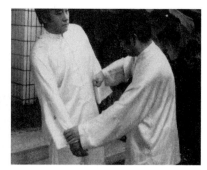

2-2: Straight Punch **2-3: Drilling Punch** **2-4: Planting Punch**

Pi quan—chopping punch: The arm should be raised, usually over the head, and the fist should strike down like an ax. Either the back of the fist or the root of the fist can be used (fig. 2-5).

 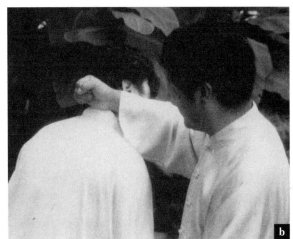

2-5: Chopping Punch Using the Root of the Fist

Fanbei quan—back-fist punch: This punch uses the elbow like an axle to turn the forearm and fist over from a palm-down to a palm-up position. Then the arm and hand move forward in a quick and sudden release of power. The back of the fist is used in this punch (fig. 2-6).

Za quan—pounding punch: The arm should be raised, usually at shoulder level, and the fist should strike downward like a hammer. Either the back of the fist or the root of the fist can be used (fig. 2-7).

Guaner quan—through-the-ear punch: This is a side punch, usually using the back of the fist to punch the left or right side of the opponent's head (fig. 2-8).

2-6: Back-Fist Punch

2-7: Pounding Punch Using the Root of the Fist

2-8: Through-the-Ear Punch

Zhang—Palm or Palm-striking

In Chinese *zhang* means either "palm" or "palm-striking." In internal martial arts there are several different palm shapes that can generate different power for different kinds of striking.

Palm Shapes

Each palm shape is used for a different function. The most common shapes are described in this section.

Liuyie zhang—willow-leaf palm: The four fingers are straight and held tightly together, and the thumb is placed on the palm. The palm and fingers are integrated so that the tips of the fingers will be hard. This integration strengthens the fingers by promoting the flow of *qi* all the way to the fingertips (fig. 2-9).

2-9: Willow-Leaf Palm

Waleng zhang—tile palm: The fingers are slightly separated and slightly bent. The thumb is allowed to stretch out naturally. This makes the palm and the back of the hand strong (fig. 2-10).

Yingzhua zhang—eagle claw palm: The shape of this palm is like a loose fist that is not fully closed. All the fingers are bent as though to grip something. The index finger, middle finger, and thumb should be very firm as though ready to pinch something (fig. 2-11).

2-10: Tile Palm

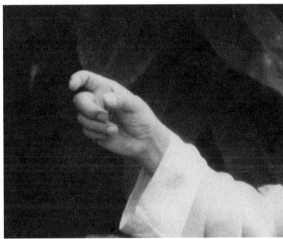

2-11: Eagle Claw Palm

Ping zhang—plate palm: In this, the most common palm shape, the palm is flat, and the thumb and fingers are straight. Power should reach to the fingers, the flat part of the palm, the edges of the palm, and the back of the hand (fig. 2-12).

Li zhang—erect palm: The fingers are close together, and the thumb is bent back to the palm. The wrist is bent so that the palm is held vertically. This shape generates power at the little-finger edge of the palm (fig. 2-13).

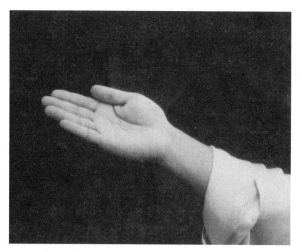

2-12: Plate Palm

2-13: Erect Palm

Palm-Striking Skills

Palm-striking is much more frequently used than fist-striking because there are many more variations of palm shapes than there are of fists. Different palm-striking skills characterize different schools of martial arts. The most common palm-striking skills are described in this section.

Cha zhang—inserting palm: The fingertips are used to strike forward, like a thrusting sword. Inserting palm is most commonly used to strike an opponent's weak point, like the eyes, throat, or acupuncture points (fig. 2-14).

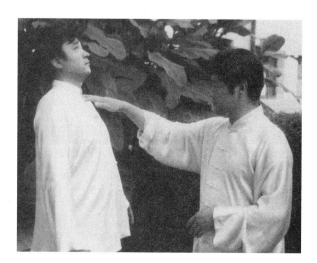

2-14: Inserting Palm

Chuan zhang—piercing palm: Piercing palm includes two main skills. The first uses the fingertips like a spear to strike directly at an opponent. This skill is similar to *cha zhang* or inserting palm. The second skill, which is more common, uses the fingertips to lead the palm a short distance forward as though it were drilling through a small space. As the palm moves, power is generated through the arm. For example, a piercing palm thrust forward under your opponent's armpit generates power at the touch-point. This power creates the forward strike (fig. 2-15).

Tui zhang—pushing palm: One or both palms can be used to push forward. To generate sufficient power for this strike, the force must come from your whole body, starting at your feet and flowing through your legs, waist, back, shoulders, and finally to your hands and fingers. If the movement is integrated in this way, the pushing-palm strike will be very powerful (fig. 2-16).

2-15: Piercing Palm

2-16: Pushing Palm

Ta zhang—stamping palm: The palm is used to push down hard and suddenly, as though stamping an imprint into a surface. Usually you can use your fingers to touch your opponent's body first and then suddenly push the root of your palm forward to strike him. In *ta zhang*, your force is released from the root of the palm. If all the force is released from the whole palm, this strike is usually referred to as *zhuang zhang* or ramming palm. In a ramming palm strike, the whole palm is pushed forward suddenly and strongly (fig. 2-17).

Pi zhang—chopping palm: This palm strike uses the little-finger edge of the palm to strike like a cutting sword. Chopping palm is usually characterized by a large and powerful downward movement (fig. 2-18).

2-17: Stamping Palm

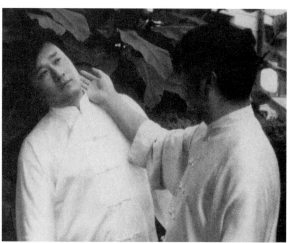

2-18: Chopping Palm

Xiao zhang—cutting palm: Cutting palm strikes also use the little-finger edge of the palm. Cutting palm is usually a quick strike like that of a sword, but it need not be very hard. If a sword is very sharp and wielded with speed, a strike can be effective without great force. There are two common cutting-palm strikes. When the

palm faces up, the strike is called *zheng xiao zhang* or obverse cutting palm (fig. 2-19a). When the palm faces down, the strike is called *fan xiao zhang* or reverse cutting palm (fig. 2-19b).

2-19: Obverse Cutting Palm   **Reverse Cutting Palm**

Gai zhang—covering palm: The whole palm is used to hit and push downward in a curving path. The hand is used like a cover that is being put over the opponent's head (fig. 2-20).

Tiao zhang—raising palm: The index-finger edge of the palm or forearm is used. Here the palm is raised directly upward or is used to lead the whole arm up. The raising palm strike involves either a quick, hard strike or a slow, powerful movement as though you were lifting something up (fig. 2-21).

2-20: Covering Palm

2-21: Raising Palm

Pai zhang—clapping palm: The palm is thrown quickly outward as though slapping something. Most of the time this strike is aimed forward and down (fig. 2-22).

2-22: Clapping Palm

Dou zhang—pocketing palm: The whole palm is used to hit upward or sideward. The center of the palm should be kept slightly hollow as though (like a pocket) it could hold something (fig. 2-23).

Fanliao zhang—turn over and strike back palm: The whole palm is used in this strike, and the usual trajectory is upward. When the palm makes contact, the arm should twist and turn over. To increase the power of this strike, it is helpful to turn the body back slightly at the outset (fig. 2-24).

2-23: Pocketing Palm

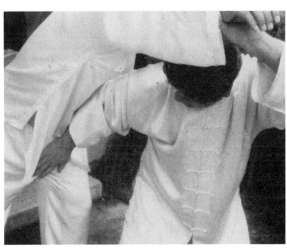

2-24: Turn Over and Strike Back Palm

The palm is used in control skills even more frequently than it is used for strikes. The ability to gain control first in a fight is very important for achieving ultimate success. In this section, several of the most commonly used combination gripping skills are described. They will be referred to often in the chapters that follow.

Zhua luo zhang—gripping and pulling palm: When an opponent reaches toward you with his hand, first stretch your hand out to

touch his wrist lightly. Your palm should face toward your body. This will allow your palm and arm to remain soft and relaxed (fig. 2-25a). Turn your hand over and use your thumb and index finger to grip your opponent's wrist (fig. 2-25b). You can use your middle finger along with your index finger to strengthen your hold. Then pull your opponent's hand quickly and suddenly downward and slightly to the side of your body. This will make him lean forward (fig. 2-25c).

2-25: Gripping and Pulling Palm

Zhua dai reng zhang—gripping, pulling, and throwing palm: When an opponent attacks you from the front, first stretch your hand out to touch his wrist lightly. Your palm should face toward your body to help maintain softness and relaxation in your hand and arm (fig. 2-26a). Turn your hand over and use your thumb and index finger to grip your opponent's wrist. You can use your middle finger alongside your index finger if you want to gain additional control. Quickly and suddenly, pull your opponent's hand simultaneously down and to the side. This will cause him to lean forward and sideways (fig. 2-26b). Then suddenly change the direction of your pull to the other side of your body, as though you were tossing something away (fig. 2-26c). After the throw, you can

increase the effectiveness of this skill by using your other hand to grab your opponent's wrist and pull it to the other side (fig. 2-26d).

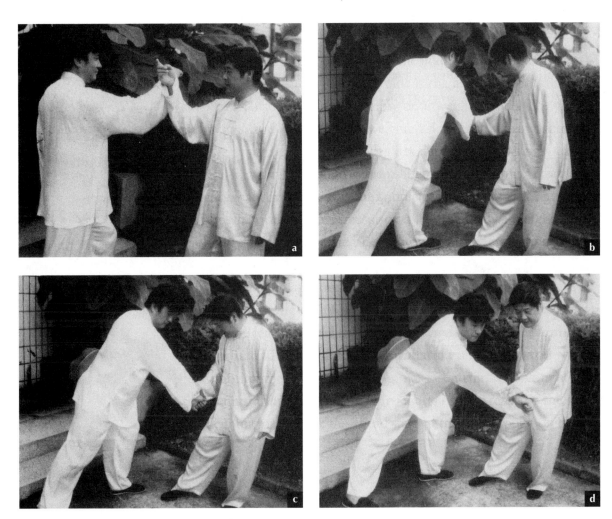

2-26: Gripping, Pulling, and Throwing Palm

Gou—Hook

In Chinese *gou* means "hook," and in martial arts it means to bend the wrist to shape the hand like a hook. There are two basic hook shapes. One is called *shi gou* or substantial hook; the other is called *xu gou* or insubstantial hook. In the substantial hook, the thumb

and fingers are gathered together until they touch each other (figs. 2-27a, 2-27b). The usual function of this hand shape is to grip and hook something. It is often used to defend against an incoming kick (fig. 2-28). In the insubstantial hook, the thumb and fingers are gathered together but do not touch each other (fig. 2-29). This hand shape, called a goose-head fist, is frequently used for wrist strikes (fig. 2-30).

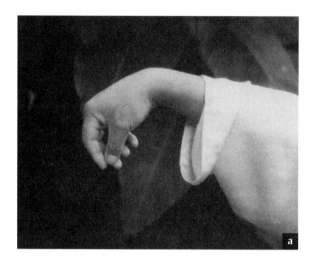
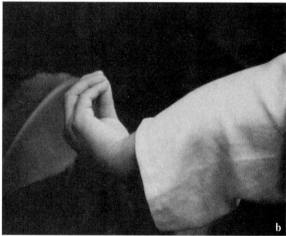

2-27: Substantial Hook

2-28: Substantial Hook Used to Grip a Leg

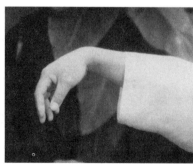

2-29: Insubstantial Hook

2-30: Strike with Insubstantial Hook (Goose-Head Fist)

✪ *Zhou*—Elbow or Elbow Strike

In Chinese *zhou* means either "elbow" or "elbow strike." Elbow-striking skills are very effective for short, powerful strikes. Because internal martial arts emphasize fighting at close range, elbow elements are of central importance. In this section, we introduce some of the common elbow-striking skills used for close-range strikes.

Ding zhou—propping-up elbow strike: The hand is used to lead the elbow strike. First the hand is raised and thrust forward. During the thrust, the arm is suddenly bent and the hand moves backward until the tiger mouth of the hand (the area between thumb and index finger) is close to the corresponding shoulder. Imagining that the tiger's mouth is touching the shoulder will cause the elbow to move forward and up and will result in a more powerful strike by the tip of the elbow (fig. 2-31).

Zhuang zhou—straight-ahead ramming strike: The arm is bent and the hand moves back toward the shoulder. Imagine that the tiger mouth of the hand touches the corresponding shoulder. This causes the elbow to move straight forward and the tip of the elbow to gain power for a straight-ahead strike (fig. 2-32).

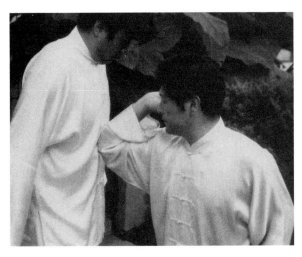

2-31: Propping-Up Elbow Strike      **2-32: Straight-Ahead Ramming Elbow Strike**

Zha zhou—pounding-down strike: In this movement, the hand is raised and the arm is bent. The elbow moves forward and then downward in a curving line. Imagining the hand moving back to touch the shoulder will cause the tip of the elbow to strike more powerfully downward (fig. 2-33).

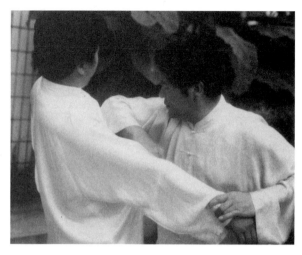

2-33: Pounding-Down Elbow Strike

No matter what skill you practice, you must always use *zhui zhou*. An internal sensation rather than a particular skill, *zhui zhou* means that you should always feel as though your elbows are slightly weighted or dropping down. This allows your *qi* and internal force to extend to your hands. As a result, your wrists will acquire greater power and will move more nimbly. Dropping your elbows will also increase the integration of your movements. The key acupuncture points on which to focus your mind for *zhui zhou* are the *Quchi* points on your elbows.

✪ *Jian*—Shoulder or Shoulder Strikes

In Chinese *jian* means either "shoulder" or "shoulder strike." Like elbow strikes, shoulder strikes are used for powerful, short-distance attacks. When your opponent is so close that an elbow strike is not possible, you can use a shoulder strike. The common shoulder strikes are *jian zhuang* or ramming striking and *jian kao* or leaning strike. In a ramming strike, the front part of the shoulder is used to strike quickly forward (fig. 2-34). It is often used after hand and elbow strikes have failed. If you miss with your hand or elbow strike, you can immediately launch a ramming shoulder strike without having to move your body back. In a leaning shoulder strike, the back part of the shoulder is used to strike backward (fig. 2-35). This strike is

powerful but requires that you turn around during the strike, so it is used only in special circumstances.

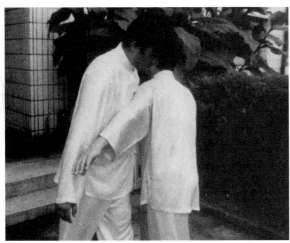

2-34: Ramming Shoulder Strike

2-35: Leaning Shoulder Strike

The shoulder is the root of the arm. If you do not master shoulder elements, your hands will never acquire full power. No matter what skill you practice, you should always maintain *song jian* or relaxation of the shoulders. This will help you relax your arms and allow your *qi* and internal force to extend through your arms to your hands. If you cannot relax your shoulders, the muscles of your arms and hands will tighten and you will be unable to move with strength and fluidity. The key acupuncture points on which you should focus your mind for *song jian* are the *Jianjing* points on your shoulders.

✪ *Kua*—Hip or Hip Strikes

In Chinese *kua* means either "hip" or "hip strike." *Kua da* or hip strikes are effective for quick, powerful hitting when your opponent is too close for effective elbow or hand strikes. Hip strikes are usually launched to the side. When using a hip strike, it is easy for

your root to be shaken, so you must be very careful to maintain your balance (fig. 2-36).

The hip is the root of the leg, and the movement of your hips strongly influences your footwork. In all footwork, it is important to maintain *chou kua* or the drawing in of the hips. This means that when you are about to take a step, you should feel as though the hip that is above the unweighted leg (the leg that will be moved) is being raised and placed on top of the hip that is over the weighted leg. This will make all your footwork quick, nimble, stable, and powerful. In *chou kua*, the key acupuncture points are the *Huantiao* points on your hips. When you step, your focus should shift first to the *Huantiao* point on the hip of your unweighted leg and then to the *Huantiao* point on the hip of your weighted leg.

2-36: Hip Strike

★ *Xi*—Knee or Knee Skills

In Chinese *xi* means either "knee" or "knee skills." The most powerful and commonly used knee strike is called *xi zhuang*. This skill is used to strike an opponent's lower abdomen, groin, stomach, chest, or ribs (fig. 2-37).

A very important function of knee skills is to control the opponent's leg movements. Knee skills can intercept the opponent's footwork and cause him to lose balance. In this section, we introduce several of the common knee skills that are used to control an opponent.

2-37: Knee Strike

Tao suo—lasso control: The foot is used to hook the opponent's foot, and then the knee is used to lock and control his shank. This combination of foot and knee movements controls the opponent's footwork by creating the effect of a lasso around his leg (fig. 2-38).

Wai cha kao—insert push from the outside: The outside of the leg controls the opposite-side leg of the opponent by pushing in on it. The outside of your left leg, for example, pushes in on the outside of your opponent's left leg. Your leg should be placed to the outside of your opponent's leg, and your foot should be behind his foot. Then, touch the outside of his knee with the outside of your knee. You can strike inward immediately or touch his leg lightly first and then push inward (fig. 2-39).

Nei cha kao—insert push from the inside: In this maneuver, the outside of the leg controls the same-side leg of the opponent by pushing out on it. The outside of your right leg, for example, is used to push out on the inside of your opponent's left leg. In this knee strike, you step to the inside of your opponent's leg and put your foot behind his foot. Then, touch the inside of his knee with the outside of your knee. You can strike outward directly or lightly touch his knee first and then push outward (fig. 2-40).

2-38: Lasso Controlling   **2-39: Insert Push from the Outside**   **2-40: Insert Push from the Inside**

✪ Foot Skills

The foot skills—sometimes called leg skills—described here are the most commonly used kicks. There are many different kinds of kicks, and they are differentiated and named according to the part of the foot and the kind of force that is used.

Dian—toe kick: The tip of the toe is used in this kick, which is quick but not very powerful. The usual target of this kick is the opponent's knee, groin, or the acupuncture points on his legs and ribs (fig. 2-41).

Ti—straight kick: The instep of the foot is used for this quick and powerful kick. The upper surface of the foot is aimed straight ahead, usually at the opponent's crotch or lower stomach (fig. 2-42).

Chuai—full-foot kick: This is a powerful kick using the sole of the foot. Usually the knee is bent first to bring the foot back in order to store energy. Then the leg is straightened out in a large motion with the sole of the foot in a vertical or horizontal position so that the toes point up or to the side. Because it involves a large movement, this kick is easy to use but it can also be easily defended against, so you must be very careful when releasing it. This kick is usually aimed at the opponent's ribs, stomach, or hip.

2-41: Toe Kick   **2-42: Straight Kick**   **2-43: Straight-ahead Full-Foot Kick**

There are two kinds of *chuai*. If the body faces forward and the kick is straight ahead, the kick is called one of the following: *zheng chuai* or straight-ahead full-foot kick, *yingmen chuai* or front-door kick, *zhuang* or ramming kick, or *deng*, which means stamping-forward kick (fig. 2-43). If the body is turned to the side and the kick is also to the side, the kick is called *ce chuai* or sideways full-foot kick (fig. 2-44). *Ce chui* can be either high or low, but it is usually not aimed higher than the opponent's waist or chest.

Cai—Stamping kick: This quick but not very powerful kick uses the sole of the foot. The toes are turned to the outside of the body, and the foot is put lightly on the point to be kicked. The force of the kick is then released forward and down, as though the foot were stamping on something. This kick is most often used to strike the front of the opponent's shank or knee (fig. 2-45).

Jie—side-cut kick: Like *Cai*, this kick is quick but not very powerful. The outside edge of the sole of the foot is used. The toes are turned toward the inside of the body, and the outside edge of the foot is aimed at the opponent's shank or knee. This kick is usually used for defense (fig. 2-46).

2-44: Sideways Full-Foot Kick   **2-45: Stamping Kick**   **2-46: Side-Cut Kick**

✪ Head

Head movements are important because they influence the movement of the rest of the body. If you move your head incorrectly, you will lose your balance. The critical factor for correct head position is *ding tou xuan,* which means that the head should be held as though it were suspended from above.

Ding tou xuan is one of the most important internal martial arts principles. It requires that you hold your head erect at all times. If this principle is not followed, no movement, skill, or technique can be effectively executed. Correctly performed, *ding tou xuan* will enhance the development of your *shen*, *yi,* and *qi* and will make your body alert and nimble. It will also adjust the balance of your body and increase your ability to focus your mind on the acupuncture points. The key acupuncture point for *ding tou xuan* is *Baihui,* which is on the top of the head. Imagine that you are using *Baihui* as a point of suspension. Put your mind on this acupuncture point and make sure that it is aligned directly above the *Huiyin* point, midway between the sexual organ and the anus.

Although head strikes are common in many external styles, they are not often used in internal martial arts.

✪ Body

Body movement is called *shen fa*, and it has two aspects. First, it includes guidelines for proper body position and alignment in any posture; and second, it involves methods for changing position from one posture to another. There are several key points that should characterize all body movements.

Han xiong—empty the chest: To empty the chest means to draw your chest back slightly so that your upper torso feels slightly concave. This will cause your *qi* to sink smoothly and easily down to

Dantian along *Renmai*, the acupuncture meridian that runs along the front centerline of your torso. Emptying the chest will also improve your footwork. For *han xiong*, you should focus your mind on the key acupuncture point *Tanzhong*, which is on the center of your chest.

Ba bei—straighten the back: You must always keep your back straight. Never let it hunch forward or sway backward. Proper alignment will help your *qi* ascend smoothly and easily along *Dumai*, the acupuncture meridian that runs along the centerline of your back. When combined with *han xiong*, *ba bei* will allow your *qi* to move around your body in a circle, extending from your head down to your toes and back up again. This circular movement of *qi* facilitates the release of internal force and is the most important element in your basic internal training. You should focus on *Jiaji*, the key *ba bei* acupuncture point located at the center of your back, to help you align your back.

Song yao—relax the waist: *Song yao* is one of the most important key points because it involves your waist, which is the center of your body and the locus of control for all your movements. If your waist is tight, you will not be able to relax any other part of your body. Your *qi* will not be able to move smoothly throughout your body, your internal force will not be sustained, your arms will not be flexible, and your footwork will not be nimble. The key acupuncture points for relaxing your waist are *Mingmen* on the center of your lower back and *Shenque* on your navel. You should alternate your focus between these two points.

Guo dang—curve and expand the crotch: In *guo dang*, the arch formed by the inside surfaces of your legs and your crotch should expand and maintain a curved shape. This will help your *qi* sink and move smoothly down to your legs without becoming dissi-

pated. *Guo dang* will also increase your root and the power in your legs. It will make your whole body very nimble. The key acupuncture points for *guo dang* are the *Yanglingquan* points on your knees. To curve and expand your crotch correctly, put your mind on these acupuncture points and make sure that each knee is aligned directly above the toes of the corresponding foot.

Liu tun—tuck the buttocks under the lower back: *Liu tun* means that you must keep your lower spine straight so that your buttocks do not protrude. This movement will allow your waist to remain relaxed and your *shen* to rise. The key acupuncture point for *liu tun* is *Weilu*, on the tailbone. Imagine that *Weilu* is pointing straight down.

✪ Stance

"Stance" refers to the position of the feet and legs when a stationary posture is assumed. It is a very important aspect of your training. If your stances are not correct, you will never achieve high-level skill and you may injure yourself. If your stances are correct, your root and balance will be improved. Proficiency in assuming correct stances will increase your ability to relax, to sense the internal components, and to acquire good fighting skills. It will also enhance the flow of *qi*. It is said that when you stand in front of a master, he can tell immediately from your stance what your *gongfu* level is.

In the majority of stances, all or most of the body's weight is borne by one leg. This allows for the clear differentiation of *yin* and *yang*. There are standards that specify the correct distance between the feet for each posture in form practice. These specifications, however, become less important in fighting situations. Generally, your stances should be smaller when fighting because smaller stances allow you to move more nimbly and quickly. Nevertheless,

2-47: Merging Stance

it is important for you to be familiar with the proper standards even if your goal is primarily to develop fighting skills. Several common stances are described in this section.

Bing bu—merging stance: In merging stance, the feet are close together and parallel to each other. Both legs bear the weight of the body evenly. In this configuration, the feet are said to be "merged" or closed. This stance can be changed to any other stance easily and quickly (fig. 2-47).

Gong bu—bow stance: In the bow stance, the feet are placed some distance apart. One leg is bent, like a bow, while the other leg is straight. The bent leg bears the full or almost full weight of the body. There are several different bow stances. The most common are *zheng gong bu* or standard bow stance and *ce gong bu* or side bow stance. In the standard bow stance, one foot is placed in front of the other. The front leg is bent and bears the full weight of the body, the back leg is straight and empty, and the toes of both feet point forward (fig. 2-48). In the side bow stance, also called *pu bu* or lay-down stance, the feet are parallel to each other and are spread apart to the right and left sides of the body to form a side stance. The weight shifts to one leg, which bends and bears the full weight of the body. The other leg is empty and remains straight (fig. 2-49).

Zuo bu—sitting stance: In the sitting stance, the back leg is bent and bears the full weight of the body, and the front leg is straight and empty with either the toe or the heel touching the ground. In this configuration, it is said that the body is sitting on the leg. Sometimes, if the toes touch the ground, this stance is called *xu bu* or insubstantial stance (fig. 2-50).

2-48: Standard Bow Stance

2-49: Side Bow Stance

2-50: Sitting Stance

Ma bu—riding horse stance: In riding horse stance, the feet are parallel to each other and spread apart to form a side stance. Both legs are bent, and each knee should be directly above the toes of the corresponding foot, as when riding a horse. There are two different riding horse stances. One is called *zheng ma bu* or standard riding horse stance; the other is called *ban ma bu* or half riding horse stance. In the standard riding horse stance, the weight of the body is evenly divided between the two legs (fig. 2-51). In the half riding horse stance, one foot points forward and bears about sixty to seventy percent of the body's weight, while the other foot points to the side (fig. 2-52).

2-51: Riding Horse Stance

2-52: Half Riding Horse Stance

Xie bu—rest stance: In rest stance, the legs are crossed and bent. The front foot is always pointed away from the body and bears almost all of the body's weight. The heel of the back foot can be raised off the ground. The knee of the back leg should touch the back of the front leg as though the back leg were resting on the front leg. In this stance, the body assumes a squatting position (fig. 2-53).

Bei bu—back step stance: In back step stance, the legs are crossed. The front foot is always pointed outward from the body. The back leg is bent and bears most of the body's weight. The front leg is almost straight and stretches out across the other leg. This stance is similar to *xie bu* but the body position is a little bit higher. This makes it more flexible than *xie bu* and as a result, it is used more often (fig. 2-54).

Duli bu—single-leg stance or balance stance: In *duli bu*, one leg is raised off the ground, and the other leg bears the full weight of the body and balances the body. There are many different kinds of single-leg stances. The leg that supports the body can be straight or bent, and the raised leg can be held in a variety of positions. In form practice, the balance stances are used more for the practice of basic abilities than for direct application to fighting situations. Single-leg stances can be very helpful in developing an awareness of internal force and for increasing one's root (fig. 2-55).

2-53: Rest Stance   **2-54: Back Step Stance**   **2-55: Single-Leg Stance**

✪ Step

Step, usually called *bu fa*, refers to the movement of the feet or to footwork in general. It is a very important part of one's training. The traditional view is that thirty percent of martial arts skill is in the hands and seventy percent is in the feet. This difference between the importance of stepping skills and that of hand skills is especially marked in fighting.

Footwork provides the foundation for all the other movements. If your steps are not correct and well executed, none of your other movements will be adequate. Good footwork is a basic component of the ability to relax and to move with agility and stability. Not only can it improve your technique, it can increase your internal force. The steps used in the form are described and illustrated in this section.

Shang bu—step forward with the back foot: *Shang bu* is a big step in which the back foot moves forward and is placed in front of the fixed foot. The distance between the two feet at the end of the step depends on the kind of stance that is being assumed. As the back foot moves forward, it follows a curved path, first being placed alongside the fixed foot and then moving forward to a position ahead of the fixed foot. Because *shang bu* is a long step, it is taken more slowly than many other steps and is used only when you need to move far forward. Figure 2-56 shows the path followed by the right foot moving forward in *shang bu*.

2-56: Step Forward with the Back Foot

Jin bu—step forward with the front foot: *Jin bu* is when a forward step is taken with the front foot, and the back foot just follows. This is a quick step commonly used in situations that require you to move forward swiftly. Usually *jin bu* does not involve a weight change or a change in stance posture. If the back foot follows quickly and moves close to the front foot, it will be easy to step forward again with your front foot. If a second forward step is taken, the sequence is called *gen bu* or following step. *Gen bu* offers a chance to make quick and continuous forward steps. In real fighting situations, *jin bu* and *gen bu* are used more often than *shang bu*. Fig. 2-57 shows the movement of the feet in *gen bu*.

2-57: Step Forward with the Front Foot

Che bu—step back with the front foot: *Che bu* is a big step in which the front foot moves back until it is behind the fixed foot. The moving foot should follow a curved path, moving first alongside the fixed foot and then to the back and side of the fixed foot. Like *shang bu*, *che bu* is a large, slow step. It is used when you need to move back a long distance. Fig. 2-58 shows the position of the feet in *che bu* when the left foot moves back.

Tui bu—step back with the back foot: *Tui bu* is when a backward step is taken with the back foot, and the front foot just follows.

2-58: Step Back with the Front Foot

Like *jin bu,* it is a quick step often used in situations that require you to move back swiftly. Usually there is no weight change or change in stance posture during *tui bu.*

Ceshan bu—side-dodge step: *Ceshan bu* is a step in which the right foot moves to the right and forward while the left foot follows, or the left foot moves to the left and forward while the right foot follows. *Ceshan bu* is frequently used for moving quickly to the side.

Figure 2-59 shows the movement of the feet in *ceshan bu*, first to the right and then to the left.

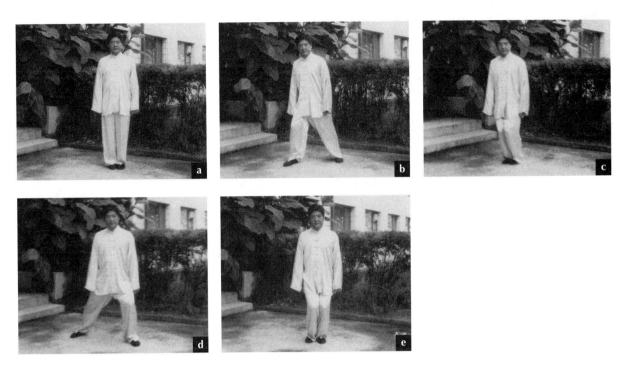

2-59: Side-Dodge Step

Gai bu or *hengbai bu*—cover step: *Gai bu*, or *hengbai bu,* is a step that turns the body slightly so that the side of the body faces slightly forward. In it, one foot is lifted up and moves forward. As it moves, it turns outward and comes to rest alongside the fixed foot. Having taken this step, the foot that moved is placed flat on the ground. *Gai bu* can result in a rest stance in which most of the body's weight is on only one leg, or in a cover stance in which the body's weight is more evenly divided between the two legs. It is a fast, often-used step for moving forward and turning quickly to the side. Figure 2-60 shows the position of the feet in *gai bu* with the left foot moving forward and turning.

2-60: Cover Step

Kou bu—buckle step: *Kou bu* is a step in which one foot moves forward, touches the ground heel-first, and then turns so that the toes face the toes of the other foot. The toes of the two feet should be closer to each other than the heels. The knees should be close to each other and may even touch. *Kou bu* is a fast and frequently used step for turning the body inward. Figure 2-61 shows the position of the feet in *kou bu* with the left foot moving forward and turning.

2-61: Buckle Step

Bai bu—swing step: In *bai bu,* one foot moves forward then swings to the outside and touches the ground heel-first. The toes of this foot point outward so that the heels are at right angles to each other. *Bai bu* is a commonly used fast step for turning the body outward. Figure 2-62 shows the position of the feet in *bai bu* when the swing step is executed with the left foot.

2-62: Swing Step

CHAPTER THREE

Basic Gongfu Training

There are many schools of traditional Chinese martial arts. Their styles are different, but they all place great importance on basic gongfu (*ji ben gong*) training. In many groups, students practice only basic *gongfu* skills for years before learning other skills. It is generally believed that without good basic *gongfu,* it is not possible to attain high-level mastery in the martial arts.

Basic *gongfu* can be likened to the foundation of a building. Viewers of the completed building may give no thought to the building's foundation, but it is this foundation that determines many of the building's visibly impressive characteristics. A tall building, for example, cannot be constructed unless it rests on a strong foundation. The same is true for developing high-level skill in the martial arts. While good basic *gongfu* does not guarantee that one will ultimately achieve high-level mastery, the lack of it certainly ensures that such mastery will be forever outside one's reach. The understanding and diligent practice of basic *gongfu* is one of the most important aspects of martial arts training. This is true for all practitioners but especially beginners.

Basic *gongfu* derives from characteristics of physical movement and body dynamics. Among the most important of these, for training in the internal martial arts, are flexibility, stability, strength, speed, agility, nimbleness, integration, coordination, sensitivity, and speed of reaction time. Correct training can greatly enhance these characteristics and release latent energy to a certain extent. *Gongfu*

practice is of great benefit throughout your training. The level of skill that a practitioner finally achieves depends on how much of his or her natural potential is brought out in the course of *gongfu* practice.

To acquire the sixteen skills that are introduced in this book, one should practice basic *gongfu* first. Because the form described here includes skills from several different schools of martial arts, I have selected several basic *gongfu* training methods from each of these schools, which are introduced in this chapter. I believe that this combination training will help people understand internal martial arts skills more comprehensively. I encourage you to practice hard and to keep in mind that it often takes a lot of time, as well as effort, to improve your basic *gongfu*. Occasionally the training may seem boring and pointless, but please be patient. You will eventually reap great benefit from it. Remember that the term *"gongfu"* refers to any activity or quality that takes a long time to develop. When it comes to *gongfu* training, nothing of value is achieved easily or quickly, but if you apply yourself with patience and commitment, time will pay you back generously. You will find that not a moment was wasted.

There are some basic *gongfu* skills that are especially important for fighting. In Taiji Quan, they are the skills of listening, dissolving, adhering, and sticking; in Bagua Zhang, they are the skills of changing, moving smoothly, and executing quick and nimble footwork; in Xingyi Quan, they are maintaining and expressing stable and integrated force; and in Tongbei Quan, the basic skill involves releasing force suddenly, quickly, and crisply. If one can perform these skills and apply them naturally and with ease, one will have understood the essence of internal martial arts fighting. In the following sections of this chapter, I describe basic *gongfu* practice methods that can help practitioners improve their skills in many different ways.

✪ *Zhuang Gong*—Pile-Standing

Zhuang gong or *zhan zhuang*, usually translated to "Pile-standing" or "Post-standing," is one of the most important training methods in traditional Chinese martial arts. If practiced over a long period of time, it will increase your ability to understand and use the internal components, like *shen*, *yi*, and *qi*, of the martial arts. You will be better able to quiet and focus your *shen*, to direct your mind, to make your *qi* sink down and move smoothly throughout your whole body, and to increase your internal force. Pile-standing is also helpful for improving the external components of your martial arts practice. It aids in relaxing your body, increasing your strength, improving integration, stability and root, and in correcting your body movements and stance positions. Post-standing is an easy and useful training method that provides many benefits.

Zhan zhuang means "to stand as a pile or post." Most post-standing exercises derive from *jing gong* or "still skill" practice in which the practitioner holds one unchanging posture for some period of time. Occasionally the posture may include a few simple changes. Standing still, however, does not mean that one is not doing anything. Pile-standing creates many internal effects that should be further developed through repeated practice. Close attention is required if your skills are to improve.

Although different internal martial arts schools emphasize different pile-standing training methods, all schools share some general principles. These are discussed in the following section.

Body relaxation: In all post-standing practice, relaxation is of central importance, and it is a basic requirement for the proper execution of almost all skills. To learn body relaxation through pile-standing practice, you must use your mind. While holding a posture, you should breathe deeply, slowly, and smoothly and focus your mind on one identified point. This point may differ

from posture to posture. After focusing your mind, you should try to relax every part of your body.

It is important to understand the meaning of relaxation as it is used in the internal martial arts. Relaxation means to use only the minimum amount of force needed to maintain the correct posture. A common and mistaken assumption is that in a state of relaxation one exerts no force at all. When you practice, it is important to pay careful attention to the amount of force that is being used in every part of your body. If in a posture, for example, you are supposed to raise an arm and hold it outstretched, you should first raise your arm to the required position and hold it there. Then you should use your mind to relax your shoulder and drop your elbow until you feel that your whole arm is about to drop down. Just when you notice this feeling, stop thinking about relaxing your shoulder and elbow. As soon as you feel that your arm has stopped dropping down, think again about relaxing your shoulder. Repeat this process for as long as you maintain the pile-standing posture. Through this process, it will seem as though your body gradually comes to recognize and remember exactly how much force is needed to keep your arm in the correct position. When you naturally use just this amount of force, your arm will be truly relaxed. When you can achieve this state throughout your whole body, you will have understood the full meaning of relaxation, and your martial arts practice will show great improvement.

Body alignment: With the exception of a few special practices, your body should always be held comfortably in an upright position during post-standing. The centerline of your body, from the *Baihui* point on the top of your head to the *Huiyin* point on the bottom of your torso, should be kept vertical and straight. The three *Dantian* (upper, middle, and lower) will fall along this vertical line. When your alignment adheres to this principle, your *shen* will become more intense, your mind will become calm and focused, your *qi* and

your internal force will flow smoothly and naturally throughout your body, and you will be able to maintain good balance. You will feel settled, stable, and comfortable.

To achieve proper alignment, you should focus your mind on the *Baihui* point and imagine that your body is suspended from above at this point. You should also make sure that your eyes gaze straight ahead and that your shoulders are level. The same should be true for your hips.

Six integrations: *Liu he* or the maintenance of the six integrations is a very important concept in internal martial arts training. There are three internal integrations and three external integrations. The internal integrations are: *xin* integrated with *yi*, which is often expressed as *shen* leading mind; *yi* integrated with *qi*, expressed as mind leading *qi*; and *qi* integrated with *jin*, expressed as *qi* leading internal trained force. The external integrations refer to physical movements of the body and involve shoulder and hip integration; elbow and knee integration; and hand and foot integration.

The essential concept of the six integrations is that the mind is used to lead your practice so that the internal and external components of the body work together in a completely coordinated way. The internal martial arts are, by definition, those martial arts in which all practice is led by the mind and in which the external components of physical movement derive from the sequencing of the internal components of *xin*, *yi*, *qi*, and *jin*.

Xin means "heart" and in the internal martial arts refers to the part of the mind that intends to do something. *Yi* refers to the part of the mind that expresses your intentions. The integration of *xin* and *yi* means that if you intend to do something, your mind will follow your intention and lead you to realize your intention. Careful training and perseverance are necessary in order to achieve this first internal integration. A very common mistake is to hesitate

when you find a chance to translate intention into action. In fighting, opportunity can quickly and easily be lost.

Yi and *qi* integration means that when your mind leads you to do something, your *qi* can immediately follow your mind and flow smoothly throughout your body so that your intention can be accomplished. As *qi* moves through your body, *jin* or internal force follows, and as a result, energy becomes readily available for physical action. This relationship between *qi* and *jin* is the third internal integration. Because *jin* includes external as well as internal features, whenever *jin* moves, the body will move.

It is said of the whole sequence of integrations that "if *xin* is thinking, the body is moving," and for the movements of your body to be maximally effective, they must be fully coordinated. Because your arms and legs are the most difficult parts of the body to integrate, these parts should be a focal point of your practice. The external integrations define the relationship between arm movements and leg movements. When *qi* brings *jin*, and *jin*, in turn, stirs your arms and legs into action, the movement of your shoulders must be coordinated with that of your hips.

To accomplish this first external integration, you should focus your mind on the *Jinjing* point on your shoulder and imagine that this point is moving in concert with the *Huantiao* point on your opposite hip. Then, focus on the *Quechi* point on your elbow and imagine that its movement is coordinated with the movement of the *Yanglingquan* point on the knee of your opposite leg. This is the second external integration. For the third integration, focus your mind on the *Laogong* point on your hand and integrate its movement with the *Yong-quan* point on your opposite foot.

With long practice in these three external integrations, your body's movements will become fully coordinated and your body will remain completely relaxed. Your acupuncture channels will be well connected so that *qi* can readily and smoothly flow along them and reach every part of your body. This will cause a very power-

ful force to be generated throughout your body. Practicing these integrations will bring out many of the latent potentialities within your body. Often a practitioner will acquire several times greater force than was originally accessible. It then becomes possible to focus all this force on one point and release it in all directions at same time. Such force is usually referred to as "six directions force" with the directions being up, down, left, right, forward, and back. Because you can still be very relaxed when you release this force, your body will be strong but not tight, like a metal bar bound in cotton. Your force will have a springy quality, like a ball full of air. It will also be incisive and instantaneous, like a touch of electricity. If you can release it from one point—a hand, for example—it will be very powerful. You can acquire this kind of force by using your mind to lead your practice.

In the internal martial arts, all movement should originate from *xin* and then derive from the sequence of *yi*, *qi*, and *jin*. The goal is to ignite your *shen*, strengthen your *qi*, increase the power of your *jin,* and make your movements flexible, your steps quick and nimble, and your root stable and deep.

In the next three sections, I will discuss several training methods of post-standing. They are selected from different schools, and each helps develop different skills.

Santi Shi—Trinity Pile-Standing

Santi Shi or Trinity pile-standing is the most important and fundamental training in Xingyi Quan practice. It is said that "*Santi Shi* is the source of all skills." In traditional training, beginners need to learn *Santi Shi* and practice it for a long time before they can be taught other skills. Practicing *Santi Shi* can help practitioners improve their movements and the integration of internal and external components. Stability and rooting can also be increased by this practice, as can relaxation and the control and use of *shen*, *yi*, *qi*,

and *jin*. *Santi Shi* training is emphasized in every Xingyi Quan group and is presented here as a foundation training for martial arts fighting skills.

Santi Shi practice includes several steps. First, you need to study the *Santi Shi* movements and stance carefully. Correct movement will facilitate the development of correct feelings—for example, feelings of *qi* flow—at all key acupuncture points throughout your body. It is important to maintain relaxation during *Santi Shi* training, especially for beginners. Second, you should learn to generate *jin* (trained force) and fully express it in your physical movements. As in all internal martial arts training, your practice should be led by your mind. Adherence to the Twenty-Four Key Points (described later) will further enhance your training.

At different stages of your training, your mind should be used in different ways. Because the training process takes a long time, you should practice daily and have patience. Beginners may be able to maintain the correct posture for only three to five minutes. When you can stand correctly for about thirty minutes, you will have developed a strong foundation for further progress in your practice. Some ancient masters were known to have required their students to practice *Santi Shi* for at least one to two hours every day. Without this discipline and the strength that such practice engendered, it was considered pointless to teach other skills.

Basic Principle

The inspiration for *Santi Shi* comes from the Daoist principle that describes the creation of the universe. It states: "Dao generates One, One generates Two, Two generates Three, and Three generates all the things of the world." The Dao originates from *xuwu* or *wuji*, the undifferentiated state of the universe. From the Dao, a *qi* force is generated that initiates change within the universe and produces *yin* and *yang*. Thus, although the *xuwu* state appeared

to be empty, it had within it a creative force that could bring order and balance out of chaos.

Taiji is the "One" referred to in the Daoist principle of creation. It describes the state of the universe just after the undifferentiated state of *xuwu* has become ordered by the emergence of Dao and the movement of *qi*. The entities of *yin* and *yang* are differentiated within *Taiji* but are not yet fully separated. *Yin* and *yang* are the basic attributes of the universe, and the existence of each depends on and is clarified by the existence of the other. Each attribute also contains part of the other within it.

Liangyi, the "Two" in the principle of creation, is the point at which *yin* and *yang* become separated into two entities, each with its own attributes. *Yin* and *yang* are qualities possessed by all objects in the universe. When *yin* and *yang* interact, a new entity is generated. So together *yin*, *yang*, and the new entity are called *Sancai*—the "Three Essentials."

Sancai is the generative point from which all perceptible things derive. *Sancai* contains within it the three most valuable treasures of the universe: sky, earth, and humans. Sky is characterized by the attributes of *yang*; earth, by the attributes of *yin*. Humankind is generated from the interaction of sky and earth.

According to Daoist principle, the *Sancai* can be found within even the smallest units of matter. In every occurrence of *Sancai*, there are three treasures or *Sanbao*, and in each treasure there are three more treasures. The sky, for example, a treasure of *Sancai*, contains the three treasures of sun, moon, and stars; the earth contains the three treasures of water, fire, and wind; and man contains the three treasures of *jin*, *qi*, and *shen*.

In Xingyi Quan, the trinity or tripartite structure is called *Santi* or *Sanjie*. This structure includes three external parts of the body and three internal components. The three body areas defined by *Santi* or *Sanjie* are: *Shao jie*, the tip section that includes the arms and hands; *zhong jie*, the middle or trunk section that includes the head

and torso; and *gen jie*, the root section that includes the legs and feet. Consistent with the tripartite principle, each of these three sections can be divided into three smaller sections. *Shao jie* includes a tip section composed of the hands; a middle section composed of the elbows; and a root section composed of the shoulders. *Zhong jie* includes the head as the tip section, the chest as the middle section, and the waist or stomach as the root section. In *gen jie*, the feet are the tip section, the knees are the middle section, and the hips are the root section. The three internal components of *Santi* or *Sanjie* are *shen*, *qi*, and *jin*.

Santi or *Sanjie* is the foundation of all skills in Xingyi Quan and the starting point for all change and development. The post-standing practice *Santi Shi*—also commonly called *Sancai Shi*—is a technique that can be divided into five component parts known as *Wuji Shi*, *Taiji Shi*, *Liangyi Shi*, *Santi Shi*, and *Shou Shi* (Closing Form). Practice of *Santi Shi*—which is a name for all the postures together as well as the name for one of the five components—incorporates the core concepts of Xingyi Quan and generates all other Xingyi Quan skills.

Movement to Form Standing Posture

Wuji Shi

Wuji Shi or *Wuji* Standing is a preparatory form that involves simply standing upright. In this form, the body should be relaxed and the mind should be empty. Everything should be quiet, with only a glimmer of intention inside the mind to initiate movement. If you are thinking about something strongly, even about your practice, you are not yet ready to move. You should maintain *Wuji Shi* until your thoughts have quieted completely.

Movement Description for Wuji Shi

Stand upright with both feet together. Your arms should rest naturally alongside your thighs with your palms facing in. Hold your

body erect and look straight ahead. The tip of your tongue should touch the upper palate behind your teeth. Your chin should be slightly withdrawn (fig. 3-1).

3-1

Focus your mind on the *Jianjing* points to encourage relaxation of your shoulders and on the *Quchi* points and *Shaohai* points to cause your elbows to drop. Then focus your mind on the *Jiaji* point to expand the middle of your upper back and straighten your spine. Focusing your mind next on the *Tanzhong* point and imagining that water is trickling down your breastbone to your navel will cause your chest to withdraw slightly and feel hollow. After using your mind to achieve these effects, forget everything and just experience the comfortable relaxed state of your body and the quietness of your mind. Your *shen* should be fully alert, and you should feel as though *qi* were gently impelling your body to begin moving.

Taiji Shi

Taiji Shi or *Taiji* standing signals the beginning of the form. Your mental intention and the flow of *qi* will cause change to occur inside your body. It is important in *Taiji* standing to distinguish between *yin* and *yang*. *Yin* is a substantial quality and represents stillness in your body. *Yang* is insubstantial and characterizes movement. Although *yin* and *yang* are separate and distinct, they should mutually embrace and support each other in all physical processes. *Taiji* standing creates an inclination to move and to keep the mind quiet. The practitioner should follow these feelings as he begins the form.

Movement Description for Taiji Shi

All physical movement starts from this point. When you move, you should always keep your body erect. Do not lean in any direction.

Focus your mind on the *Baihui* point on top of your head and imagine that your body is suspended from this point. Turn your right foot on your right heel about forty-five to sixty degrees to the right. Relax your shoulders and drop your elbows. This will cause your hands to feel like moving. Follow this feeling and slowly move both hands in front of your abdomen. Your left hand should be over your right hand, and the pad of your left middle finger should be over the nail of your right middle finger. Look at the nail of your left middle finger.

Relax your hips and knees. This will cause a feeling in your legs of wanting to move. Follow this feeling and slowly bend your knees and lower your body until your knees are over your toes. At the same time, drop your elbows down and slightly back. This will cause your hands to move slightly up. Let your fingers point forward and your palms face the ground while you slowly shift your weight to your right leg (fig. 3-2).

3-2

Liangyi Shi

It is said that *Liangyi Shi* is generated by the changes in *Taiji Shi*. These changes result in the separation of *yin* and *yang* and end when *yin* and *yang* become integrated and generate *Santi Shi*. *Liangyi Shi* embodies the dual principles of motion and stillness, rising up and dropping down, stretching out and drawing back, going forth and moving back. Although *yin* and *yang* remain separated in *Liangyi Shi*, they are always in balance. When your body is moving, for example, your heart should be quiet; as your body rises up, your *qi* should sink down. When *yin* and *yang* are balanced and become integrated in the *Liangyi* posture, *Santi Shi* arises.

Movement Description for Liangyi Shi

Imagine using the nail of your right middle finger to hold up your left middle finger. This will cause your left middle finger to move forward. Relax your left shoulder and drop your left elbow. Then stretch your left hand up and forward. Simultaneously, step forward with your left foot and pull your right hand—which is in front of your abdomen—back to touch your body lightly (fig. 3-3).

3-3

Look straight ahead and stretch your left hand out until the tip of your index finger is at the level of your nose. Your left palm should face forward. Keep your left elbow slightly bent. Pull your right hand back until the *Yuji* point on your right wrist touches the *Shenqie* point on your navel tightly. Your right palm should face down. Step forward about two to three feet with your left foot. Shift about thirty to forty percent of your weight to your left leg. Keep your left knee slightly bent (fig. 3-4a).

3-4a

Keep your body erect and stable. Imagine that your waist is pushing your shoulders and hips; that your shoulders, in turn, are pushing your elbows; and that your elbows are pushing your hands. Be careful during this sequence that you do not lean forward. Imagine that your hips are pushing your knees, which are then pushing your feet. The movements of your upper and lower body should be fully coordinated. Internal and external components should be integrated. If this posture is done correctly, *yin* and *yang*, though still separate, become integrated. Physically, *Liangyi Shi* is a dynamic posture that generates *Santi Shi* through the integration of *yin* and *yang*.

Santi Shi

It is said: Dao came from *xuwu*, the insubstantial and empty state, and generated *qi;* then *qi* generated *yin* and *yang,* which became integrated and generated *Santi.* Finally, *Santi* generated all things in the world. In Xingyi Quan, *Santi Shi* is called "the source of all skills."

When *Santi Shi* or Trinity Standing is generated from *Liangyi Shi,* there is no overt physical movement. (Figs. 3-4b, 3-4c, and 3-4d show this posture from different angles, but no actual movement has taken place.) The *Santi Shi* posture should be held for at least several minutes. This will help develop strength, particularly in your legs, and will also help train your mind to integrate the different parts of your body.

3-4

Although there is no physical movement during *Santi Shi,* strict attention should be paid to the various postural requirements. It is important to keep your body and head upright, your neck and spine straight, and your shoulders and hips level. It is also important not to lean in any direction.

If done correctly, *Santi Shi* will improve many of your *gongfu* skills because it will significantly increase your leg strength. To hasten the strengthening of your legs, imagine that you are trying to raise your front knee slightly. This will create a feeling of expansion and a very hot, burning sensation in your back leg.

The internal feelings that develop through *Santi Shi* are com-

plex, and so this practice can be very helpful for learning to focus your mind so that it can lead the internal components that direct your physical movements. The mental aspects of *Santi Shi* training should be developed step by step.

Changing-Side Form

When your left hand and left foot are in front during *Santi Shi*, the posture is called left-side *Santi Shi*. The opposite situation is referred to as right-side *Santi Shi*. You should practice equally on both sides.

Movement Description for Changing-Side Form

In left-side *Santi Shi*, focus your mind on the right *Jianjing* point to relax your right shoulder and on the left *Huantiao* point to relax your left hip. Then imagine moving your tailbone over your left heel. This will cause your weight to shift forward onto your left leg. While your weight is shifting forward, relax your left hip. This will cause your left foot to turn on the heel about forty-five to sixty degrees to the left. At the same time, pull both hands back slightly.

Focus your mind on your left shoulder. This will cause your right hip to relax as your weight shifts to the left. Touch your right foot to the ground in preparation for stepping forward but keep your weight on your left leg.

Focus your mind on your left elbow. This will cause your left arm to drop down and move back until it is in front of your right hand.

Then focus your mind on your left shoulder. This will relax your left shoulder and cause your right foot to step forward lightly. At the same time, pull your left hand back until it is in front of your stomach, with your left palm facing the ground. The fingers of your left hand should point to the right and forward. The *Yuji* point on your left wrist should touch the *Shenqie* point on your navel. At the same time, push your right hand forward until your right index finger lines up with your nose and your right palm faces forward. Shift your weight forward until about thirty to forty percent of

your weight is on your right leg. Keep both knees bent slightly. Look straight ahead.

Shou Shi—Closing Form

When it becomes difficult to focus your mind on maintaining the correct body positioning and intention, you should stop *Santi* Standing. Continuing to hold the posture beyond this point can increase your leg strength, but it will not benefit your internal practice. When you are ready to end your standing practice, use the ending form, also called the ending form for Trinity Standing or, more simply, the closing form. This form will provide a feeling of refreshed completion to your practice.

Movement Description for the Closing Form

If you have been standing in the left-side posture, relax your left shoulder. This will cause your arms and legs to withdraw. Follow this feeling and withdraw your left foot and left arm. Bring both feet together. When your left hand pulls back, raise your right hand slightly until both hands meet in front of your chest. Then push your hands down slowly in front of your stomach. Keep both knees bent (fig. 3-5).

Turn your right foot on the heel until your feet are parallel. At the same time, straighten your legs slowly until you are standing upright (fig. 3-6). Continue moving both hands down and gradually separate them so that each hand rests along the corresponding

3-5   3-6   3-7

thigh as your legs straighten up. Relax your whole body and breathe deeply, smoothly, and slowly several times (fig. 3-7).

Six-Direction Force

When you have developed the physical ability to hold the *Santi Shi* posture correctly, you should begin to train your mind in more detail. Although your body will appear to an outside observer to be motionless during *Santi* Standing, many changes and feelings of movement will be occurring inside your body. It is said of this state that "Outside there is stillness but inside there is movement."

Typically, six-direction practice is the first step in training your mind during *Santi* Standing. It provides a simple way to focus your mind so that your mind can lead your *qi* and your internal force. Diligent practice of the six-direction force will stabilize and coordinate all aspects of your external posture. It will also integrate your internal force and develop an internal state of comfort and clarity.

The six-direction force practice is of central importance for the development of *jin*. In this practice, internal force is developed simultaneously in six directions: forward, backward, left, right, up, and down. Often, training in *Santi Shi* emphasizes force primarily in one direction, but unless one develops the ability to support or express force in all directions, it will be difficult to change and maintain balance during movement, especially when fighting.

Internal force should be expressed in all directions, but for convenience of training, only six directions are delineated. If you can express force in these six basic directions, you can quite easily expand your skill to the release of internal force in all directions. Internal force should follow the flow of *qi* and fill your body as air fills a ball. When inflated by air, a ball becomes springy and strong, and equal pressure is exerted at every point on its surface. Internal force should similarly affect your body.

The following instructions for six-direction force practice assume

that you are in the left *Santi Shi* posture—that is, your left hand and left foot are in front. Each directional force is described individually.

Upward Force: Focus your mind on *Baihui,* the acupuncture point at the top of your head. Imagine that it is pushing upward. Imagine, too, that your feet are being inserted into the ground. This will create a reverse-direction force that will push your body up. The greater the feeling of your feet being inserted into the ground, the more upward power you will feel. Be careful that the force is directed straight upward. It is important that your body always be upright, especially your neck and head.

Downward Force: Focus your mind on the *Dantian* in the center of your lower abdomen. Think about relaxing every part of your body and about your *qi* sinking down to the *Dantian.* This will cause your body to feel heavy and drop slightly. Imagine also that your legs are pushing down into the ground.

Forward Force: Focus your mind on the *Laogong* point in the center of your left palm and feel as though your left palm were pushing forward. Feel power coming up from your back foot. Your right rear foot should press down into the ground, and power should feel as though it were flowing up through your right leg to your waist, then through your back, your left arm, and finally out through your left palm. You should feel a forward-pushing force from your back foot (in this case your right foot) all the way up to your front or left hand. At the same time, imagine that your right shoulder is chasing your left hand.

Backward Force: Focus your mind on the *Jiaji* point in the center of your back and imagine that it is pushing backward. This feeling is often characterized as "leaning on the mountain." Imagine that your left foot is pressing down into the ground. This will create a feeling that your torso is pushing toward your back. At the same time, imagine that your right hand is pulling something back,

and then coordinate this feeling with the downward force in your left foot. The integration of the feeling in your right hand with the downward press of your left foot will augment the backward force.

Leftward Force: Focus your mind on the *Shangyang* point in your right index finger and imagine pointing with this finger to the left side of your body. This will enhance the integration of your right arm and left leg and will create a feeling that your body is twisting to the left. The sense of twisting will generate a feeling of power rotating to the left inside your body.

Rightward Force: Focus your mind on the *Shaoshang* point in your left thumb and imagine your thumb twisting to the right. This will enhance the integration of your left arm and right leg and create a feeling that your body is twisting to the right. This twisting feeling will generate a force that seems to rotate to the right inside your body.

In the beginning of your practice, you should concentrate on only one of the six directions of force. When you feel comfortable with one direction, proceed to work on the next one. Remember that this training involves using only your mind to lead your practice and to create internal feelings. There is no overt physical movement. Sometimes a strong, clear feeling inside your body may cause some slight movement. You should neither seek to increase such a feeling nor struggle to stop the involuntary movement. Just maintain a relaxed state and continue with your six-direction training.

When you can practice each direction of force separately with confidence, you can practice pairs of force. First, practice upward and downward forces together, then forward and backward forces, and finally leftward and rightward forces. This gradual process is recommended because most practitioners find it difficult to focus on more than one point or direction at a time. When practicing pairs, concentrate on each side of the paired force directions. Initially, change your mental focus slowly and with clear intent from one

force in the pair to the other. Eventually you will be able quickly to switch your mental focus back and forth between the two different directions. Ultimately it will come to seem as though you are focusing on the two directions simultaneously. When you can do this routinely, your mind will generate a powerful, clear feeling.

Acquiring this ability takes a great deal of practice, so be patient. With sustained practice over a long period of time, focusing your mind on a pair of directions will seem almost effortless. Then you can extend your practice to include all three paired-force directions. The goal of such training is to increase your ability to generate or withstand power from any direction instantaneously and without conscious thought.

Integration Force

Basically, the six-direction force is an expanding force. *He jin* or integration force is the other important force that can be cultivated in *Santi Shi*. It balances your energy, makes you more stable, and allows your internal components to be comfortably coordinated. Integration force can also increase your internal power. As with six-direction force, integration force concerns mental intention and physical awareness but does not involve overt physical movement.

Integration force in your arms works to coordinate the use of both arms so that they can work harmoniously together as one. Integration force flows from your back to your arms and hands. To feel this force, first imagine strongly pushing your front hand forward. At the same time, imagine pulling your rear hand backward as though trying to tear a stiff and resistant piece of paper in half. Next, imagine pulling your front hand back and pushing your rear hand forward as though trying to put two heavy things together. Remember that all these "actions" should occur only in your mind. The images should not be accompanied by overt physical movement or by isometric tensing of your muscles.

Integration force in your legs is also a coordinating force. It can

help develop rooting. To practice leg integration force, first imagine that your body is sinking down. This will create a feeling that your feet are being inserted deeply into the ground. Your front foot should slant down and forward, and your rear foot should slant down and backward. Next, imagine that you are standing on an icy surface. The surface is so slippery that your feet feel as though they are about to slide apart. Imagine that your front foot is sliding forward and your rear foot is slipping backward. In order to maintain your balance and avoid falling down, you will feel as though you need to use force to bring your feet together. Once again, all of this occurs only in your mind. There should be no overt physical movement and no isometric tensing of your muscles.

Integration force in your arms and legs results in the coordination of your upper and lower body. A simple way to practice integration force is to use three specific points on your arm and a corresponding set of three points on your opposite leg. The three points on your arm are: the *Jianjing* point on your shoulder, the *Quchi* point on your elbow, and the *Laogong* point on your hand. The three coordinating points on your opposite-side leg are: the *Huantiao* point on your hip, the *Yanglingquan* point on your knee, and the *Yongquan* point on your foot.

The first step in integration force training is to mentally connect one arm with the leg on the opposite side of your body. Focus first on the *Laogong* point of your left hand and then expand this thought to the *Yongquan* point on your right foot. Then focus your mind on the *Quchi* point on your left elbow and connect that thought to the *Yanglingquan* point on your right knee. Next, focus your mind on the *Jianjing* point on your left shoulder and make a connection in your mind to the *Huantiao* point on your right hip.

Then shift your mental focus to the other *Jianjing* point—that is, the *Jianjing* point on your right shoulder—and connect it to the *Huantiao* point on your left hip. Continue by focusing next on the

Quchi point on your right elbow and connect it to the *Yanglingquan* point on your left knee. Complete this part of your practice by focusing on the *Laogong* point on your right hand and connecting it to the *Yongquan* point on your left foot. Repeat these six steps until all the connections feel natural.

In the second part of integration force practice, you should try to coordinate the feelings in both arms with the feelings in both legs, at each of the three sets of points. This integration training is commonly called *bao* or "holding and embracing." In *bao* practice, you should focus your mind first on both left and right *Laogong* points and then connect the feelings at these points to those at your right and left *Yongquan* points. Then, mentally focus on both left and right *Quchi* points and make connections to your right and left *Yanglingquan* points. Third, focus on both left and right *Jianjing* points and connect them to your right and left *Huantiao* points. Next, focus on your right and left *Jianjing* points and connect them to your left and right *Huantiao* points. The fifth step is to focus on your right and left *Quchi* points and connect them to your left and right *Yanglingquan* points; and the sixth step is to focus on both right and left *Laogong* points and connect them to your left and right *Yongquan* points. Repeat these steps until the paired connections feel natural at each set of points.

Integration force practice will strengthen your *qi*, increase your mental control, and concentrate your *shen*. The physical training of movement in your arms and legs will gradually cause internal changes. This is what is meant by the traditional adage that "outside training leads to inside training." As training improves sufficiently, the internal and external can be integrated. At this point, you can reduce your concentration on external movement and focus more on training the internal components. Gradually, your internal feelings will grow stronger, and any internal change will automatically cause an external change. At high levels of mastery, it is possible to focus exclusively on *shen* because everything else—that is, mind *(yi)*,

qi, jin, and physical movements—will follow naturally. With this ability, you will have fully achieved the integration force.

Twenty-Four Key Points

For more detailed practice of *Santi Shi,* one should keep in mind and conform with the Twenty-Four Key Points in order to achieve high-level skill.

The Twenty-Four Key Points come from *Ba Zi Ge*—the Eight-Word Song—which is one of the most important traditional formulations in Xingyi Quan. One should be mindful always of these essentials throughout one's practice. Before one can apply all these considerations in one's moving practice, one should learn and practice them well in *Santi Shi,* a stationary posture.

The eight words of *Ba Zi Ge* are: *ding, kou, yuan, min, bao, chui, qu,* and *ting.*

Most people believe that the "Eight-Word Song" was written by Master Li Luo Neng. It should be used everywhere in Xingyi Quan. It is very important for all movements. Sometimes people refer to it as "the twenty-four key points in *Santi Shi*" because each of the eight character/words includes three points, resulting in a total of twenty-four ideas.

Xingyi masters traditionally introduce the Twenty-Four Key Points when students start to practice *Santi Shi,* which is the first focus in traditional training.

The Twenty-Four Key Points include some internal and external ideas. Even so-called external points actually should be done internally, i.e., using internal components to lead external training. Some of these ideas look similar on the outside but are different inside. Some of these ideas may appear to be opposites; however, they describe how to balance these points in practice. One should practice and then try to understand all of them in detail.

Because *Santi Shi* is a stationary practice, students may find it easier to learn and feel each point in the right way. When every point

can be done well in *Santi Shi,* finally all points should be applied to all moving skills.

Below is some explanation of the Twenty-Four Key Points:

Ding

Ding means "go against," "push forward or upward slowly but hard," "withstand," "support," or "stand up."

- Head (back of skull) should be *ding* (pushing up), as if to fly up and smash the sky. This will cause one's *qi* to ascend along the back to the upper *Dantian,* which is on the point inside and between the eyebrows and underneath the *Baihui* point.
- Palms should be *ding* (pushing outside or around), as though pushing downward on a big mountain. This will cause one's *qi* and internal force to extend to the tip of the hands and feet.
- Tongue should be *ding* (pushing up to the gums behind the incisors), as if one were a lion trying to swallow an elephant. This will cause one's *qi* to sink to *Dantian.*

Kou

Kou means "withhold," "suppress," "restrain," "hold," "keep," "control," "lock up," or "button up."

- Both shoulders should be *kou* (held a little bit forward), as though slightly enfolding something on the chest. This will make one's chest comfortable, and *qi* can go to the elbows with internal force.
- Back of palms and feet should be *kou* (suppressed), as though gripping something with one's hands and gripping the earth with one's feet. This will make one's hands really strong and one's steps very stable.
- Teeth should be *kou* (suppressed), as though one were gritting them. This will make all one's bones, muscles, and tendons withdraw and become more integrated.

Yuan

Yuan means "circular," "round," "smooth," or "flexible."

- Back should be *yuan* (round), as if internal force were pushing the body forward. This will keep one's tailbone in the center of the body and make one's *shen* rise to the top of the head.
- Chest should be *yuan* (round), as though sunken slightly. This will make one's elbows stronger and one's breathing smoother.
- Tiger mouth (the area between thumb and forefinger) should be *yuan* (round), causing the hands to open like eagle talons. This will train one's binding and controlling force.

Min

Min means "quick," "nimble," "agile," "sharp," "acute," "alert," or "sensitive."

- Heart should be *min* (nimble and quick), like an angry cat that wants to catch a mouse. This will make one's mind alert and sensitive, increasing the nimbleness of one's movement.
- Eyes should be *min* (sharp), like a hungry eagle seeking to catch a rabbit. This will train one to capture the best chance (timing) in combat.
- Hands should be *min* (quick), like a starving tiger wanting to spring on a goat. This will train one to move just before the opponent moves.

Bao

Bao means "hold," "carry in arms," or "embrace."

- *Dantian* should be *bao* (embracing), as though holding *qi* in *Dantian* so that it cannot be destroyed. This will train one to concentrate, collect, and use one's *qi*.
- *Xin qi*—*qi* of heart (mind and *shen*) should be *bao* (kept quiet), holding the mind and *shen* in a steady, concentrated and relaxed state. This will train one never to be nervous and never to be confused in combat.

- Both sides of the chest should be *bao* (held in), as though carrying something in the chest. This will train the use of one's *qi* to protect one's body.

Chui

Chui means "droop," "hang down," or "vertical."
- *Qi* should be *chui* (sinking down), as though always moving back to *Dantian*. This will make one's body stable like a mountain.
- Both shoulders should be *chui* (slightly drooped and relaxed), as if the shoulders were chasing the elbows. This will make one's arms become longer and more agile, and *qi* will be able to move to the arms and hands more smoothly.
- Both elbows should be *chui* (dropped down), so that *qi* can move along the inside of one's arms. This will make both sides of one's chest stronger and train side-to-side force.

Qu

Qu means "curve," "bent," "crooked," or "winding."
- Arms (elbows) should be *qu* (curved), like a crescent moon. This will make one's internal force in the arms become strong, like a bow.
- Legs (knees) should be *qu* (bent), like a crescent moon. This will make one's internal force in the legs more springy and dense.
- Wrists should be *qu* (curved), like a crescent moon. This will concentrate one's internal force in the hands so that they are capable of continuously moving forward and backward freely and smoothly.

Ting

Ting means "press onward," "upright," "erect," "stiff," or "straight."
- Neck should be *ting* (upright), and the chin should be tucked in slightly. This will enable one's *qi* to rise to the *Baihui* smoothly.

- Spine and waist should be *ting* (erect) and kept straight. This will make one's internal force move smoothly, extending through the arms and legs freely, and also exciting one's *qi* to permeate every part of one's body.
- Kneecaps should be *ting* (stiff), as if made of a sturdy material. This will make one's *qi* comfortable, extend one's *shen*, and deepen one's rooting.

There are a lot of things on which one should focus during practice, but no one can focus on all of them simultaneously. It is also important to note that one cannot fight while focusing on these points. Each point should be practiced separately until it becomes ingrained, i.e., the skill comes naturally without requiring focused thought. Then one can move to the next practice point.

When all points have become ingrained and can be applied spontaneously and without forethought, one will experience a totally new feeling. Only when one reaches this level can it be said that mastery of these points has been achieved.

From the above description of *Santi Shi*, it becomes understandable why people traditionally refer to it as the source of all skills. This practice establishes a good foundation for Xingyi Quan training. With internal and external practice, each of the Twenty-Four Key Points is trained, and the benefits of this training can then be applied everywhere in one's movements and applications. How well one can perform internal skills will determine how high a level one can reach in Xingyi Quan. Thus, *Santi Shi* skill is emphasized greatly.

Seven-Star Pile-Standing

In traditional Taiji Quan practice, pile-standing is a common training method, especially for beginners. *Qixing Zhuang* or Seven-Star Pile-Standing, is the most frequently practiced Wu-style Taiji Quan training stance. Careful practice of Seven-Star Pile-Standing can significantly enhance the development of rooting, internal energy,

relaxation, sensitivity, body integration, and control of the internal components.

Basic Principle

In Taiji Quan practice, each side of the body is considered separately, as *yang* and *yin* sides. The *yang* side is the active and insubstantial side. It can also be called the empty or unweighted side. The *yin* side is the quiet and substantial or weighted side. Each side includes a leg and the arm on the opposite side of the body. *Yin* and *yang* qualities are exchanged whenever movements involve weight shifts. This changing of *yin* and *yang* sides is the source of all Taiji skills.

The *yin*-side leg holds most or all of the body's weight, while the *yang*-side or empty leg bears none or only a relatively small amount of weight. The arm on the side of the body opposite the *yin* leg is the *yin* arm, and the *yang* arm is on the side of the body opposite the *yang* leg. When the right leg is weighted, it is the *yin* or *yin*-side leg, and the left leg is the *yang* leg. The right arm is the *yang* arm, and the left arm is the *yin* arm.

Although the original meaning of "seven-star" is "plough," the phrase in traditional Chinese martial arts usually refers to the seven key acupuncture points: the "head star" at the *Baihui* point on the top of the head; the "shoulder star" at the *Jianjing* point on the *yang*-side shoulder; the "elbow star" at the *Quchi* point on the elbow of the *yang*-side arm; the "hand star" at the *Laogong* point on the *yang*-side palm; the "hip star" at the *Huantiao* point on the *yang*-side hip; the "knee star" at the *Yanglingquan* point on the knee of the *yang*-side leg; and the "foot star" at the *Yongquan* point on the ball of the *yang*-side foot.

Because the *yang* side is the active side, the focus of your mind during a stationary posture such as Seven-Star Pile-Standing is always on this side. Six of the seven stars that your mind will focus on are on the *yang* arm and leg. *Baihui,* the head star—also called *Ding Pan Xin* or "criterion star"—is not associated with either side of

the body. It is of primary importance for maintaining *Zhong Ding* or central equilibrium. One of the foremost goals of Seven-Star Pile-Standing is to increase the smooth, free-flowing movement of the internal components, *shen, yi,* and *qi,* through the seven key points.

Movement Description

The basic movements for Seven-Star Pile-Standing are the same as those for holding the seven-star posture in the empty-hand form. This posture is one of the most important in the form. In the seven-star posture, a sitting stance is used and one hundred percent of your weight should be kept on your back leg. When you hold this posture, if your weight is on the right leg and your left arm is extended in front of your body, you are in a "left posture"; otherwise, you are in a "right posture." The left posture will be used for the movement description in this section. The movements for the right-posture are the same except that the sides are reversed.

Preparatory Movements

Stand Erect

Stand facing forward with your feet parallel. Relax your mind and body. Make your breathing slow, deep, and smooth (fig. 3-8).

From *Baihui,* bring your mind to the left *Jianjing* point and let your left shoulder fully relax so that your left arm feels as though it could effortlessly be detached from your body.

Lower Your Body, Extend Your Left Arm, and Shift Your Weight to Your Right Leg

3-8

Next, focus your mind on the left *Quchi* point on your left elbow and then move it down to the left *Laogong* point on your left hand. As your mind moves down to your left hand, you will feel like bending your legs. Follow this feeling and bend your knees, letting

your body sink down. Your body will feel heavy, and your stance will become very stable. In spite of the sensation of heaviness, you should feel as though there is a spring inside your legs that balances the downward push of your body. Your left hand should also feel heavy and as though the palm were reaching down to touch the floor. At this point, the fingers of both hands should point forward, and both palms should face down.

Keep your mind on your left hand until you feel as though your left arm wants to move up. Then follow this feeling by letting your arm move forward and up. Remember that it is always important in Taiji Quan practice to concentrate your mind and then wait until the feeling to move arises before you actually perform the movement. As expressed in a classic tenet of Taiji practice, movement always occurs "first in mind, then in body."

As your mind continues to focus on the left *Laogong* point of your left hand, your weight should start to shift to your right leg. Then bring your mind to the left *Quchi* point on your left elbow and continue shifting your weight to your right leg as your left arm continues to move up and forward on a slight diagonal to the right.

As your mind moves to the *Jianjing* point on your left shoulder, your weight should shift completely to your right leg, and

3-9

your left arm should be extended in front of you with the elbow slightly bent and the left thumb opposite your nose. Throughout the movement of your left arm, you should feel as though your shoulder has been chasing your elbow, which in turn has been chasing your hand.

At the end of this movement, your right leg should be fully weighted and your right toes, right knee, and nose should be aligned vertically. Your left leg should be completely empty (fig. 3-9).

Extend Your Right Arm, Extend Your Left Leg,
and Turn Your Left Palm Up

Move your mind from the left to the right *Jianjing* point and feel
your right arm become relaxed. Only when you feel as though your
right arm wants to move up should you let this movement occur.

As your mind moves down to the *Quchi* point on your right elbow
and then to the *Laogong* point on your right hand, your right arm
should continue to move up and forward on a slight diagonal toward
the center of your body. Touch the crook of your left elbow with
your right middle finger. Your right thumb should point to the
Tanzhong point in the middle of your chest at the level of your breast.

Next, focus your mind first on the *Tangzhong* point and then
down to the *Dantian,* which is inside your abdomen about three
inches behind your navel. Let your mind remain briefly at *Dantian* before moving to the *Huiyin* point on the perineum at the midway point on your crotch. Focus your mind next on the *Huantiao*
point on your left hip.

When your mind is focused on your left hip, wait until your left
leg seems ready to move of its own accord before letting it extend
forward.

From your left hip, bring your mind to the *Yanglingquan* point
on your left knee and then to the *Yongquan* point on your left foot.
Your left leg should continue to move forward and when it is fully
extended, your body will have assumed a sitting stance with your
left heel touching the floor and your toes pointing up.

While your left leg moves forward, your left palm—which had
been facing to the right—should turn up in a counterclockwise direction. It is important when you turn your palm that your left thumb
does not move but instead remains opposite your nose, having
acted as a pivot point for the upturn of your palm. Figures 3-10a
and 3-10b show this posture from different angles.

When your mind focuses on the *Yongquan* point of your left
foot, it will have moved through all seven "stars," three of which—

3-10

the shoulder, elbow, and hand—are on the *yang* arm and three of which—the hip, knee, and foot—-are on the *yang* leg. The seventh or "criterion" star is *Baihui* at the top of your head. To complete the opening circle, you should bring your mind from the left foot star back to *Baihui*. This ensures that your *shen* will be active and alert. This creates a sense of nimbleness that provides a counterpoint to the stability that has been generated by the stance.

Having assumed the Seven-Star Pile-Standing, you can begin to move your mind and *qi* through as many circuits around the seven key points as possible. Gradually try to increase the length of time you can hold the stance and maintain the flow of mind and *qi* through the seven-star acupoints.

Closing Form

When you feel that you can no longer maintain enough focus to move your mind smoothly through the seven-star circuit, it is time to close your pile-standing practice.

As your mind returns to *Baihui* at the end of the last seven-star circuit, withdraw your left foot and place it alongside your right foot with both legs bent. Be careful not to raise your body as you bring your left leg back.

At the same time, bring your arms back toward your body, letting your hands cross in front of your chest, slightly above the line of your breast. Your palms should face the ground. Your gaze will naturally lower and you will be ready for the last mind and *qi* circle practice, called *Xiao Zhoutian* or microcosmic orbit. Separate your hands to both sides and let your thumbs, index fingers, and middle fingers touch each other. Then slowly push your hands down until they reach the level of your stomach. At the same time raise your body slightly (fig. 3-11).

Continue to push your hands down and then separate them to the sides of your legs. Touch each thigh with the middle finger of the hand resting alongside it. Raise your body until you are standing erect. Look straight ahead (fig. 3-12).

3-11

3-12

Circling of Mind during Seven-Star Pile-Standing

Remember that pile-standing is an internal practice and although it involves no physical movement, all of the internal components should be in continuous movement inside your body during the stance. The internal movement of *shen, yi,* and *qi* will always bring some feeling or tendency toward physical movement. It is said that to intend

something will lead or direct the mind, and that the mind can then be used to lead *qi*. *Qi*, in turn, can be used to generate movement.

To begin the first small circle of Seven-Star Pile-Standing, move the focus of your mind from the "head star" *Baihui* to the right "shoulder star" *Jianjing* and then to the right "elbow star" *Quchi*. Move it next to the right "hand star" *Laogong* and from here through your right thumb to *Tanzhong*. The flow of *qi* will follow the movement of your mind.

To begin the first big circle, bring your mind from *Tanzhong* to *Dantian* and then to the left "hip star" *Huantiao*, the left "knee star" *Yanglingquan*, and then to the left "foot star" *Yongquan*. Then your mind should move immediately from the big toe of your left foot back to *Baihui* in a large imaginary circular path.

At this point, your mind should move straight down from *Baihui* to the *Yongquan* point on the bottom of your right foot. Your body will feel heavy, and there will be a strong sensation of compression in your right leg. Bring your mind to your extended left palm and imagine that your right foot is resting on that palm so that your left hand is holding up your whole body. This will lead you to feel that your body is sinking down more and more heavily onto your right leg. As this occurs, imagine the force increasing on your left hand as it supports your sinking body.

Maintain this thought until you feel as though your right leg is very hot and you cannot hold your body up any longer. Then let your mind return to *Baihui*. This will cause you to feel more relaxed and your right leg will become more comfortable. Then begin another circuit of your mind through the "head star" acupoints.

Repeat the circling of your mind as many times as your skill and strength allow. Maintain a sense of physical relaxation and stability while also experiencing internal excitement and springiness. Through this practice you will be enhancing your capacity for nimbleness as well as increasing your root.

Conclusion

Seven-Star Pile-Standing can improve your understanding of Taiji Quan principles and the internal sensations that underlie the proper execution of many basic skills. This understanding will refine your form practice. In this way, pile-standing and form practice can supplement each other. A traditional saying in Taiji Quan is "One step, one pile," which means that every movement in the Taiji form can be used as a pile-standing practice, and that every movement in the form should be practiced as though it were pile-standing. Although pile-standing is very important as a training method, it should generally be combined with form practice for advanced study. When so combined, form practice is usually called *dong zhuang* or "moving pile-standing." Thus, pile-standing becomes a dynamic rather than a static expression of Taiji Quan skills.

Kan-Li Zhuang—Kan and *Li* Pile-Standings

Kan and *Li* are two trigrams of Bagua. The two post-standing practices used in Bagua Zhang training correspond to the principles of these two trigrams and can be used to develop special *jin* or internal trained force.

Kan Zhuang—Kan Pile-Standing

Basic Principle

The three bars of the *Kan* trigram are Yin, Yang, and Yin. This is called *Kan Zhong Man* or full (substantial) in *Kan,* which means that Yin contains Yang. According to the basic Bagua principles, the Yin bar represents softness and the Yang bar represents hardness. The bars of the *Kan* trigram convey that softness contains hardness. *Kan*'s attribute is water. Water is considered to be soft on the outside because it assumes the shape of its container and hard on the inside because it cannot be compressed. In terms of its attributes

as well as its bars, *Kan* describes the principle of hardness within softness.

In martial arts, the principle that softness contains hardness is a very important feature of internal trained force. Defense skills, in particular, frequently require the use of this kind of force. In defense skills, you should move in a smooth and relaxed way and show softness by effortlessly following the movements of your opponent. At the same time, you must maintain your ability to change the direction and speed of your movements. You should retain hard force inside to prevent your opponent from compressing or controlling you. If you can remain soft on the outside, you will give your opponent the impression that you are not resisting his attack and that he will be able to defeat you. This impression will lure him toward you, and if you have maintained a firm strength internally, you will be able to attack him effectively. The combination of external softness with internal hardness is easy to describe but difficult to accomplish. Most of the time, practitioners are either soft or hard in their movements but unable to combine these two qualities. *Kan Zhuang* practice will help you develop the kind of *jin* that expresses hardness within softness.

3-13

Movement Description for *Kan Zhuang*

Stand erect and look straight ahead. The distance between your feet should match your shoulder width. Relax your body and breathe deeply, slowly, and smoothly (fig. 3-13).

Relax your shoulders, drop your elbows, and relax your abdomen. This will create a readiness in your arms to rise up. Follow this feeling and raise your arms in front of your body until your hands reach shoulder level. Both palms should face toward your chest

with your thumbs facing up. Your middle fingers should point at each other and be held very close to each other without touching. Your arms should form a circle in front of your chest. Withdraw your chest slightly and round your back. Look at a point between your middle fingers. Bend your legs slightly (figs. 3-14a, 3-14b). Hold this *Kan Zhuang* posture for the duration of your practice.

3-14

Mind Practice

Kan Zhuang practice requires that you hold this posture and use your mind to train your internal force. Imagine that there is water inside the circle created by your arms. Your arms hold the water and must not let it flow out. Then imagine that more water is pouring in. Feel pressure building up against your arms, forcing the arm circle to expand in order to contain the water. This will cause your middle fingers to move slightly further apart, and your arms to lengthen slowly and very slightly. Then your middle fingers will move slightly toward each other again. You should feel energy flowing along your arms from your back to the tip of your fingers. Your mind should register all of these feelings in detail, but your overt physical movements should be very slow and almost imperceptible.

Repeat the cycle of pressure and expansion until you can no longer maintain your mental focus. Then end this part of your practice.

Li Zhuang—Li Pile-Standing

Basic Principle

The three bars of *Li* are Yang, Yin, and Yang. The trigram is called *Li Zhong Xu* or "insubstantial in *Li,*" which means that Yang contains Yin or hardness contains softness. The attribute of *Li* is fire. Because fire is very hot and can destroy everything, it is characterized as hard on the outside. On the inside, however, it is soft and insubstantial because nothing exists within it. *Li* represents softness contained within hardness.

In martial arts, this relationship is a very important feature of internal trained force. Most attack skills require a *Li* kind of force. When attacking, your movements should be strong and powerful, but if your movements are only hard, your force will be too straight, and you will find it difficult to relax and follow changes in your opponent's movements. It will also be difficult to quickly modify the direction or timing of your attack, and you may miss your opportunity to win. If you can keep a quality of softness within your powerful movements, your attack will be more balanced and more likely to succeed. When you make a hard and powerful attack, you should always maintain a quality of softness and relaxation internally. This is easier said than done but *Li Zhuang* training will help you develop the kind of internal force that retains softness within hardness.

Movement Description for *Li Zhuang*

Stand erect and look straight ahead. Separate your feet so that the distance between them is about shoulder width. Relax your body. Keep your breathing slow, smooth, and deep. The beginning stance for *Li Zhuang* is the same as the starting posture for *Kan Zhuang* (fig. 3-13).

Relax your shoulders, drop your elbows, and relax your abdomen. This will cause you to feel that you want to raise your arms. Follow this feeling and raise your arms in front of your body until your hands reach shoulder level. While raising your arms, imagine that you are pushing the center of your palm outward. This will cause your arms to twist. Both palms will face forward, and your thumbs will face down. Point your middle figures toward each other and hold them very close to each other but do not let them touch. Your arms should form a circle in front of your chest. Your chest should be slightly concave and your back slightly rounded. Look at the point between your middle fingers. Bend your legs slightly as you assume the *Li Zhuang* stance (figs. 3-15a, 3-15b).

3-15

Mind Practice

You should stand almost completely stationary in the *Li Zhuang* posture throughout this part of your practice, the purpose of which is to improve your mind's ability to lead your *qi* and *jin*. Imagine that the inside of your arm circle is empty, but that a substance such as water is pressing in on the circle from outside. Imagine responding to this compression force by expanding your arm circle. Then

imagine that additional pressure is applied at the front part of the circle and focus on the *Jiaji* point on the center of your upper back. Feel as though your back is moving slightly outward. This will create a feeling of expansion in your arms. Then imagine that there is pressure against your back and that your arms lengthen slightly and move slightly forward. The more pressure you imagine, the more your shoulders should relax and your elbows drop. This will cause you to feel that your arm circle is expanding. Any actual physical movement that results from this series of images should be slight and slow. The activity in this practice should be generated only by detailed mental imagery and should remain almost completely internal.

Repeat the imaginary cycle of pressures coming from the front and initiating slight movement of *Jiaji* backward, thus enlarging your arm circle and then coming from behind and initiating a movement forward by your arms that also enlarges your arm circle. Repeat this sequence for as long as you can clearly maintain your mental focus.

Movement Description for Alternating Kan Zhuang and Li Zhuang

Practitioners usually like to alternate *Kan Zhuang* and *Li Zhuang* postures during training sessions. To change from *Kan Zhuang* to *Li Zhuang*, continue from figure 3-14 by revolving both forearms so that your thumbs point to your body, then to the ground (fig. 3-16), and finally away from your body. You will now be in the *Li Zhuang* posture shown in figure 3-15.

To change from the *Li Zhuang* to the *Kan Zhuang* posture, continue from figure 3-15 by revolving both

3-16   3-17

forearms so that your thumbs first point down, then toward your body (fig. 3-17), and finally up to form *Kan Zhuang*, as shown in figure 3-14.

Closing Form

When you feel that you can no longer maintain enough focus to move your mind smoothly through the correct sequences, it is time to close your practice of *Kan Zhuang* and *Li Zhuang*. Begin by shifting your weight to your right leg and moving your left foot toward your right foot until your feet are close together and parallel. Keep both legs slightly bent. At the same time, bring your arms back toward your body, letting your hands cross in front of your chest with your palms facing down. Your hands should be a little bit higher than your breasts. Your gaze will lower naturally. Separate your hands slightly so that your thumbs, index fingers, and middle fingers touch each other. Then slowly push your hands down until they reach stomach level. At the same time, begin slowly to straighten your legs (fig. 3-18).

Continue to push your hands down and then separate them and move each to the corresponding thigh. Touch the outside of each thigh with the middle finger of the hand resting alongside it. Stand erect and look straight ahead (fig. 3-19).

3-18

3-19

✪ *Bu Fa*—Application Steps

As mentioned earlier, it is said that thirty percent of the skill needed to win a fight involves the hands and seventy percent involves the feet. This adage indicates the importance of footwork for training applications in the internal martial arts. In martial arts, footwork is called *Bu Fa* or step training for applications.

In fighting, you will need to step forward, backward, or sideways and be able quickly to dodge, turn around, or jump. If you cannot move your body in the right way, you will not be successful. Effective body movement depends on correct footwork. Good step training can increase the power and speed of leg movements and the coordination of your hand and body skills. Correct footwork is the foundation of all skills.

There are two main aspects to step training. One emphasizes nimbleness, and the other emphasizes stability. It is important that your step training focus on these two aspects in a balanced way. To focus on either one more than the other is a common training mistake. If you focus on post-standing or lower-level form practice almost exclusively, you may develop very good root and become adept at skills that do not require much footwork, but you will never achieve nimbleness of movement. In real fighting, your movements will be too slow, especially when your opponent can move quickly away from you. If you focus almost solely on learning to step quickly, your movements may become very nimble but you will easily lose stability. This will make it difficult for you to deal well with powerful attacks at short distances. Without stability, you will lose your balance and none of your skills will be effective. Without nimbleness, you will be unable to move quickly, and the opportunity to win or to mount a successful defense will often be lost.

Post-standing practice is a common training method for developing stability. Form practice can also be very helpful. For nimbleness training, there are many special step-training methods. These can be grouped into two main types. One type of step-training method

is designed to increase the basic abilities that underlie fighting skills. These abilities are not, themselves, directly used in fighting. The other method focuses on improving the skills that are actually applied in fighting situations. Several methods for each type of step-training are discussed in this section.

Mo Jing Bu

Mo Jing Bu is a fundamental basic footwork training. *Mo* means "rub," and *Jing* refers to the inside of the shank. Because this step practice requires that your shanks lightly touch or rub against each other when you walk, it is called *Mo Jing*.

Movement Description for Mo Jing Bu

Start by standing erect and looking straight ahead (fig. 3-20). Bend both knees until they are over your toes. At the same time, bend your wrist so that your palms face down and your fingers point forward (fig. 3-21). Gently shift your weight to your right leg and step forward with your left foot until your left knee is straight. Keep your left foot flat and lightly touch the ground with it as you step out. Do not immediately shift your weight onto your left leg (fig. 3-22). Keep your body erect and your head level as you move forward and shift your weight to your left leg (fig. 3-23). Then step forward with your right foot until it is alongside your left foot. Keep the full weight of your body on your left leg (fig. 3-24). Continue

Figs. 3-20 to 3-29: Mo Jing Bu   **3-21**   **3-22**

3-23   3-24   3-25

3-26   3-27

to move your right foot forward until your right knee is straight (fig. 3-25) and then shift your weight completely onto your right leg (fig. 3-26). Step forward with your left foot until it is alongside your right foot, but keep your weight on your right leg (fig. 3-27). Continue to move your left foot forward and follow the same sequence until you are ready to end this part of your practice. When you make your steps, your feet and legs should pass close together. When the legs pass each other, the shanks should keep touching or rubbing each other.

Closing Form

Stop your practice when your feet are beside each other. Place both hands in front of your stomach (fig. 3-28), then lower them together and separate them so that they come to rest along the outside of your thighs. While lowering your hands, slowly straighten your

3-28

3-29

knees. As your hands touch the outside of your legs, you should be standing upright and looking straight ahead (fig. 3-29).

When practicing *Mo Jing Bu,* it is essential that you shift your weight one hundred percent to your front foot before moving your rear foot. Only when one foot is fully weighted can you test your balance and develop root and stability, and only when one foot is totally empty can you feel what it is like to move nimbly. With repeated weight shifts, you can experience stability and nimbleness in both legs and develop these skills in a balanced way. At the beginning of your training, you should practice your steps and weight shifts very slowly. Allow five to ten seconds for each step. When you can step comfortably and shift your full weight smoothly from foot to foot, you can gradually speed up your steps until they become very quick. Although *Mo Jing Bu* is fundamental to all footwork, it is rarely perceptible as a skill in real fighting.

Jiao Cha Bu

Jiao Cha means "crossing," and *Jiao Cha Bu* refers to the method for training crossing steps. Crossing steps are a basic skill used frequently in fighting. Imagine that there are six points on the ground.

The distance between any two consecutive points is about one-and-a-half feet. You can set the distance longer if you want to practice in a lower posture. Start at the first two points and move your feet along the route shown in figure 3-30. The route can also be followed in the reverse direction.

```
        4   5
      3           6
        2   1
```

Fig. 3-30: Step Routine for *Jiao Cha Bu*

Movement Description for Jiao Cha Bu

Stand with your right foot on point one and your left foot on point two. Bend your legs slightly. Keep your body erect and look forward (fig. 3-31). You should face forward throughout this routine. Step forward and to the left with your right foot, letting it cross in front of your left foot as you move it to point three (fig. 3-32). Then, step forward to point four with your left foot, letting it cross from behind to in front of your right foot in a curving line (fig. 3-33). Step to the right with your right foot, letting it cross behind your left foot as you move it onto point five (fig. 3-34). Step backward and to the right with your left foot, letting it cross behind your right foot so that you can place it onto point six (fig. 3-35). Step backward and to the left with your right foot, letting it move from in front of your left foot to behind your left foot in a curving line and place it onto point one (fig. 3-36). Step backward and to the left with your left foot, letting it cross your right foot as you move it onto point two (fig. 3-37).

In *Jiao Cha Bu* practice, it is essential that you maintain a constant speed throughout the stepping route. *Jiao Cha Bu* should be performed very quickly, and to do this you must be relaxed and keep your body erect so that your center of gravity remains stable. Your feet must move quickly, but the body must be calm and still.

Figs. 3-31 to 3-37: *Jiao Cha Bu*   3-32   3-33

3-34   3-35   3-36

3-37

Wuxing Bu

Wuxing refers to the five elements, which are metal, wood, water, fire, and earth. *Wuxing Bu* is a footwork training method for learning to step forward and backward while dodging sideways. In fighting, your steps and body movements should be coordinated, or as

it is described in a traditional saying, "body follows step to move, and step follows body to change." To practice this in *Wuxing Bu,* imagine that there are five points on the ground. The distance between any two consecutive points is about one-and-a-half feet although you can set the distances longer if you want to practice in a lower posture. Start at the first two points and move your feet along the route shown in figure 3-38. You can also practice this step sequence in the reverse direction.

```
    4       5

        3

    1       2
```

Fig. 3-38: Step Routine for *Wuxing Bu*

Wuxing Bu can be done as a solo practice and as a two-person practice. The solo practice is the basic training method and should be learned thoroughly before you advance to the two-person practice.

Movement Description for Wuxing Bu

Solo Practice

Stand with your left foot on point one and your right foot on point two. Keep your body erect and look forward. Face forward throughout the routine. Bend your legs slightly and distribute your weight evenly (fig. 3-39). Shift your weight to your left leg and then step forward and to the left with your right foot to point three (fig. 3-40). Shift your weight to your right leg and step forward, placing your left foot alongside your right foot. Let your feet touch but keep all your weight on your right foot (fig. 3-41). Continue by stepping forward and to the left with your left foot to point four (fig. 3-42). Shift your weight to your left leg and step forward and to the left with your right foot until your right foot is alongside your left foot (fig. 3-43). Continue by stepping to the right with your right foot to point five. Shift part of your weight onto your right foot so that

your weight is distributed evenly on both legs (fig. 3-44). Then shift all your weight to your right leg and step to the right with your left foot until it is alongside your right foot (fig. 3-45). Step backward and to the left with your left foot to point three (fig. 3-46). Shift your weight onto your left leg and then step backward and to the left until your right foot touches your left foot (fig. 3-47). Keep your weight on your left leg and step backward and to the right with your right foot to point two (fig. 3-48). Shift your weight to your right leg and step backward and to the right with your left foot until it is alongside your right foot (fig. 3-49). Keep your weight on your right leg and step to the right with your left foot to point one. When your left foot touches the ground, shift half your weight onto it to form a riding horse stance (fig. 3-50)

The primary goal of this practice is to coordinate your body movement with your footwork. During *Wuxing Bu* training, your

Figs. 3-39 to 3-50: Solo Practice of *Wu Xing Bu*

3-40

3-41

3-42

3-43

3-44

3-45   3-46   3-47

3-48   3-49   3-50

body should not sway from side to side, and your step should never falter.

Two-Person Practice

When you can do the solo practice well, you should find a partner and practice the two-person routine. In the two-person practice, both people do exactly the same routine, but each one starts from a different point. If, for example, you start with your left foot on point one and your right foot on point two, your partner should start with his left foot on point five and his right foot on point four (fig. 3-51). From then on, all movements are the same for both people.

Bend your legs slightly and step to the left with your right foot next to your partner's right foot and your left foot next to his left foot (fig. 3-52). Each person should continue by stepping forward with his right foot to point three. The right side of your right foot

should be very close to the right side of your partner's right foot; your toes should be next to his heel and his toes should be next to your heel (fig. 3-53). Shift your weight forward onto your right leg. At that time, your body should be very close to your partner's; your right shoulder should be next to his right shoulder (fig. 3-54). Step forward with your left foot and place it next to your right foot (fig. 3-55). Continue to step forward and to the left with your left foot to point four; your partner's left foot should be on point two (fig. 3-56). Step forward with your right foot and place it next to your left foot (fig. 3-57). Continue to step to the right with your right foot to point five; your partner's right foot should be on point one (fig. 3-58). Step to the right with your left foot and place it next to your right foot (fig. 3-59). Continue to step backward with your left foot and place it on point three. The left side of your left foot should be very close to the left side of your partner's left foot;

Figs. 3-51 to 3-64: Two-Person Practice of *Wu Xing Bu*

3-52

3-53

3-54

3-55

3-56

3-57

3-58

3-59

3-60

3-61

3-62

3-63

3-64

your toes should be next to his heel and his toes should be next to your heel (fig. 3-60). Shift your weight back onto your left leg and then step backward with your right foot and place it next to your left foot (fig. 3-61). Continue to step backward and to the right with your right foot and place it on point two; your partner's right foot should be on point four (fig. 3-62). Shift your weight back to

your right leg and step back with your left foot, placing it next to your right foot (fig. 3-63). Continue to step to the left with your left foot and place it on point one; your partner's left foot should be on point five (fig. 3-64).

This routine can be practiced in one direction and repeated in the other direction; that is, each partner would step forward with his left foot rather than his right at the beginning of the routine. Be careful in this routine that when you and your partner step onto the center point, you do not bump into each other. Your bodies should be very close, but the feeling should be that you want to avoid touching him at all costs.

Ca La Bu

Ca La Bu is the step used most often in fighting. It involves stepping forward with your front foot and simply letting your back foot follow. *Ca* means "mop," and *La* means "pull." In *Ca La Bu,* the step forward should be like a mop pushed forward on the ground. You should not raise your front foot off the ground as you step. Your back foot should follow as though it were being pulled forward by your front foot. The step by your front foot should be quick and nimble; the step by your back foot should be heavy and stable. *Ca La Bu* is a quick and easy step that is frequently used for attack.

Movement Description for Ca La Bu

Start from a posture in which your right foot is in front and your left leg bears about sixty to seventy percent of your weight. This is a common fighting stance (fig. 3-65). Use your left foot to push against the ground and step forward with your right foot. At the same time, shift your weight slightly to your right leg (fig. 3-66). As soon as your right foot touches the ground, pull your left foot forward. Keep your left foot in touch with the ground while it is being pulled forward. Because part of your weight is still on your left leg, your left foot will seem to be mopping the ground when it

is pulled forward (fig. 3-67). As soon as your left foot pulls close to your right foot, shift sixty to seventy percent of your weight onto your left foot and use it to push your body forward again. This will cause your right foot to step forward (fig. 3-68).

Figs. 3-65 to 3-68: Ca La Bu

3-66

3-67

3-68

In the *Ca La Bu* routine, it is essential that most of your weight be kept on your back leg because your back leg must push your front leg forward. When your front leg steps and has pulled your

back leg forward, your weight should shift to your front leg slightly (about twenty percent) and then should shift back immediately to your back leg. This will allow your front foot to take another step forward very quickly and continue your forward momentum without interruption.

Shan Zhan Bu

Shan Zhan Bu is another step that is often used in fighting. *Shan* means "to dodge," and *Zhan* means "to fight" or "spread out." *Shan Zhan Bu* is a step forward with a sideways dodge. It is always used to defend against a powerful frontal attack. This step creates a sudden change of angle when you move forward. It is much quicker than many other sideways steps because its movement is small and always sudden. Usually the step is used in order to evade an attack by side-stepping and then quickly turning around.

Movement Description for Shan Zhan Bu

Start from a posture in which your left foot is in front of your right foot. Keep about sixty percent of your weight on your right leg (fig. 3-69). Bring your left foot back slightly and then step forward in a small curving line to the front and right side of your right foot. It should seem as though your left foot has gone around a post from one side to the other (fig. 3-70). As soon as your left foot touches the ground, step forward with your right foot and move it around your left foot until it is in front. Turn the toes of your right foot to the left. Turn your body slightly to the left as well (fig. 3-71).

Continue turning your body to the left and shift your weight slightly back (fig. 3-72). Bring your right foot back slightly and then step to the left and forward in a small curving line until your right foot is to the front and left of your left foot. It should seem as though your right foot has gone around a post from one side to the other (fig. 3-73). As soon as your right foot touches the ground, step forward with your left foot, bringing it around your right foot

from back to front. At the same time turn your body slightly to the right (fig. 3-74). Continue turning your body to the right and turn your left foot on the ball of the foot so that the toes of your left foot point to the right (fig. 3-75).

Figs. 3-69 to 3-75: *Shan Zhan Bu*

3-70

3-71

3-72

3-73

3-74

3-75

San Jiao Huan Shi Bu

The most common standing position for fighting is a posture in which one foot is in front of the other. Most people have a preference for putting either the right or the left foot forward, so they become adept at using their skills on one side more than the other. It is preferable, of course, to be able to use your skills equally well on both sides. If you are stronger on one side than the other, your opponent may be

able to discover and take advantage of your weakness. Good training should develop skills on both sides so that you can change your standing position often when fighting and use your skills on either the right side or the left with equal effectiveness.

This *San Jiao Huan Shi Bu* triangle position changing-step is a common and useful step for changing your standing position. Imagine that there are three points forming a triangle on the floor with a distance of about one-and-a-half feet along the edges of the triangle (fig. 3-76).

1

2   3

Fig. 3-76: Step Position for *San Jiao Huan Shi Bu*

Movement Description for San Jiao Huan Shi Bu

Stand upright with your left foot on point one and your right foot on point three. Turn your body slightly to the right (fig. 3-77). Step backward and to the left and place your left foot on point two. As soon as your left foot lands on point two, jump up and move your right foot to point one and turn your body to the left (fig. 3-78).

Figs. 3-77 to 3-78: *San Jiao Huan Shi Bu*—Triangle Position Change-Step   **3-78**

Zhi Zi Jin Bu

Zhi Zi Jin Bu is a zigzag step forward. It is used for avoiding a direct attack by your opponent and quickly moving in to counter-attack. It is a sideways step that is frequently used in fighting. If you were only to move to the side without moving forward, you would be able to dodge your opponent's attack, but you would not easily be able to cause trouble for him and mount an attack of your own. In internal martial arts, a dodge without a coordinated attack is not generally considered a good idea. It is usually best to combine defense and offense. *Zhi Zi Jin Bu* is a step that reflects this principle. In *Zhi Zi Jin Bu* practice, you should always be moving forward, even when you are also moving to the side.

Figs. 3-79 to 3-83: *Zhi Zi Jin Bu*   **3-80**   **3-81**

3-82   **3-83**

Movement Description for Zhi Zi Jin Bu

Stand erect and bend your legs slightly (fig. 3-79). Step forward and to the left with your left foot (fig. 3-80). Let your right foot follow your left foot lightly and nimbly until it is next to your left foot. Touch the ground lightly with only the toes of your right foot. You should feel energy urging you to move your right foot forward (fig. 3-81). Follow this feeling and step forward and to the right with your right foot (fig. 3-82). Let your left foot follow your right foot lightly and nimbly until it is next to your right foot. Touch the ground lightly with only the toes of your left foot, feeling as though you want to move your left foot forward (fig. 3-83).

Zhi Zi Tui Bu

Zhi Zi Tui Bu is a zigzag step backward and to the side. When your opponent's attack is too hard, your best response is usually to withdraw—which is sometimes called "leaving the touch"—and wait for a chance to counterattack. In this situation, many people tend naturally to step straight back, but because backward steps are usually slower than forward steps, this is not a good idea. The better skill for stepping back is to move sideways at the same time. It will not feel natural to do this, so you should practice *Zhi Zi Tui Bu* to develop this skill.

Movement Description for Zhi Zi Tui Bu

Start from the posture shown in figure 3-83. Step backward and to the left with your left foot and shift your weight back at the same time (fig. 3-84). Lightly and nimbly step back and to the left with your right foot until your right foot is next to your left foot. Keep lightly touching the ground with your right foot (fig. 3-85) as you continue to step back and to the right with your right foot (fig. 3-86). Shift your weight back and bring your left foot back lightly until it is next to your right foot (fig. 3-87).

Figs. 3-84 to 3-87: *Zhi Zi Tui Bu*   3-85

3-86   3-87

Zhuan Shen Bu

Zhuan Shen Bu is a useful step when you need to turn around. Although not used frequently in fighting, it is nevertheless an important skill to have. Because the movement of this step is often quite big, it may be difficult to keep your balance. The main point of *Zhuan Shen Bu* practice is to make your movements as quick and small as possible.

Movement Description for Zhuan Shen Bu

Stand erect with your right foot in front of your left and about sixty percent of your weight on your left leg (fig. 3-88). Shift your weight forward to your right leg and step forward with your left foot. When it passes over your right foot, start to turn the toes of your left foot to the right. When your left foot is about one foot in front of your right foot, touch the ground with your left heel (fig. 3-89). As soon as your left heel touches the ground, point your left foot to the right and simultaneously shift your weight to your left leg. As your left foot turns, turn your body to the right. At the same time, relax your right leg and let it naturally follow your body by turning slightly to the right. Touch the ground lightly with your right foot throughout this move (fig. 3-90). Continue turning your body to the right until you have turned 180 degrees around from your starting posture.

Keep your right leg relaxed and slightly turn your right foot on the ball of the foot, keeping it in contact with the ground (fig. 3-91). Step forward with your left foot. When it passes over your right foot, start to turn the toes of your left foot to the right. When your left foot is about one foot in front of your right foot, touch the ground with your left heel (fig. 3-92). As soon as your left heel touches the ground, point your left foot to the right and simultaneously shift your weight to your left leg. As your foot turns, turn your body to the right. At the same time, relax your right leg and let it naturally follow the turn of your body to the right. Keep your right foot lightly in touch with the ground (fig. 3-93). Continue turning your body to the right until you have returned to the starting posture. Keep your right leg relaxed, slightly turn your right foot on the ball of the foot, and keep the ball of your right foot touching the ground (fig. 3-94).

Figs. 3-88 to 3-94: *Zhuan Shen Bu*   **3-89**   **3-90**

3-91   **3-92**   **3-93**

3-94

Dao Cha Bu

Dao Cha Bu is an insert step from the back that results in a snake-like forward motion. In this quick and hidden step, the back foot moves forward from behind the front foot and is difficult for an opponent to detect. Because this step allows you to change direction quickly and easily, it is very useful in fighting situations.

Movement Description for Dao Cha Bu

Stand erect with most of your weight on your left leg. Turn your head to the right about forty-five degrees. In this practice, you will always be moving in the direction toward which you are facing (fig. 3-95). Move your left foot to the

right behind your right foot so that your legs cross. Imagine that you want to insert your left leg into the ground behind your right leg (fig. 3-96). As soon as your left foot touches the ground, step quickly to the right with your right foot until it is in front of your left foot, similar to its position in your starting posture (fig. 3-97). When you do this step, the essential point is to keep your body stable. You should also minimize any overt movements or changes in the upper part of your body. Internally, you should feel as though you can move or change your position easily.

Figs. 3-95 to 3-97: *Dao Cha Bu*   **3-96**   **3-97**

Ce Shan Bu

Ce Shan Bu is a side dodge step that is very useful. It is similar to *Dao Cha Bu* but moves in the opposite direction. It is always used to move suddenly away from your opponent.

Movement Description for Ce Shan Bu

Start from your posture in figure 3-97. Step to the left with your right foot and move it in front of and across your left foot (fig. 3-98). Step to the left with your left foot and let it pass behind your right foot. Shift your weight to your left leg and keep your right leg relaxed (fig. 3-99).

Many additional steps are introduced in the sixteen-posture form. Any one of them can be practiced separately and can provide the basis for routines similar to those described here.

Figs. 3-98 to 3-99: Ce Shan Bu   3-99

✪ *Tui Shou*—Pushing Hands

Different schools of internal martial arts emphasize different principles and training methods for fighting, but the goal of all schools is the same—to win in the most efficient way possible. To fight efficiently, you should not use force directly against your opponent's force. You should always use your strong point to beat your opponent's weak point, and you should always conserve your energy. You should also develop your sensitivity so that you can accurately gauge your own balance as well as the balance of your opponent and so that you can feel the force, direction, and timing of the defense and attack moves that you and your opponent make. You should remain relaxed so that your movements can be nimble, and quickly and smoothly changed. *Tui Shou*, or push hands, is the best method for training these abilities.

Push-hands training is used in many martial art styles, but it is in Taiji Quan that this method has been researched in great detail and developed to a very high level. In this section, we describe some of the basic push-hands training methods used in Taiji Quan. These methods can help you develop your sensitivity, body relaxation, and sense of balance and distance.

Push hands is a two-person training method. In the photographs that follow, imagine that you are the person on the left and your partner is the person on the right. Although there are many push-hands skills that can be directly applied to fighting situations, the push-hands routines discussed in this section are designed to develop your basic abilities. In these routines, both you and your partner should avoid the use of force. You should stay relaxed, follow each other's movements closely, use as little pressure as possible at the touch point, and keep all your movements smooth and even. Your goal should be to help each other rather than to compete. All push-hands routines should be practiced many times. For each of the routines presented in this section, only one complete sequence of moves is described. You and your partner should practice the sequence many times. Each sequence is described for either the right side or the left, but all the routines should be practiced on both sides. Try to practice on one side for at least five minutes before switching to the other side.

Push-Hands Routine with Horizontal Circle and One-Hand Pushing

You and your partner should stand and face each other at a distance of about two feet (fig. 3-100). Each of you should raise your right hand and stretch it out in front of you so that the back of your right wrist touches the back of your partner's right wrist (fig. 3-101). Both of you should bend your legs and step forward with your right foot, letting your right heel touch the ground and your toes point up to form a sitting stance (fig. 3-102).

Figs. 3-100 to 3-107: Push-Hands Routine with Horizontal Circle and One-Hand Pushing

3-101

3-102

3-103

3-104

3-105

3-106

3-107

Maintaining contact with your partner's wrist, turn your right hand to the right and push forward toward your partner's left shoulder. At the same time, shift your weight forward to form a bow stance. Your partner should relax his arm and follow your push, turning his right hand slightly so that his palm faces his shoulder

(fig. 3-103). Your partner should move his right hand from in front of his left shoulder to the front of his right shoulder, turning his right hand over as it crosses his body so that his right palm faces toward you. You should stay relaxed and follow his movement (fig. 3-104). Your partner should then push his right hand toward your left shoulder and shift his weight forward to form a bow stance. You should continue to relax and follow his push, turning your right hand over to face your body as your right hand moves to the front of your left shoulder. At the same time, shift your weight back to form a sitting stance (fig. 3-105).

Move your right hand across your body from the front of your left shoulder to the front of your right shoulder. Turn your right hand over while it moves across your body so that by the time it is in front of your right shoulder, your palm is facing your partner. Your partner should stay relaxed and follow the movement of your arm as it moves across your chest (fig. 3-106). Push your right hand forward toward your partner's left shoulder as you shift your weight forward to form a bow stance. Your partner should relax, turn his hand around so that it faces his body, and follow your push while shifting his weight back to form a sitting stance (fig. 3-107). Repeat and continue this sequence of movements starting from figure 3-104.

Push-Hands Routine with Vertical Circle and One-Hand Pushing

This routine begins in the same way as the routine with the horizontal circle. When you and your partner have touched right wrists, and each of you has assumed a sitting stance (fig. 3-108), you should turn your right hand over and use your thumb and middle finger to lightly grip your partner's right wrist. Pull downward and to the right until your right hand is next to your right hip. Your partner should stay relaxed and follow your movement as he shifts his weight forward to form a bow stance (fig. 3-109). Release your

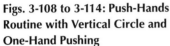

Figs. 3-108 to 3-114: Push-Hands Routine with Vertical Circle and One-Hand Pushing

3-109

3-110

3-111

3-112

3-113

3-114

right hand and raise it up in a vertical, counterclockwise arc. Your partner should follow the arc of your hand's movement so that his right wrist remains in contact with your right wrist (fig. 3-110). Your right palm should face toward your partner and push slantingly up toward your partner's face. Simultaneously shift your weight forward to form a bow stance. Your partner should stay relaxed and keep his right wrist in contact with your right wrist as he follows your movement and shifts his weight back to form a sitting stance (fig. 3-111).

While following your movement, your partner should move his right hand slightly to the right side of his head and then lead your right hand so that it moves past the centerline of his body (fig. 3-112). He should shift his weight forward to form a bow stance and at the same time push his right hand down and forward toward your left hip. You should relax, shift your weight to your back leg to form a sitting stance, and follow his push. At the same time, you should turn your right palm over to face your body (fig. 3-113). Then turn your right hand over and use your thumb and middle finger to grip his right wrist and pull it across your body at stomach level until it is next to your right hip. Your partner should stay relaxed and follow your movement (fig. 3-114). Repeat and continue this sequence starting from figure 3-110.

Push-Hands Routine for Moving-Step Stick-Hand Pushing

You and your partner should stand erect and face each other at a distance of about three feet (fig. 3-115). Each of you should raise your right hand and stretch it out in front of your face so that the back of your wrist touches the back of your partner's wrist (fig. 3-116). Keep the touchpoint light and even. Each of you should step forward with your right foot so that the toes of your right feet are close together (fig. 3-117). Then, each should move his left foot forward until it is next to his right foot. Your bodies should be very close, and each of you should bend your right arm so that you can keep the touchpoint of your right wrists light and even (fig. 3-118). Then each of you should step back with your left foot (fig. 3-119) and move your right foot back until it is next to your left foot. This will cause your right arms to stretch out in order to maintain a light and even touch at your wrists (fig. 3-120). Each of you should step forward with your right foot until the toes of your right foot are close to those of your partner (fig. 3-121). Repeat and continue the sequence starting from figure 3-118.

Figs. 3-115 to 3-121: Push-Hands Routine for Moving-Step Stick-Hand Pushing

3-116

3-117

3-118

3-119

3-120

3-121

The essential element of this practice is always to keep the touchpoint of the wrists light and even, regardless of the distance between you and your partner.

Push-Hands Routine for Moving-Step Stick-Hand Pushing with Position Shift

Stand facing your partner and touch right wrists as in figures 3-115 and 3-116. The directions for this routine, as in the routine just described, are the same for both partners. Each of you should step forward and slightly to the left with your right foot until it is close to the right side of your partner's right foot. Turn slightly to the right (fig. 3-122) and move your left foot forward until it is next to your right foot.

Your bodies should be very close. Each of you should bend your right arm in order to maintain a light and even touch on the other's wrist. Turn slightly to the right (fig. 3-123) and step to the left and slightly forward with your left foot. Continue turning to the right (fig. 3-124). Then, step back and to the left with your right foot until it is next to your left foot. Turn your body and feet to the right so that you and your partner switch starting points. At the same time stretch your right arm out so that a light touchpoint at the wrists can be maintained (fig. 3-125). Repeat and continue the

Figs. 3-122 to 3-125: Push-Hands Routine for Moving-Step Stick-Hand Pushing with Position Shift

3-123

3-124

3-125

sequence of movements starting from figure 3-122, but this time you will be starting from your partner's original position and he will be starting from yours.

In this practice, when you step back and move away from your partner, you should turn your body and feet so that you and he exchange standing positions. As in the routine for moving-step stick-hand without a change of position, the most important aspect of this routine is always to keep the touchpoint of the wrists light and even, regardless of the distance between partners.

✪ *Fa Jin*—Releasing Trained Force

Knowing how to release force is one of the most important fighting skills. Mastering it can increase dramatically your chances of winning. The usual term for this skill is *fa jin*. *Fa* means "release" or "launch," and *jin* means "power" or "force." In internal martial arts, the force used in *fa jin* refers to a kind of force that is acquired only by special training, so we refer to it as "trained force." It does not refer to the natural kind of force that is used in everyday life. Much of the training in internal martial arts is devoted to acquiring and using this kind of force.

There are many different types of *jin*. For example, there are thirty-six kinds of *jin* in Taiji Quan. Each is expressed and used in a different way, and each requires a different kind of training.

Jin can be separated into two general groupings. One is called *wai jin* or external trained force, and the other is *nei jin* or internal trained force. *Wai jin* is considered to be external because when it is used, it is always with some big or obvious physical movements, which can be clearly seen. *Nei jin* is not visible when applied but is derived from the movement of internal components, like mind and *qi*. Because *wai jin* is much easier to understand and learn than *nei jin,* internal martial arts training emphasizes *nei jin* more than *wai jin*. This does not mean that nei jin is more important

than *wai jin*. Both should be used, but in different ways and for different reasons.

Today many people in internal martial arts groups do not understand *nei jin* well. Even most of the time when you say *jin* or *nei jin*, actually it is *wai jin*. So there is a widespread but mistaken assumption that training in the internal martial arts focuses too much on *wai jin*. Often *nei jin* training and applications are downplayed or ignored because they are difficult to understand. This has resulted in the interesting situation whereby people can emphasize *nei jin* training a lot, but they are actually training *wai jin*. Furthermore, the two kinds of *jin* are often confused because the term "*jin*" is generally used to refer only to *nei jin*. Differentiating *wai jin* and *nei jin* is an important aspect of internal martial arts training.

Wai Jin Training

Some kinds of *wai jin* are used frequently. They include *bao fa jin*, *cun jin*, *jie jin*, and *chuang jin*. These *wai jin* can be launched in vigorous and quick ways, so they are always used in hard strikes and as final attacks. They should be sudden and powerful, like thunder. *Wai jin* is a hard force that contains a soft force inside. Once *wai jin* force has been released, it cannot easily be changed, nor can it be maintained for long. Unless you are sure that your strike will hit its target, you should not attempt *wai jin*. Also, you should not release *wai jin* if it will be directed straight at your opponent's force. You must be able to exercise control before you use *wai jin*. In external martial arts, the ability to control *wai jin* is not considered to be as important as it is in the internal martial arts. This is a major point of difference between the two schools of martial arts.

Some kinds of commonly used *nei jin* are *chang jin*, *chen jin*, *peng jin*, *zhan jin*, *nian jin*, *lian jin*, and *sui jin*. These *nei jin* can be more easily controlled than *wai jin*. Once launched, they can be changed and controlled throughout their course, and their effects last

for a longer period of time. It is said that they should emerge like water from a spring—that is, water that flows forth without end. *Nei jin* is a soft force that contains a hard force within it, and it is used far more often than *wai jin* in internal martial arts. If you cannot do *nei jin* well, you will not be able to use the full range of internal martial arts skills.

In this section we describe several *wai jin* and *nei jin* training methods. Basically there are two parts to *jin* training. The first training goal is to increase force by learning how to generate and store strength in the body, and the second training goal is to apply the force by launching it through movement. In *wai jin* practice, the two kinds of training are usually combined; in *nei jin* practice, they are presented separately. First we will discuss several *wai jin* combined training methods.

Basically *wai jin* training is not very difficult because it follows quite closely the ways force is naturally used in everyday activities. It is relatively easy to demonstrate and so can be quite readily learned. It is about how to tap your potential. If you practice hard enough, you should be able to develop excellent *wai jin* skills. The key points in *wai jin* training are to relax and integrate all parts of your body, to smoothly coordinate your movements, to focus your *shen* and *yi*, and to move your *qi* evenly throughout your body. Be patient and do not try to use large amounts of force at the beginning of your training. You should do everything softly, smoothly, and in a state of relaxation.

Pu Mian Zhang

Pu mian zhan, or palm strike to the face is a simple but useful skill. Start this practice by standing erect and staying relaxed (fig. 3-126). Bend your legs slightly and stretch your right hand out in front of your face with your right palm facing your body (fig. 3-127). Step forward with your right foot and at the same time pull your right hand down and slightly to the right until it is next to your right

hip. Turn your body slightly to the right and sink down. In this movement, your body will move forward with your step, while the movement of your right hand will generate force in the opposite direction. The resultant force will increase the pulling power of your right hand (fig. 3-128).

Raise your right hand suddenly and quickly in a curving path until it is on the right side of your head. Shift your weight forward. The force should come from your legs, which should feel compressed like coiled springs when you lower your body. This compression provides a force that pushes your body up. Follow this feeling when you raise your right hand (fig. 3-129).

Step forward with your left foot and shift your weight to your left leg. At the same time, push your right palm forward and slightly down in a curving path and pull your left palm back toward your body. Your left palm should face your torso at the level of your

Figs. 3-126 to 3-130: Pu Mian Zhang   3-127   3-128

3-129   3-130

stomach. The movements of your right and left hands should be coordinated, as though they were rotating a large ball. Imagine that your right hand is on your opponent's face and push it forward and down. At the same time, imagine that your left hand is on your opponent's waist and pull it back and up. These forces should be integrated and should rotate when applied (fig. 3-130).

Shuang Zhuang Zhang

Shuang zhuang zhang or double palm ramming strike is a frequently used skill. In Xingyi Quan it is well known as the "tiger." Start this practice by standing erect with your right foot in front and about sixty percent of your weight on your left leg (fig. 3-131). Push off with your left foot and step forward with your right foot. At the same time, raise both palms up to chest level and turn your palms outward. Your body, arms, and hands should form a circle. Your body, legs, and feet should stay in the same position throughout the execution of this skill. Your whole body should move together as your back foot pushes off from the ground. Also, you should feel your arm circle expand slightly. This will create a powerful force in your palms (fig. 3-132).

Figs. 3-131 to 3-132: Shuang Zhuang Zhang   **3-132**

Ye Zhuang

Ye zhuang or single palm ramming strike is a difficult but useful skill. In this training exercise, you can learn how to launch a straight force from a soft circle and how to launch two powerful continuous strikes. Start by standing erect (fig. 3-133). Raise your left hand up to the left side of your head and your right hand up in front of your chest. Both palms should face up. Bend your right elbow so that your right arm forms a circle in front of your chest. At the same time, bend your legs and take a small step forward with your right foot and touch the ground with the toes of your right foot. Stay relaxed and soft. Withdraw your chest and stomach slightly to create a hollow feeling in your body (fig. 3-134).

Turn your right hand over and stretch your right palm out in front of your body with your palm facing forward and your fingers pointing up. At the same time, step forward with your right foot and shift your weight forward to form a bow stance. Keep your right arm very soft so that you can dodge any kind of block (fig. 3-135). Move your left palm forward to strike the back of your right palm, and shift your weight forward slightly as you stamp the ground with your right foot. The strike by your left palm and the stamp of your right foot must be integrated. Imagine that your right palm is soft and moving forward to touch your opponent's chest, and that a sudden strike by your left palm goes through your right palm to hit your opponent. This force will shake your opponent's body to its core (fig. 3-136).

Continue to push your left palm down and then pull it back until it is in front of your left hip. At the same time, shift your weight back to form a half riding horse stance and turn your body to the left. Despite the fact that your left palm moves a long distance and your right palm moves very little, you should feel as though these two movements are connected. It should feel as though the downward push and backward pull of your left palm cause your right

Figs. 3-133 to 3-137: Ye Zhuang

3-134

3-135

3-136

palm to strike forward. The weight shift to your back leg causes more power to flow to your right palm from your legs, and this creates a second, much more powerful strike. The first and second strikes should be continuous. The first strike shakes the inside of your opponent's body, and the second sends power directly into his body and can hurt him badly (figs. 3-137a, 3-137b).

3-137: Ye Zhuang

Pian Xun Zhang

Pian xun zhang or whirlwind cutting palm is a quick and flexible strike in which a cutting strike results from a revolving movement of the body that shakes the opponent's balance. Start by standing erect (fig. 3-138). Step forward with your right foot but do not shift your weight forward. At the same time, raise your hands so that your right hand is at face level with your right palm facing down, and your left hand is at stomach level with your left palm facing up. Raise both hands softly in a curving path (fig. 3-139). Continue to raise your right hand and twist your right forearm until your right hand is over your head with your palm facing up. At the same time, lean slightly back and raise your right knee a little bit. The movements of your right arm and right knee must be closely coordinated or you will lose your balance (fig. 3-140). Drop your right hand behind your head in a curving motion and simultaneously shift your weight forward to your right leg to form a bow stance. The movement of your right hand back should be coordinated with your weight shift forward; in this movement, your body moves forward while your hand moves back (fig. 3-141).

Throw your right hand forward in a circular movement and twist your right forearm until your right palm faces up. Imagine using the outer edge of your palm to chop straight ahead. Your right arm should move in a revolving motion that is controlled from your waist and derives its power from your legs (fig. 3-142).

Figs. 3-138 to 3-142: Pian Xun Zhang   3-139   3-140

3-141   3-142

Nei Jin Training

The training for *nei jin* applications is much more difficult than that for *wai jin* because *nei jin* skills are subtle and hidden, and more difficult than *wai jin* skills to discern or demonstrate. Also, *nei jin* skills are not practiced or applied in ways that feel intuitive or natural. For these reasons, both the teaching and the acquisition of *nei jin* skills are challenging.

Training designed to increase *nei jin* skills is not easy because the use of *nei jin* depends on the practitioner's feeling. The use of your mind to lead your *qi* and the ways to move your *qi* through your body are internal processes that are invisible to observers. In the beginning of your training, it will be especially difficult for you to assess whether you are executing *nei jin* skills correctly. The best way to acquire these skills is through the practice of forms such as those in Taiji Quan.

Learning to apply *nei jin* is also complicated by the need for a knowledgeable master who can practice with you. The master should explain and demonstrate what it feels like to have the force applied to your body so that you can understand the desired effect of each application. Then you should apply your force to the master's body and let him check that you are using *nei jin* properly. With many repetitions of this process, you will have a chance to understand and master *nei jin*. This kind of training, called *Shuo Jin* or *Shuo Shou*—which means "explaining how to apply *jin*"— is the only method that can help you learn *nei jin* applications. Push hands is the focus of such training and is the best way to practice *nei jin*.

Because *nei jin* is internal and therefore not visible, it would be pointless to provide photographs of *nei jin* skills. Pictures would more likely promote misunderstanding than provide useful information. We suggest that you find an experienced teacher to train you face to face in *nei jin* skills.

~

There are many basic *gongfu* training methods in traditional internal martial arts. Although generally different methods will bring you different benefits and develop different *gongfu* skills, there are many points of overlap among them. Post-standing practice, for example, is good for generating power as well as for developing root. Diligent practice should include a variety of training methods

so that you can increase all aspects of your skill. Each basic *gongfu* training method can help you build your foundation and this, in turn, will help you increase your understanding of fighting skills more quickly and easily.

The Movements and Applications of the Sixteen-Posture Form

The sixteen-posture form is designed to help middle-level practitioners understand and master the fighting principles and skills of the internal martial arts. In this chapter, we describe in detail the movements of the sixteen-posture form and the direct applications of each movement. Variations of applications that have multiple uses also are described.

✪ How to Learn and Practice the Sixteen-Posture Form

When you begin learning the sixteen-posture form and its applications, please be patient. You will have to practice each movement many times in order to understand its meaning. As repeated practice enhances your understanding, you will be better able to appreciate the structure of each movement and the way each serves its purpose. This will sharpen your mind and make your physical responses more appropriate and effective in fighting situations. It will increase your ability to transfer the skills you gain in training to conditions of real fighting.

You should practice each movement slowly, smoothly, and with complete relaxation in order to achieve mastery. Practicing the movements slowly will allow you to pay close attention to each detail; practicing the movements smoothly will allow you to train

internal components like *qi* and *yi* (mind) so that your internal power will increase. Relaxation will help you understand external and internal integrations. When doing your solo practice, you should imagine that you are fighting with an opponent. Think how each movement, even in its smallest detail, might be used.

Then, practice the applications of each movement with a partner. In this phase of your training, pay careful attention to the timing, angle, and direction of each skill so that you will be able quickly to determine how each skill is best applied in different fighting situations. You should know the differences between the movements as they are practiced in the form and as they appear in the applications. In many cases, the movements as practiced in the form are somewhat different from the movements when they are applied in real fighting. For this reason, your practice must always include the training of variations for each technique as well as form training.

After you have learned the various applications for each movement, you should turn your attention to how your internal power can be used. The goal here is to differentiate and use clearly each kind of force, such as controlling, throwing, or striking. You should focus on learning how to increase your power and then how to release your force in a natural and relaxed way.

When you practice, you should think deeply about your movements and reflect carefully on your internal responses. You should always summarize your experience and make frequent adjustments. Because people have varying physical characteristics, habits, and personalities, the movement applications may be expressed very differently from person to person. This is to be expected and should not be considered a problem. You must be very clear, however, about the basic principles you are following, and you must follow these principles without variation. It is essential that you train diligently and according to correct principles.

The sixteen postures of the form are preceded by a preparation

form and followed by a closing form. For each of the sixteen postures, a posture name and a skill description are given. The posture name is provided in the traditional way; that is, it includes a brief discussion of the literary sources from which the name of the posture is derived as well as some cultural background information. This traditional name makes it easier for the practitioner to remember and understand the postures. The skill description for each posture is a long name, made up of the main movements that appear in the posture. The skill name is designed to make it easier for people, especially foreigners, to remember all the movements.

Each posture in the form includes several skills. These can be used separately or in a continuous sequence. In order to master each technique, you should begin by practicing them separately. Perform each movement many times. Such repetition will give you ample opportunity to experience the meaning of each movement. This is the only way you will be able to truly master each skill. Also, you should practice each posture on both the left and right sides, even though most of them are done on only one side in the form.

Along with written explanations for each posture, photographs are included to help the reader understand the movements. Some movements and applications are shown from different angles. In these instances, the same figure number is used for the movement, and the notations (a), (b), etc., indicate different angles of view. Separate sets of photographs are provided for movement and application sequences. Variations for many of the applications are also provided. Finally, because some movements in the form are not performed in exactly the same way when applied in fighting situations, the photographs for a given movement may look quite different in the two sets of pictures, so please be careful. Do not be concerned when the related photographs in the movement and application sequences appear to be different.

Because people have different styles of movement and different feelings and dispositions, skills that are easy for one person may

be problematic for another. Although you should practice each skill thoroughly, it is important to discover which skills feel most natural to you. When you begin your study of the sixteen-posture form, you should focus on mastering those skills that feel most comfortable for you—the ones you really like. This will help you avoid a common problem for most beginning internal martial artists, which is the likelihood that lengthy practice may produce little or no improvement in skill level. The development of understanding and feeling in your movements is a very important and difficult step in the successful practice of internal martial arts. Focusing first on skills that are compatible with your particular characteristics and inclinations will help you accomplish this task and will deepen the effectiveness and meaning of your training.

✪ Name List of the Sixteen-Posture Form

预备式 Preparatory Form

1. 扬鞭催马 **Brandish a Whip at the Horse**
   蹲身进拍掌横扇 Step forward and crouch down, slamming back and clapping palm

2. 三仙聚会 **Three Immortals Gather Together**
   双贯拳下栽反背 Double punch, downward punch, and turn with fist punching back

3. 二郎担山 **Er Lang Carrying the Mountain**
   缠抱势横担前顶 Entwine and embrace, carry on, and withstand by striking forward

4. 飞虎拦路 **Flying Tiger Blocking the Road**
   捋手进踩跺连撞 Pull hand and charge in, stamp-kick, side-kick, and knee strike

5. 御铡除恶 **Rid Evil with a Hay Cutter**
   后撤步立身压肘 Step back, straighten body, and press elbow down

6. 苍龙摆尾 **Black Dragon Swaying Its Tail**
   侧身进上劈下扶 Step forward with body turned to the side, chop above and press below

7. 霸王抖甲 **Ba Wang Shaking His Armor**
   挑肘上回身侧摔 Raise elbow, turn around, and side-throw

8. 野马奔腾 **Wild Horse Galloping**
   侧身进立身直栽 Step forward with your body turned to the side, straighten your body, and punch straight down

9. 饿虎扑食 **Hungry Tiger Pounces on Its Prey**
   进步冲双掌前撞 Step forward, both palms ramming forward

10. 周仓扛刀 **Zhou Cang Shouldering the Big Sword**
    问心肘转身扛臂 Elbow strike to the heart and turn around to press arm down over the shoulder

11. 栽花移木 **Plant Flower and Move Tree**
    栽捶势抱肩反搬 Downward punch and turn around to hold shoulders and move backward

12. 醉卧苍松 **Sleeping Off the Wine Under a Pine Tree**
    侧身上转身搬靠 Step forward with body turned to the side and turn around to pull and lean on arm

13. 猛虎出洞 **Fierce Tiger Leaping Out of Its Lair**
    上掐嗉进步掖撞 Choke and step in to tuck and ram with palm

14. 风轮飞旋 **Wind-and-Fire Wheel Spinning Swiftly**
    肩撞进勾手削掌 Step in with shoulder strike, hooking hand and chopping palm

15. 猿猴入洞 **Monkey Jumping in Its Lair**
掖拿势转身腕打 Grip wrist and tuck back, and turn body back with wrist strike

16. 朔风扑面 **Cold Wind Caresses the Face**
捋手势搂腰盖掌 Pull hand, hold waist, and cover palm

华陀问脉（收势）**Hua Tuo Feeling the Pulse (Closing Form)**
回身走拧腕归原 Turn around, twist wrist, and return to starting position

✪ The Movements and Applications of the Sixteen-Posture Form

预备式 Preparation

Before practicing, you should prepare yourself by adjusting your mind, breath, and body for the movements of the form and their applications. You should keep your mind quiet and focused, your breath deep and smooth, and your whole body naturally relaxed. Imagine that opponents surround you so that your spirit becomes stimulated and alert and your body becomes quiet in anticipation of quick movement. Even while looking forward, become aware of any change around you; and even while standing still, feel ready to move at any time in any direction. Imagine that you are in danger, but feel confident that you will be able to win any fight. Be focused but not nervous. Maintain this feeling throughout your practice.

Movement

Keep your body erect and your feet parallel and close together (fig. 4-1, page 238). Look straight ahead. Relax both arms and let them rest naturally along the sides of your body. Focus your mind on the *Jianjing* point (on your shoulder). This will cause both shoulders to relax. Move the focus of your mind to the *Quchi* point (on the

outside of your elbow) and then to the *Shaohai* point (on the inside of your elbow). This will cause both elbows to relax and drop down naturally. Both palms should face inward toward your legs, and your middle fingers should touch the *Fengshi* points (on the outside of your thighs). This will cause *qi* to move to the tip of your fingers. Keep your neck straight and the top of your head up, as though your body were suspended from the ceiling. This will animate your spirit. Let the tip of your tongue touch the hard palate just behind your front teeth. This creates a connection between *renmai* and *dumai,* the acupuncture channels on the front and back centerlines, and forms *xiaozhoutian,* which is the microcosmic orbit, the most basic orbit of qi flow in *qigong* practice.

The objective of this posture is to focus your mind by dismissing distracting thoughts and to let both your body and mind attain an insubstantial, quiet, and empty state. At the same time, all the muscles of your body should be relaxed and prepared for anything. This creates an internal sense of stability, alertness, and comfort and is displayed externally as quiet receptivity and gentleness.

1. 扬鞭催马 Brandish a Whip at the Horse

Posture Name

"扬鞭催马 *yang bian cui ma*" means to whip a horse in order to encourage it to exert more force. Usually this sentence is used when a new move is initiated, and so it also means "beginning." It is applied here, quite logically, to the first posture of the form. When you practice this skill, you should imagine that your arm is a whip and your opponent is a horse.

In this posture, which mimics the action of brandishing a whip, imagine that your body is the handle of a whip, your arm is a whip, and your hand is the tip of the whip. Imagine that the handle of the whip is being held at waist level, so when you brandish this whip the force comes from your legs, is controlled by your waist,

and reaches to your fingertips. The movement should generate a powerful, quick, and sudden action without causing your body to tighten up.

4-1

Movement Name and Description

蹲身进掩击拍掌 — *dun shen jin yan ji pai zhang:* Step forward and crouch down, slamming back and clapping palm

Stand erect with both feet parallel and close together, as in figure 4-1. Extend your right hand in front of your body (fig. 4-1-1).

Imagine that your right wrist is gripped by an opponent while you relax your right shoulder and drop your right elbow. At the same time, bend both legs slightly. Raise your left hand over your right forearm and let your left forearm cross to your right forearm. Look at your right wrist (fig. 4-1-2).

Quickly move your left forearm down along your right forearm as though brushing something off your arm. This movement is called *ma luo,* and it should be quite energetic. At the same time, twist your right forearm to the right, and move your right elbow back as though you were pulling something back toward your body. Withdraw your chest and stomach. Continue to bend your legs until your body assumes a squatting position. Keep moving your left forearm down until it loses touch with your right arm. Look down in front of your left hand (fig. 4-1-3).

Stretch your left hand forward. Imagine that you are using the outside of your left wrist to touch and stick to the inside of your opponent's right forearm. Step forward with your left foot. Raise your right hand to ear level, close to the right *Ermen* point (on the side of your ear), and form an empty fist with your right hand. Look forward (fig. 4-1-4).

Step forward with your right foot until it is parallel with your

4-1-1   4-1-2   4-1-3

4-1-4   4-1-5   4-1-6

left foot. Open your right empty fist to make a palm and at the same time hit forward with your right palm. This movement is called *pai zhang*. Simultaneously bring your left hand back with the palm first touching the inside of your right wrist and then moving along your right forearm near the elbow, where it should remain. Look into the distance (fig. 4-1-5).

Step back and about forty-five degrees to the left with your left foot. Turn your right palm toward the left. At the same time, imagine that you already grip the inside of your opponent's right wrist. Bend your right arm and move your right hand toward your left foot (fig. 4-1-6). Shift your weight to your left leg and move your right hand back slightly in a curving motion. Look at your right hand (fig. 4-1-7).

Step back with your right foot until it is parallel with your left foot and let only the toes of your right foot touch the ground.

Keep moving your right hand from left to right until it is slightly in front of and to the side of your right hip. At the same time, bend both knees and make sure that your full weight is still on your left leg. Look at the tiger mouth between the thumb and index finger of your right hand, and then turn to the left slightly (fig. 4-1-8).

Take a half step forward with your right foot and then shift your weight to your right leg. Raise your right hand in front of your body and relax your left arm so that the fingers of your left hand point to the ground. Step forward with your left foot, letting only the toes of this foot touch the ground, and imagine that you have used your left leg to lock your opponent's right leg. Raise your left arm slightly and turn your left palm to face your right palm. The tip of your right index finger should point forward and then down. By now you should feel as though you could attack your opponent at will (fig. 4-1-9).

Raise your right hand, twist your right forearm, and pull back slightly. Pierce forward with your left palm and simultaneously twist your left arm counterclockwise until the palm faces up. Look forward and far away. When you pierce forward and twist your left palm, the movement of your left hand should follow your eyesight. At that time, raise your body slightly and make a half step forward with your left foot. Your right foot should just follow the movement of your left foot (fig. 4-1-10).

Drop your left arm down and turn your body toward the right. Bend both legs slightly. Keep your right hand in the same position (fig. 4-1-11). Continue to turn your body to the right and look to the right and slightly back. Move your left arm in the same direction as your eyes. Your forearms should cross each other, with your right arm on top of your left. Point your left index and middle fingers to the right and back as you shift your weight onto your right leg. Squat down and make a sneak step with your left foot, letting only the toes of this foot touch the ground. Turn your head as your body turns and look to the right (fig. 4-1-12a, 4-1-12b).

4-1-7   4-1-8   4-1-9

4-1-10   4-1-11   4-1-12

4-1-13

Raise your right hand up and pull back slightly. Your left arm led by your index and middle fingers should draw a horizontal circle counterclockwise from right to left in front of your body. Feel the force come from your right foot and increase in your waist to accelerate your movement. At the same time, shift your weight to the left a little bit to form a riding horse stance. Stretch

both arms out to each side of your body, and focus your mind on your right hand. Look far away toward the left. This movement is called *chuan zhang* (fig. 4-1-13). It requires that the hand follow the body, the body follow the waist, and the waist follow the eyes. This sequence should be done as quickly as possible and should flow smoothly as one movement. It is said of such movement that the eyes look simultaneously where the hand reaches.

Application

When your opponent grips your right wrist with his right hand (fig. 4-1-14)

Focus your mind on the right *Jianjing* point (on your right shoulder). This will cause your right arm to relax so that you do not use your force directly against your opponent's force. Move your left arm up and put the lower part of your left forearm on the gripped part of your opponent's right wrist, with your left palm facing your body (fig. 4-1-15). Then use the edge of your left palm to chop at your opponent's right hand or wrist by turning your left forearm and moving it down along your right forearm toward the toes of your left foot and toward the tiger mouth of your opponent's right hand. At the same time, slightly bend your right elbow and move your right forearm up in a clockwise twisting motion. Bend both legs, relax your right shoulder, and drop your elbow as you pull your stomach in and squat down slightly. This will cause your right wrist to be freed from your opponent's grip. Then move your right hand up with your palm facing your opponent. Look forward. While maintaining contact with your opponent, step forward with your left foot and raise your right hand up to the side of your right ear and form a fist. The fist should be relaxed and empty (figs. 4-1-16a, 4-1-16b). The most important feature of this application is that all movements be quick, continuous, and smooth. The separate movements should flow together as one. Each movement will create a strong and heavy internal force called *ma luo jin,* which is used

4-1-14

4-1-15

4-1-16

to free your right wrist. Your opponent will have difficulty resisting this kind of force.

Ma luo jin is different from the muscle force that is usually exerted by your body. If you exert force through your muscles, the power will be directed straight against your opponent's force. This is called *shuangzhong* or "double-weighting" in Taiji Quan. In this situation, you must exert a force greater than that of your

opponent if you are to succeed in freeing your wrist, and even if you succeed, the result will not be achieved in an efficient way.

The best time for a *ma luo jin* strike is when your opponent has just gripped your wrist but has not yet applied much force. You should be very careful to sense this point. It is important that you twist your right arm and pull it back at the same time. Both movements should be smoothly coordinated.

After freeing your wrist, keep your left wrist in touch with your opponent's right arm or wrist and follow his movement so that you can move in close for a possible attack. Maintaining the touchpoint will allow you to sense any changes in the timing or direction of your opponent's movement. This is called *ting jin* or "listening force" in Taiji Quan.

A strong and heavy internal force will be generated automatically as soon as your left arm touches your opponent. This internal force will extend down the left side of your body. It is called *cai an jin* or "stamp and push downward" force, and it will cause your opponent to lean forward slightly and move back in an effort to keep his balance. You must take advantage of this opportunity.

Relax your left arm. This will cause your opponent to lose his support point. Then step forward with your right foot, open your

4-1-17

right fist as you bring your arm forward, and beat your opponent's face or chest with your right palm (fig. 4-1-17). Imagine as you strike that you are using a whip. Your torso becomes like the handle of the whip, and your right arm becomes like the whip. Imagine that you are using your hand to hold your waist—the handle of the whip. The force, which should be powerful, quick and sudden, should come from your feet and legs, be controlled by your waist, and extend through your body to your fingertips.

When your opponent punches you with a center punch using his right fist (fig. 4-1-18)

Follow your opponent's punching movement and use your right hand to touch lightly the inside of his right wrist. Then close your right hand to grip his wrist. Step back and at an angle of about forty-five degrees to the left with your left foot. Use your right hand to control your opponent's right wrist continuously and keep moving back with your left foot. The movement of your right hand and left foot must be integrated. At this point, your right hand should be in front of the left side of your body (fig. 4-1-19).

Bend both legs so that your body sinks down. Withdraw your stomach and shift your weight to your left leg. Step back with your right foot until it is almost parallel to your left foot. Let only the toes of your right foot touch the ground. Then step slightly forward with your right foot and shift your weight onto it. At the same time, turn your body to the right and use your right hand to pull and lead your opponent in a half-circle from the left to the right in front of your body. This will shake your opponent's root and cause him to lean forward (fig. 4-1-20).

Continue raising your right hand without interruption and twist it slightly outward. This will cause your opponent to shift his weight back slightly. Maintain your grip so that you can maintain control of your opponent's right arm. Continually shift your weight

4-1-18

4-1-19

4-1-20

to your right leg quickly and step forward with your left foot. Place your left foot down parallel with or in back of your opponent's right foot and use your *Yinlingquan* point (on the inside of your knee) to touch your opponent's *Yanglingquan* point (on the outside of his knee). At the same time, move your left arm under his right armpit (fig. 4-1-21). Then turn your right hand until the palm faces up and at the same time push your left shoulder forward toward the back of your opponent's right shoulder. Simultaneously twist and pull your right hand back to make your opponent straighten his right arm so that it is totally under your control. Then use your left palm to pierce upward at an angle under your opponent's right armpit. Make sure your left shoulder touches his armpit and your left arm touches his chest (fig. 4-1-22).

Look far into the distance in the direction of your left hand as it moves, and let your mind follow your *shen* immediately to the distant point. Your whole body should be integrated. When your left palm pierces forward, your left arm should twist outward until the palm faces up. This movement is called *chuan zhang* or "piercing palm," and if your movements are well integrated, they will generate a powerful internal force that throws your opponent down.

4-1-21

4-1-22

When the opponent punches your chest or grips your chest with his right hand (fig. 4-1-23)

Take a half step back and to the left with your left foot. Turn your body slightly to the right and at the same time use the outside of your right wrist to touch your opponent's right wrist (fig. 4-1-24).

Turn your right hand to grip your opponent's wrist and pull it down in a slanting motion toward your left foot. At the same time, step back with your right foot and place it down close to the side of your left foot. Raise the heel of your right foot so that only the toes of that foot touch the ground. Step back and toward the left at about a forty-five-degree angle with your left foot. Hold your opponent's right wrist in your right hand (fig. 4-1-25).

Pull and push down toward the back of your right foot. Your body should turn to the right at the same time, so that your left shoulder touches your opponent's right armpit. At this point, your weight should be on your right leg. This will create a powerful and heavy internal force in your right hand. Your right hand should lead your opponent's right arm to the left side of your body and then should quickly change direction to lead his arm to the right side of your body and downward. This force will shake your opponent's root and make him lean forward (fig. 4-1-26).

Continue without interruption to squat down and at the same time raise your right hand. Keep your left shoulder in touch with your opponent's armpit. If you feel the opponent use his force against you—for example, if he uses his right arm or shoulder to push you back—relax your waist, turn your body slightly to the right, and look back. This will cause a soft force that will eliminate the problem and give you more control of your opponent's body. Then take a sneak-step forward with your left foot and let your left knee touch the back of your opponent's right knee to lock his right leg (fig. 4-1-27).

Look back to the left of your body. Following your line of sight, move your left arm in a big circle to the right and back, then up,

and finally left and forward. At the same time, use your waist to turn your body to the left and use your left arm like a whip to strike your opponent down to the ground (fig. 4-1-28).

In this movement, the main force starts from your right foot. You should use your waist to allow the force to move into your left arm, which then leads the movement of your left forearm. Finally, the force should extend through your left index finger, which should straighten out and point far away.

In this skill, it is important to keep the left side of your body in touch with your opponent so that you and your opponent become like one person. You must also make sure that your left leg really locks your opponent's legs. When you whip your left arm, you should look far away and your mind should follow your line of sight to the distant point. Then you will be able to throw your opponent far.

4-1-23   4-1-24   4-1-25

4-1-26   4-1-27   4-1-28

2. 三仙聚会 Three Immortals Gather Together

Posture Name

"三仙聚会 — *san xian jue hui*" means three immortals gathering together. There are many traditional myths about what happens at gatherings of the immortals. There are always displays of magic power and demonstrations of special, often incredible skills. In this posture, three very useful techniques are shown and because of this, the posture is considered reminiscent of the skills displayed by the three immortals. The main skills are: double punches to the front and back of your opponent's body; a strike that metaphorically knocks a hat off the back of your opponent's head; and a turn back to chop your opponent with the back of your fist.

Movement Name and Description

双贯拳下栽反背 — *shuang guan quan xia zai fan bei*: Double punch, downward punch, and turn with fist punching back

Continue with the movement from figure 4-1-13.

Imagine that your opponent kicks your left leg. You should then use your left toes to press into the ground and generate the force needed to spring back at him. Shift your weight fully onto your right leg and raise your left knee. Keep your left leg bent so that your left knee can be raised as high as possible. Relax your left ankle and move your left hand forward. At the same time, turn your right palm downward and then push it down toward the ground. The movement of pushing your right palm down has to be coordinated with the movement of raising your left knee. This will cause your left palm to become powerful. Look forward and down while executing this movement (fig. 4-2-1).

Make a fist with your left hand and move it forward

4-2-1

4-2-2   4-2-3   4-2-4

4-2-5   4-2-6

until there is about a forty-five-degree angle between your arm and your body. Imagine that you are using the inside of your left forearm to touch the outside and top of your opponent's right forearm. Put your left foot down on the ground under your left forearm and keep your left heel raised off the floor. Turn your left forearm slightly counterclockwise and downward, and then stretch it forward and bend it back a little bit. Imagine that your left forearm has already moved to the inside of your opponent's right arm and is positioned between his right arm and his body. At the same time, think about putting your left fist on the back of the opponent's lower back and step forward with your left foot. Shift your weight to your left leg. Bend your left leg and lower your body. Look at your inner left forearm (fig. 4-2-2).

Completely shift your weight to your left leg to form a left bow stance. Move your left fist along an axis that would correspond to

the spine of an opponent, and raise your fist until it would be at the level of the back of his head. At the same time, move your right fist down along what would be the centerline of an opponent's body from his face to his chest and then to his stomach. Thus, your right fist moves down while your left fist moves up. It should seem as though the two fists will meet each other, the left by moving upward along the back of the opponent's body and the right by moving simultaneously downward along the front centerline of his body. The movement of both fists should be powerful and coordinated (fig. 4-2-3).

Continue the punching motion of your left fist by moving it first downward, then upward on the right side of your body and then downward again. The movement of the fist traces a large circle. Your body should follow the movement of your left fist by turning about three-quarters to the right. At the same time, think about using your left fist to punch downward toward your right heel. This will cause you to squat down on your right leg. Bend your right arm and let the right forearm move close to your body until it rests in a horizontal position. Look at the point on the ground just under your left fist (fig. 4-2-4).

Continue punching downward with your left fist. Let your body follow the direction of the punch by turning to the right. As you turn, move your left foot to the left side of your right foot. Bend both legs more deeply so that your stance lowers slightly. Imagine that your left fist is striking deeply into the ground. Look downward (figs. 4-2-5a, 4-2-5b).

Raise your body. Imagine that you are using your left hand to lift a very heavy object from the earth. Step to the right and forward with your right foot. Look to the right and forward. Move your right fist up and forward to trace a big circle in front of your body with a chopping and pounding punch using the back of your right fist. At the same time, shift your weight to your right leg to form a right bow stance (fig. 4-2-6).

4-2-7

Application

If your opponent kicks your left leg with his right foot

Withdraw your stomach and raise your left knee up. At the same time, stretch both arms out and imagine pushing your right palm back and your left palm forward. Both hands should be coordinated. Your left hand should move suddenly and powerfully to strike the inside of your opponent's right shin or ankle. Look at the point hit by your left hand (fig. 4-2-7). You can also use your left hand to make a substantial hook to grip your opponent's right shin or ankle with this movement.

If your opponent punches you in the stomach with his fist

Step back slightly with your right foot. Raise your left arm and use your left forearm to touch your opponent's right forearm and to feel any changes that may occur at this touchpoint. Shift your weight to your back leg. The toes of your left foot should touch the ground lightly. Look at the touchpoint on your left arm (fig. 4-2-8).

If the opponent keeps punching you, continue using your left forearm to adhere to his right forearm and sink down. At the same time, turn your left arm and move to the left. This will change the direction of his punch and cause his body to lean forward slightly. Relax your waist and lower your body slightly. Step forward with your left foot to move to the right side of your opponent. Simultaneously, following the turn of your body, move your left forearm around your opponent's right arm and then toward his back between his right arm and his body. Continue this movement until your left hand touches the *Mingmen* point on the center of

your opponent's lower back. Your left hand can be either a palm or a fist. At the same time, make a fist with your right hand and prepare to punch your opponent's face. You should look directly at his eyes (fig. 4-2-9).

Punch your opponent's face and then keep moving your right fist downward along a vertical axis, from his face to his chest and then to his stomach. You can release your force in any point along this line. At the same time, punch with your left fist from your opponent's *Mingmen* point up to the back of his head (fig. 4-2-10). In this movement, your right fist punches down in front of your opponent's body and your left fist punches up along the back of his body. This is called *qian zai hou dou* or "punching downward in front and upward in back." Imagine that your fists punch each other from opposite directions.

These two punches generate a very powerful resultant force. To avoid getting hurt, your opponent can only bend his body forward, but this will cause him to lose his balance. So, if you miss your punch, you can use your left shoulder to touch your opponent's right armpit and keep moving your left fist up until it is higher than the top of his head. Then continue to throw your left punch to the right of your body and downward, as though punching at your own right heel (fig. 4-2-11). This will cause your opponent's arm and shoulder to become very tightly locked by your left arm. At this point you are in full control of your opponent and can easily throw

4-2-8

4-2-9

4-2-10

4-2-11   4-2-12

him down face-first into the ground (figs. 4-2-12a, 4-2-12b). When your left hand moves up from your opponent's back, imagine that you are taking a hat off from the back of his head.

When your opponent punches you with his right fist

Step forward with your left foot in a buckle step. Turn back and look at your opponent. Make a right swing step and let only the toes of your right foot touch the ground. Continue turning your body and use your right hand to hold your opponent's right wrist (fig. 4-2-13, same as fig. 4-1-25).

Continue to control his wrist while moving your right hand to the left side of your body and pulling down slightly on your opponent's wrist. This will cause him to change the direction of his movement and miss his punch. He will also lean forward and

4-2-13   4-2-14   4-2-15

readily lose his balance. At the same time, withdraw your right foot, and as soon as possible shift your hands so that you are grabbing and controlling his wrist with your left hand (fig. 4-2-14).

Step forward with your right foot. Use your left hand to pull your opponent slightly toward you. At the same time, make a fist with your right hand and move that hand in front of your body in a half circle to throw a punch directly at your opponent's face. Look at your right fist (fig. 4-2-15). This punch uses the back of the fist and is usually called a "back-chopping" fist.

3. 二郎担山 **Er Lang Carrying the Mountain**

Posture Name

"二郎担山 — *er lang dan shan*" is from an ancient Chinese story in which Er Lang is a warrior. It is said that he was a very powerful man and could carry two big mountains on his shoulder even while being chased by others. When executing this posture, imagine that you are as powerful as Er Lang, and that however big and strong your opponent may be, even if he is as strong as a mountain, you can still deal with him. The main skills are *chan wan*—entwine the wrist; *bao na*—embrace by holding; *heng dan*—carry on; and *ding zhou*—withstand by using an elbow strike.

Movement Name and Description

缠抱势横担前顶 — *chuan bao shi heng dan qian ding:* Entwine and embrace, carry on, and withstand by striking forward

Continue the movement in figure 4-2-6.

Change your right fist to a palm and relax your right arm. Turn your right hand over until the palm faces forward and is angled slightly downward. Look at your right wrist and imagine that your opponent is gripping it with his right hand. Relax your left arm, raise it in front of your body, and place your left palm on the

outside of your right wrist. Imagine that your left hand is on top of your opponent's right hand (fig. 4-3-1).

Relax your right wrist and turn it in a full clockwise circle, with your right palm and fingers following the wrist, until the right palm again faces down at stomach level. Bend the fingers of your right hand and imagine that you are turning your right hand over to grip your opponent's right wrist. Look at the tiger mouth of your right hand (fig. 4-3-2).

Step forward with your left foot. Move your left hand from the top of your right wrist to underneath that wrist. Then turn your left palm upward at an angle to the left. Your forearm should turn until your left palm faces up. This will make your opponent lean back. Imagine using your left palm to strike your opponent's face. Your left hand should move along the line between your right hand and your opponent's right arm. As your left arm moves, let it twist and stretch so that it is out of the way of your right hand. At the end of this movement, your left palm should be facing up and your body should be in a half riding horse stance with about sixty percent of your weight on your left leg. Look forward to a point in front of your left hand (fig. 4-3-3).

Bend your left arm and move it back to grasp your right hand. Push both hands back and down to your chest and stomach, as though you are holding or hugging something tightly. Form a riding horse stance and look at the back of your left hand (fig. 4-3-4).

Do not move your right hand. Look to the left and forward at a distant point. Imagine that your left hand wants to follow quickly the movement of your eyes. This will cause you to move your left arm in an outward arc and thrust your left palm forward. Your left arm should be almost straight, and your left palm should face down. At the same time, shift your weight forward to your left leg to form a left bow stance (fig. 4-3-5).

Let your left hand move in a rolling motion back to the right side of your right ear. The fingers of the left hand should point

to the sky, and the palm should face out. Step forward with your right foot by moving it behind your left leg. This is called a steal step (fig. 4-3-6).

Turn both feet in place so that your body turns 180 degrees clockwise. Turn your left hand over until the palm faces up. This will allow you to control and raise your opponent's left wrist. Your

4-3-1

4-3-2

4-3-3

4-3-4

4-3-5

4-3-6

4-3-7

index finger should point to the outer end of your left eyebrow. Bend your right arm to prepare for an elbow strike. Your right palm should face the ground, and the tip of your right elbow should point forward and to the right. Look to the right and form a riding horse stance. Imagine a connection between the right *Hegu* point on your right hand and the right *Jianjing* point on your right shoulder (figs. 4-3-7a, 4-3-7b).

Application

If your opponent grips your right wrist with his right hand (fig. 4-3-8)

Use your left palm to touch your opponent's right hand lightly (fig. 4-3-9). Relax your right wrist and twist the palm and fingers of your right hand from the lower left to the upper right so that you can grip the top of your opponent's wrist (fig. 4-3-10). When making this twist, your right little finger should lead the movement, and the other fingers and palm of your right hand should just follow. At the same time, put your left palm on your opponent's right hand to prevent him from withdrawing his hand.

When you grip your opponent's right wrist, you should apply slight pressure and think about turning to the right. This will hurt his wrist, weaken his knees, and cause him to fall down (fig. 4-3-11). This movement is called *chan* or "entwine." If you feel that

4-3-8

4-3-9

4-3-10

your opponent is using a lot of power against you when you apply this skill, relax your right hand to create a sense of emptiness in your right palm, raise your wrist slightly, and point downward with your right middle finger. As a result, his resistance force will meet emptiness, and you will have another chance to apply this skill. Usually, *chan* can be applied more strongly the second time.

If your opponent is not well controlled and remains standing after you have gripped his wrist, like in figs. 4-3-9 and 4-3-10

Relax your right hand, elbow, and shoulder. Turn your body slightly to the right, raise your right hand, and pull your opponent slightly to the right (fig. 4-3-12). Step forward with your left foot. Release your left hand from your opponent's right hand and move it under his right arm. Turn it toward the inside of his right arm. Raise your left hand and use the fingers of this hand to thrust at your opponent's face (fig. 4-3-13).

If your opponent leans back to avoid the attack to his face, bend your left arm immediately so that it moves back to the front of your chest. Put your left palm over your right hand and let it also grip your opponent's right hand. Then push both hands down to the level between your chest and stomach, as though you were holding something close and hugging it tightly (fig. 4-3-14). When you push both hands down, your body should sink down also.

4-3-11

4-3-12

4-3-13

4-3-14

4-3-15

This allows you to apply the force of your whole body to your opponent's wrist. His wrist will become very painful, and you will be in control of the situation.

This movement is called *bao* or "embrace." It is said that by using it, one can control an opponent's whole body from just one point. If you use this controlling skill well enough, you will be able to achieve complete control of your opponent. You can raise your body slightly and move your opponent by carrying him (fig. 4-3-15). By using bao, you can make your opponent follow you anywhere you want.

If your opponent is still not under your control after your second attempt

If you missed your chance to control your opponent's right wrist with your left hand, or if your opponent has used a very powerful force against your control (fig. 4-3-16), keep your right hand in the same position and relax your left hand (fig. 4-3-17). At the same time, quickly move your left arm so that the fingers of that hand point upward and to your left. This will cause your

4-3-16   4-3-17   4-3-18

left arm to straighten out under your opponent's right arm like a big carrying pole, the bamboo or wooden poles used in China to transport heavy objects. At the same time, step to the left and forward with your left foot and form a left bow stance. Apply a leg lock by using the inside of your left knee to touch the outside of your opponent's right knee. Look to the left and upward, and imagine that your left hand is chasing the movement of your eyes. This will cause a powerful force that pushes forward from your body through your left arm. This force and the leg lock will cause your opponent to lean back and then fall down (fig. 4-3-18). The movement comprising this skill is called *dan* or "carry on."

If the opponent punches your center with his right fist

Take a half step back by moving your left foot back and to the left. At the same time, relax your waist and let your body follow with a turn to the left. Swing your right arm in a circle so that your right wrist touches the lower part of your opponent's right forearm. Feel your opponent's movement and follow it as his punch continues to come in. Withdraw your hip and stomach, and turn your right hand over to grip your opponent's right wrist. When you grip his wrist, drop your right hand down and to the right side of your body and turn your right hand slightly to the right. At the same time, point toward the earth with the tip of your right foot. Pull in your

stomach, raise your right knee slightly, and move your right hand down sharply toward the ground. This movement is called *xia cai* or "stamp down with hand." If these movements of leg and arm are well coordinated, they will create a very heavy force on your opponent's arm and make him lean forward and lose his balance. This force should also cause him to miss his punch (fig. 4-3-19).

Then quickly raise your right hand, which is gripping your opponent's wrist, until it is above your head. This movement is called *ti*, or "raise up." It is important to maintain *jin* or internal force so that this movement does not become weak. If *ti* is done correctly, your opponent will suddenly feel as though the "stamp down" force on his arm has disappeared and there is no pressure at all on his arm. This abrupt change will cause his balance to become precarious. He will feel as though he is about to fall down into a deep void, and he will feel some nervousness. At that moment, move your right hand up and back slightly. Immediately shift your weight to your right leg. This will cause your opponent's center of gravity to move up, and his heels will lift off the ground (fig. 4-3-20).

Step forward with your left foot and put it behind your opponent's right foot. Bend your left arm to form an elbow strike. Point the tip of your left elbow at your opponent's right ribs. Form a riding horse stance and let your body sink down slightly. Your right hand should still be gripping your opponent's right wrist.

4-3-19

4-3-20

4-3-21

Turn your right hand until the palm faces up, raise your right hand slightly, and pull your opponent to your right. Look at your opponent's right ribs (fig. 4-3-21). This movement is called *ding* or "withstand."

4. 飞虎拦路 Flying Tiger Blocking the Road

Posture Name

"飞虎拦路 — *fei hu lan lu*" means a flying tiger blocks a road. In ancient times, people believed in a flying tiger that had magical powers. It could move quickly and suddenly. If it blocked the road, nothing could pass. When practicing this posture, you should imagine that your movement is like that of the flying tiger— quick, powerful, and able to interrupt or block your opponent's movement. The posture includes three main skills: a lower stamp-kick, a side kick, and a knee strike. The purpose of these skills is to block your opponent's attack powerfully and suddenly, to pull him forward, and at the same time to use your foot or knee to impede his forward movement.

Movement Name and Description

将手进踩跺连撞 — *luo shou jin cai duo lian zhuang:* Pull hand and charge in, stamp-kick, side-kick, and knee strike

Continue the movement from figure 4-3-7.

Shift your weight to your left leg. Turn your body to the right. Let your left hand drop down and your right hand stretch forward. Imagine using your right hand to grip your opponent's right wrist. Look at an imaginary point in front of your right hand (fig. 4-4-1).

Step forward with your left foot to form

4-4-1

a left bow stance. Bend the fingers of your right hand as though to grip your opponent's wrist, and then pull to the left and downward (fig. 4-4-2).

Then turn your body to the right and pull your right hand to the right and downward, and at the same time put your left hand in front of your right hand with the tiger mouth facing forward (fig. 4-4-3).

Raise your right foot and turn the toes clockwise to point toward the outside of your body. Imagine that your right hand is gripping your opponent's right wrist, that your left hand is placed on the outside of his right elbow, and that the sole of your right foot is stamping down on his right knee (fig. 4-4-4).

Pull both hands back to your right. Stamp down on the ground with your right foot. Bend your right knee and shift your weight to your right leg. Look forward and down (fig. 4-4-5).

Pull both hands back continuously and turn your body slightly to the right. Bend your left leg and raise your left knee until it is close to the left side of your ribcage. Look forward and to the left (fig. 4-4-6).

Continue to pull both hands back. Straighten your left knee and stamp your left foot forward. Focus your mind on your right hand. This will increase your kicking force and help maintain your balance. Look at an imaginary point in front of your left foot (fig. 4-4-7). This movement is called *ce chuai* or "side-kicking."

Relax your left leg and let it drop to the ground in front and to the left of your body. Turn your body to the left. Relax both your arms and let them drop down in front of your body. Look forward (fig. 4-4-8).

Shift your weight to your left leg. Raise both hands in front of your body with your left hand under your right. Imagine gripping your opponent's left wrist with your left hand and holding his left elbow with your right hand. Step forward with your right foot (fig. 4-4-9).

Shift your weight to your right leg. Pull both hands back and down, and at the same time raise your left knee and use it to strike forward. Look forward and down (fig. 4-4-10). This move is called *xi zhuang* or "knee-striking."

4-4-2

4-4-3

4-4-4

4-4-5

4-4-6

4-4-7

4-4-8

4-4-9

4-4-10

Application

If your opponent throws a right center punch at you

Step toward the left with your left foot. Use your right palm to touch the inside of your opponent's wrist. Grip his wrist and pull toward your left foot. This will cause him to miss his punch and lose his balance (fig. 4-4-11).

Turn your body to the right and pull your right hand back and toward the right side of your body until your opponent leans forward. At that moment, put your left hand on the outside of his right elbow (fig. 4-4-12).

Raise your right foot to stamp on your opponent's right knee. The toes of your right foot should be pointing toward the right. At the same time, push your left hand down on your opponent's right elbow and simultaneously pull back and push down on your opponent's right wrist with your right hand. Be sure that you have control of his right elbow when you stamp down on his right knee. These two moves must be accomplished together. Shift your weight to your right leg. This will create a strong and injurious force to your opponent's right knee (fig. 4-4-13).

4-4-11   **4-4-12**   **4-4-13**

If your opponent throws a right center punch at you

Use your right palm to touch the inside of your opponent's right wrist. If you feel that his punch is still coming in, close your palm

to grip his wrist. This will immediately cause a change in the direction of his punch. Take a small step to the left with your left foot and pull your right hand down and to the left side of your body. This pull must be integrated with your step to the left (fig. 4-4-14, same as fig. 4-4-11).

Take a small step back and to the right with your right foot. Continue to pull your opponent in order to jar his balance and cause him to lean forward (fig. 4-4-15). Put your left hand on your opponent's right elbow with your palm touching the tip of his elbow and your thumb pushing on the *Quchi* point on the outside of his elbow.

While keeping your weight on your right leg, turn your right foot until the toes point to the right (fig. 4-4-16). Bend your left leg. Raise your left knee until it is close to the left side of your ribcage and your left foot is close to your opponent's right ribcage

4-4-14   **4-4-15**   **4-4-16**

4-4-17   **4-4-18**

(fig. 4-4-17). Pull back with your right hand and stretch your left leg forward so that the sole of your left foot strikes at your opponent's right ribcage (fig. 4-4-18).

4-4-19

If your opponent punches at you with his left fist (fig. 4-4-19)

Touch your opponent's left wrist with the outside of your left wrist. At the same time, step forward with your left foot so that it is positioned to the outside of your opponent's right foot. Follow your opponent's punching movement, and turn your left hand over to grip his left wrist. Put your right hand on his left elbow (fig. 4-4-20).

Step forward with your right foot. Use your left hand to pull your opponent's left hand down. This will cause his body to lean forward in the direction he is facing. Let your right hand follow the movement of your left hand so that the force of the pull is increased. This will cause your opponent to lean forward more and start to lose his balance (fig. 4-4-21). At the same time, raise your right knee to strike at his chest or ribs (fig. 4-4-22). These two movements should be done quickly and as a single action so that the knee strike will have maximal power.

If your opponent lowers his body in an attempt to maintain balance when you pull him forward, release your right grip and continue using your left hand to pull him toward you. Use your

4-4-20

4-4-21

4-4-22

right hand to grasp his neck from the back and pull him down. At the same time, strike with your knee at his chest or face.

5. 御铡除恶 Rid Evil with a Hay Cutter

Posture Name

"御铡除恶 — *yu zha chu e*" refers to the story of Bao Gong, who was the most righteous and honest government official in the Song Dynasty. In his time, many high-level officials and even the Emperor's family members used their connections to gain unfair influence and to commit crimes. Corruption pervaded the government. To show that he was serious about pursuing the wrongdoers and bringing them to justice even though some of his own relatives were implicated, the Emperor put Bao Gong in charge of finding the culprits and meting out justice. This was widely thought to be a thankless, if not impossible, task.

When Bao Gong accepted the responsibility, he asked the Emperor to give him extra resources and powers. The Emperor obliged by giving Bao Gong three large haycutters—big cleavers—and the right to execute anyone who broke the law. No one believed that Bao Gong would really use a hay cutter against the Emperor's relatives—that is, until he killed several of the criminals including the Emperor's son-in-law and one of his nephews. As a result of his successful campaign, Bao Gong gained renown as a great judge who stood against injustice wherever it was found.

Here "*yu zha chu e*" means that when you know you are doing the right thing, you should hold to your decision resolutely and act without hesitation. You should be insistent and brave. Imagine that you are using a big cleaver to attack your opponent, and that your opponent's arm is the cleaver's handle. When you push down on the cleaver's handle, you should keep your body erect and use its full force on the arm of your opponent.

Movement Name and Description

后撤步立身压肘 — *hou che bu li shen ya zhou:* Step back, straighten body, and press elbow down

Continue the movement from figure 4-4-10.

Move your right hand forward with your right palm facing to the left. Bend both legs. Step to the left and back with your left foot and let only the toes of your left foot touch the ground. Turn your right hand over and bend your fingers while imagining that you are gripping your opponent's right wrist. Then pull toward your left foot. At the same time, let the sole of your left foot touch the ground and shift your weight to your left leg. Your right foot should follow the weight shift naturally by moving back one step. The movement of your right hand and left foot must be integrated. Look at an imaginary point just ahead of your right tiger mouth (fig. 4-5-1).

Step back with your right foot and let only the toes of that foot touch the ground. Stretch your left hand forward and up until it is at face level. The palm of your left hand should face up. Then turn over your left palm until it faces down, and move your left hand down at a slight angle to the right until your left hand is at shoulder level in front of your right hand. Imagine that you are placing your left hand on your opponent's right elbow (fig. 4-5-2).

Continue to move your right foot back and shift your weight onto it. At the same time, turn your right foot on its heel and let your toes point to the right. Your body should follow the turn of your foot to the right. The toes of your left foot should continue to point forward so that the angle between your feet is 90 degrees. Keep about sixty percent of your weight on your right leg. This position is called *mading bu* or half riding horse stance. At this point, the fingers of your left hand should be pointing forward, and your left palm should be facing the ground. Relax your left shoulder and drop your left elbow. These movements will create a force as if using a file—a force that presses downward and at the

same time pushes forward. Imagine that you are using your left hand to file the opponent's arm. Imagine that your right hand is gripping your opponent's right wrist and then twist and raise it. Look directly down in front of your left hand (fig. 4-5-3).

Relax both shoulders. Move your hands down and raise your body up slightly. Keep your weight on your right leg and straighten your left leg. Look straight ahead. Take a small step with your left foot. While your foot is moving, turn your left foot to the left.

4-5-1

4-5-2

4-5-3

4-5-4

Turn and move your left hand forward with the palm facing up. At the same time, turn your body to the left. Imagine using your left hand to grip your opponent's left wrist. Look directly in front of your left hand (fig. 4-5-4).

Turn your left hand over and pull it down and toward the left. This movement is called *chen ci jin*, which means to apply a heavy force that pulls sharply downward. Take a step forward with your right foot in a curving path from the back of your left foot to the front of your opponent's right foot. Look at the tiger mouth of your left hand (fig. 4-5-5).

Step forward with your right foot and place it in front of your left foot. Raise your right arm, stretch your right hand forward, and let your right palm face up as though it were striking at your opponent's face. The fingers of your right hand should be level with your head. At the same time, step back with your left foot, letting only the toes of that foot touch the ground (fig. 4-5-6).

Close your left hand as though to grip something, and then pull it to the left and back. Relax your waist, sink your left shoulder, and drop your left elbow. Turn your body to the left and use your waist to lead the movement of your right hand. Twist your right forearm clockwise until your right palm faces up. Assume a half riding horse stance. Move both your arms together toward the left and back of your body until your left hand rests along the outside your left knee and your right hand is on the inner side of

4-5-5

4-5-6

4-5-7

your right knee. Imagine using your right shoulder to touch your left hip. Twist your left hand and raise it up slightly. Then roll and press down with your right forearm. Look to the right and down at your right forearm (fig. 4-5-7).

Application

If your opponent punches at you with his right fist (fig. 4-5-8)

Use your right palm to touch the outside of your opponent's right wrist and then grip his wrist. Step back and to the left with your left foot at about a forty-five-degree angle (fig. 4-5-9). Your right hand should follow the movement of your left foot smoothly and naturally so that a side-by-side force is generated. This force can be used to direct your opponent's incoming straight force away from you and also to pull him forward and toward his left. This will cause him to miss his punch and lose his balance (fig. 4-5-10). In this move, a "following" force is included within a side-by-side force, and a "lure" force is included within a *hua* or defense force.

Continue your movement by taking a big step back with your right foot, putting your left hand on the outside of your opponent's right elbow, and gripping his right wrist with your right hand. Pull back and thereby change the side-by-side force of your right hand to a straight force. This will shake your opponent's root and cause him to lean forward, perhaps making him lift his back foot completely off the ground (fig. 4-5-11).

Keep gripping your opponent's right wrist with your right hand and continue to twist it toward you and raise it up. This will cause his right elbow to point upward toward the sky. At the same time, turn your body slightly to the right and push your left hand down on your opponent's right elbow. Assume a half riding horse stance and direct your gaze to an imaginary point in front of your left hand (fig. 4-5-12).

There are several important points to remember when executing this skill. Keep your head up, relax your waist and sink your shoulders. Keep your hips turned under so that your tailbone points down. Push and press down with your left hand to create a filing force on your opponent's arm as though you were pulling a file across it. Use your right hand to pull upward and twist your opponent's forearm. If you perform all of these movements correctly, you will generate a powerful releasing force, *zheng jin*. In applying this force, imagine that your body has been tightly bound up and then you use the force gathered within your whole body to throw off your bonds. If you feel as though your opponent wants to move against your force, raise your right hand slightly and simultaneously push your left hand down (fig. 4-5-13).

4-5-8   4-5-9   4-5-10

4-5-11   4-5-12   4-5-13

If in the last skill you did not do everything perfectly and could not gain full control of your opponent's elbow, he will have a chance to raise his elbow and throw you off or punch at your face with his left hand

Release your left hand from your opponent's right elbow. Make a small curving step with your left foot and turn your body slightly to the left. Your left foot should trace a small curve from right to left in front of your right foot. Use the outside of your left wrist to block your opponent's left hand and then turn it over to grip his left wrist (fig. 4-5-14).

4-5-14

Keep gripping your opponent's left wrist with your left hand and twist your left hand and forearm counterclockwise while pulling your opponent's wrist to the left of your body and simultaneously pressing down on it. At the same time, step forward with your right foot so that it is in front of your left foot. This step should be a curving step forward, and your right foot should move from behind your left foot to the left side of your opponent. Release your right hand, which has been gripping your opponent's right wrist, and then strike his face with your right palm. If he wants to avoid your strike, he will have to move his head back, and this will cause his left arm to move forward automatically (figs. 4-5-15a, 4-5-15b).

Step back with your left foot while keeping hold of your opponent's left wrist. Your movement will pull your opponent back and cause his body to move forward and lean forward. Take your right palm away from your opponent's face and move it down along his right arm from the shoulder to the elbow. At the same time, turn your right palm up. This is called "striking, pressing, and rolling." Keep gripping your opponent's left wrist with your left hand. Twist it counterclockwise and lift up on it

while pulling it slightly back. Your hands should work together in a fully coordinated way, and your whole body should be integrated. Assume a half riding horse stance and keep your body stable. Look at a point in front of you and to the right and down (fig. 4-5-16 from the back).

4-5-15   **4-5-16**

6. 苍龙摆尾 Black Dragon Swaying Its Tail

Posture Name

"苍龙摆尾 — *canf long bai wei*" means a black dragon swaying its tail. In Chinese mythology, the black dragon was considered to have magical powers. When it stirred its tail, it could shake mountains and make waves on the sea. In this posture, imagine that you are the dragon and that your arm is the dragon's tail. Your opponent is a mountain or ocean. However big and strong he may be, imagine that you are much more powerful. Imagine, too, that if you snap your tail up, you can chop the mountain up and destroy it. If you snap your tail down, you can create waves in the ocean. Compared to your power, all other forces are small and light.

This posture includes two main skills. The first, *pi*, is a quick and hard chop downward. The second, *fu*, is a sideways force using twisting arms and then a downward press. Both skills should be done with total body integration.

Movement Name and Description

侧身进上劈下扶 — *ce shen jin shang pi xia fu:* Step forward with body turned to the side, chop above and press below

Continue the movement from figure 4-5-7.

Imagine that your opponent punches at your face with his right fist. Shift your weight to your left leg. Raise your body up slightly. Move your right foot in front of your left foot. Raise your right arm and stretch your right wrist straight out in front of you (fig. 4-6-1).

Shift your weight to your right leg. Step forward and to the left with your left foot. At the same time, turn your right hand over and move it to the right and down. Look to the right and at a point just below your right hand (fig. 4-6-2). When you turn your right hand over, imagine that you are gripping something with your right hand and pulling it down.

Shift your weight to your left leg. Raise your left arm up and move your left hand forward as though it were gripping something and then pulling it down (fig. 4-6-3). At the same time, form a fist with your right hand and raise the fist over your head. At this point, imagine that you are transferring the object being gripped from your right hand to your left. At the same time, step forward with your right foot and place it beside your left foot. Look forward, along the line of your right arm (fig. 4-6-4).

Raise the heels of your feet off the floor as you raise your right hand up, and then stamp down hard with both feet. Following the stamp, slide your right foot forward. Sink your body and relax and drop your waist as you assume a half riding horse stance. At the same time, chop down with your right fist and forearm and raise your left palm up to generate a force that is coordinated with the stamping movement. This will provide balance during the chop. Look at the spot toward which your strike is aimed (fig. 4-6-5).

Lift your left foot up so that only the left toes touch the ground and then stamp down with that foot. You should feel as though

you are stamping on a spring and getting a bounce from the earth. Shift your weight to your left leg. Move your right foot back and put only the toes of your right foot on the ground in the front of your left foot. At the same time, drop your left hand and stretch your right hand forward and imagine that you are gripping your opponent's wrist. Look straight ahead at a point in front of your right wrist (fig. 4-6-6).

Turn your right hand over and pull down. Stamp down with your right foot so that the whole sole of this foot rests on the ground. Step forward with your left foot. Stretch your left hand forward and then raise it up until it is over your head and the palm faces up. Imagine that your opponent's head is just below your left hand. Look straight ahead (fig. 4-6-7).

Chop down with your left palm and pull back with your right hand. The movement of both hands should be fully coordinated. Turn your body about ninety degrees to the right, and cross both hands in front of your chest with your left palm facing up. Look forward in front of your left palm (fig. 4-6-8).

Turn your waist to the left. Turn your left hand and arm over. Use your waist to lead your left shoulder, arm, and palm in a forward strike. Your right hand should follow the movement of your left hand. Shift your weight to your left leg and form a left bow stance. Look straight ahead (fig. 4-6-9).

Drop your left arm and move your body back. Shift your weight to your right leg. Step forward with your left foot and put it down in front of your right foot. Do not let the heel of your left foot touch the ground. Raise your left hand and stretch your left wrist forward with your left palm facing in (fig. 4-6-10). Imagine that you are using your left hand to grip your opponent's wrist.

Turn your left hand over as though to grip something and then pull down. Step slightly to the right with your left foot in a curving line. Look at your left tiger mouth. Then step forward with your right foot in a curve from behind your left foot and form a right

4-6-1

4-6-2

4-6-3

4-6-4

4-6-5

4-6-6

4-6-7

4-6-8

4-6-9

4-6-10

4-6-11   4-6-12

4-6-13   4-6-14

bow stance. Lift your right hand up until it is over your head with your right palm facing to the left and up. Look forward and up (fig. 4-6-11).

Turn your body to the left and chop down and back with your right hand. Bend both legs and shift your weight to your left leg. Imagine that your left hand is gripping something. Cross both arms in front of your chest with your right arm over your left. Turn your body to the left and chop down with your right arm. The turn and the chop should be smoothly coordinated. Look at your right palm (figs. 4-6-12a, 4-6-12b).

Turn your head back and turn your body slightly to the right. At the same time, raise your left hand and imagine that it is pushing slightly upward (figs. 4-6-13a, 4-6-13b).

Move your arms toward the sides of your body at waist level. Your left hand should move to the left side of your body and

around toward your back. Your right hand should move toward the right side of your body and forward. Imagine that your left arm is pulling something back while your right arm is moving something from the left to the right side of your body. Look forward and far away in the direction to which your right fingers point (fig. 4-6-14). When both arms separate to your sides, you should feel as though your hands are pulling one object in opposite directions.

Application

If your opponent punches at you with his right fist

Use the outside of your right wrist to meet your opponent's right wrist. At the same time, step back with your left foot and to the left at about a forty-five-degree angle. This will allow you to avoid the punch your opponent is aiming directly at your body. Look at the touchpoint of your wrist and your opponent's wrist (fig. 4-6-15).

Turn your right hand over to grip your opponent's right wrist and pull him down to the right and back. As you apply this downward force, step forward with your right foot, keeping your right heel raised off the ground. At the same time, move your left hand forward and place it on your opponent's right elbow (fig. 4-6-16).

Hold your opponent's right elbow with your left hand. Use your left thumb to press down on your opponent's *Quchi* point on the outside of his right elbow. At the same time, use your left hand to help your right hand as you continue to pull your opponent to the right and exert a downward press. This will cause him to lose balance and lean forward. As soon as you feel that your opponent is unsteady and has begun to move, release your right hand from his right hand and make a fist. Raise your fist up to punch his chin first and then continue to raise your fist up until it is over your opponent's head. At the same time, raise your body up slightly. The pulling and pressing movement of your left hand and the

punch with your right hand must be completely coordinated. This will create a strong pressing force in your left hand and will help you maintain control of your opponent (fig. 4-6-17).

Look at the right side of your opponent's neck or back. Relax your waist and let your body sink down. Let the force of your whole body be focused in your right hand as you chop down toward the point at which you are looking. At the same time, stamp both feet hard on the ground and imagine that you are using your toes to grip the earth (fig. 4-6-18).

4-6-15

4-6-16

4-6-17

4-6-18

If your opponent punches at you with his right fist

Step slightly to the left and back with your left foot. Raise your right wrist up to touch the outside of your opponent's right wrist (fig. 4-6-19).

Turn your right hand over to grip your opponent's right wrist and then pull and press down to the right. Step back with your right foot. At the same time, raise your left hand over your head and use your left palm to hit your opponent's face (fig. 4-6-20).

4-6-19

4-6-20

4-6-21

4-6-22

If your opponent dodges back to avoid your attack, use your waist to lead your left hand and left arm around to the right and toward the back of your body. Put your left forearm on your opponent's right arm and then press and roll back. At the same time, pull your right hand back and turn your body to the right. This will cause a powerful pull and roll-back force that will make your opponent lose his balance and lean forward (fig. 4-6-21). All the movements in this skill must be done smoothly and continuously. The force of your arm must come from your waist. When your body turns to the right and back, turn your left palm up to face the sky.

Pull your right hand back and rise up continuously. This will make your opponent lean forward. In his effort to maintain balance, your opponent's movements will become leaden, and he will move back slightly. Then shift your weight to your left leg to form a left bow stance and use your waist to lead your left arm in a strike to the left and forward at your opponent's chest. Look forward at your opponent's chest. This strike is called *dou zhang* or "get around palm" (fig. 4-6-22).

If your opponent pushes against you with his right arm and attacks you with his left arm, you will not be able to use *dou zhang*

Raise your left hand and put the back of your left wrist on your opponent's left wrist (fig. 4-6-23). Turn your left hand over to grip your opponent's left wrist and pull him to the left. Shift your weight to your right leg. Move your left foot back and touch the ground in front of your right foot with only the toes of your left foot. Step with your left foot across to the right side of your right foot and to the left side of your opponent. Look at your left hand (fig. 4-6-24).

Then step forward with your right foot quickly and put it down in front of your left foot. Use your left hand to pull your opponent's

left wrist. Step back with your left foot to form a high riding horse stance. Put your right knee between your opponent's legs and then use your right leg to "stick" to your opponent's left or right leg in order to lock him. Sink your body down slightly and stretch your waist forward. Raise your right hand to strike at your opponent's face (figs. 4-6-25a, 4-6-25b).

Let your body sink down suddenly to form a riding horse stance. Stretch your right arm around your opponent's body to create a pushing and twisting force. Then move the fingers of your right hand in the direction pointed to by the toes of your right foot. Keep gripping your opponent's left wrist with your left hand, and then turn your left hand over and push up until your opponent's arm is over your head. Continue to move your right palm back until it is in front of your chest and then use the tip of your right elbow to hit your opponent's left ribcage (figs. 4-6-26a, 4-6-26b).

4-6-23   **4-6-24**   **4-6-25**

4-6-26

Stretch your right arm forward and then around your opponent's body as though to touch your right foot. Imagine that your right leg and right arm are like a pair of scissors cutting your opponent's body in half. Your body and arms should move like a snake as you dodge, extend your arm, and stretch forward from your waist. This movement sequence is called "white snake lies on the grass" (figs. 4-6-27a, 4-6-27b).

4-6-27

7. 霸王抖甲 Ba Wang Shaking His Armor

Posture Name

"霸王抖甲 — *ba wang dou jia*" is a powerful movement. The term "Ba Wang" means "king of kings." It was the special title of General Xiang Yu, one of the most renowned heroes in Chinese history. General Xiang was a big, strong man who was very brave and had excellent martial arts skills. Twenty-two hundred years ago, he and other kings fought long and hard against the rulers of the Qin Dynasty. Finally, they prevailed and overturned the Qin Dynasty. Because of his courage and effectiveness as a fighter, many people were afraid of him and called him Ba Wang, "the

king of kings." The famous Chinese song "Ba Wang Took Off His Armor" describes Ba Wang's coming back to his tent after an arduous fight and taking off his dusty armor and shaking it to clean it.

When you practice this skill, you should imagine that you are Ba Wang and that your opponent is your armor.

In the first of the two parts of this skill, imagine that you are gently removing your armor. The important point is to change the direction of your internal force smoothly. The second part of the skill mimics the shaking of the armor. This should be done quickly and suddenly. In terms of application, the first part of this skill is an elbow strike to your opponent's ribs, and the second part is a turn and low side-throw.

Movement Name and Description

挑肘上回身侧摔 — *tiao zhou shang hui shen ce shuai:* Raise elbow, turn around, and side-throw

Continue the movement from figure 4-6-14.

Stamp your right foot and shift your weight to your left leg. Straighten your body and step back with your right foot until it is in front of your left foot. Drop both arms down along the sides of your torso. Look straight ahead. Stretch your right arm forward with your palm facing toward you. Imagine using the outside of your right wrist to touch your opponent's right wrist (fig. 4-7-1).

Turn your right hand over and pull down toward the right side of your body. At the same time, touch the ground with your right toes and move your right foot back slightly. Then shift your weight to your right leg to form a right bow stance. Look just to the right of your right small toe (fig. 4-7-2).

Raise your right hand and turn it over so that your right palm faces the sky. Drop your left arm down and point your left index finger forward and toward the ground. Prepare to move forward. Step forward with your left foot and turn your body to the right.

4-7-1

4-7-2

4-7-3

4-7-4

4-7-5

4-7-6

Bend your left arm and make a left fist with your left palm facing up. Position your left fist in front of your left shoulder to deliver a left elbow strike. Let your body sink down to form a riding horse stance. Keep your right hand over your head and pull your hand back. Look forward to the point at which your elbow will strike (fig. 4-7-3).

Step forward and to the right with your left foot. Drop your left arm down in front of your left leg. Do not change the position of your right hand. Look at an imaginary spot just in front of your left foot (fig. 4-7-4).

Turn your left foot around on the heel. This will cause your body to turn to the right and back. Raise your right hand slightly and move it a small distance to the right. At the same time, shift your weight to your left leg. Straighten your right leg and swing it back. Move your right hand in a curve over your head and then downward from in front of your right shoulder toward your left foot (figs. 4-7-5a, 4-7-5b).

While your right hand is moving down, reach up with your left hand to meet your right hand as though both were holding something. Pull down with both hands from the upper right side of your body to the lower left. Step to the left with your left foot and sink your body down to form a left side bow stance. Imagine that both hands are pulling something down to touch your left foot. Look down and to the right in front of your hands (figs. 4-7-6a, 4-7-6b).

Application

If your opponent punches your chest with his right fist

Step backward and to the left with your left foot. Place the outside of your right wrist lightly on your opponent's right wrist (fig. 4-7-7).

Use the touchpoint to determine the direction of your opponent's punch. If the punch is directed forward, turn your wrist over to pull his wrist down. At the same time, step back with your right foot so that it is in front of your left foot, and touch the ground with only the toes of your right foot. This will cause your opponent to miss his punch, lose his balance, and lean forward (fig. 4-7-8).

Turn your right hand over and quickly raise it above your head. This will abruptly stop your opponent's forward motion and will

4-7-7   4-7-8   4-7-9

raise his center of gravity so that his heels are lifted off the ground. He will feel frightened and unstable. Stamp your right foot and shift your weight to your right leg. Continue to hold your opponent's wrist with your right hand and pull it back slightly. Maintain the upward force on your opponent's wrist while you pull back. This will expose your opponent's chest area. Step forward with your left foot. Bend your left elbow and make a left fist with your palm facing up. At the same time, use your left elbow to strike at the right side of your opponent's ribcage. The tip of your left elbow should follow an upward path. Lower your body slightly to form a riding horse stance. Look at the point on your opponent's body toward which your elbow strike is directed (fig. 4-7-9).

If your opponent attempts to hit or grip your face or chest with his right hand

Step to the left with your left foot to avoid your opponent's forward thrust. Put your right wrist on your opponent's right wrist (fig. 4-7-10).

If you feel at the touchpoint that your opponent continues to direct his attack straight at you, turn your right wrist over and pull your opponent down. At the same time, keeping your weight on your left leg, move your right foot close to your left foot and let only the toes of your left foot touch the ground (fig. 4-7-11).

4-7-10   **4-7-11**   **4-7-12**

4-7-13   **4-7-14**   **4-7-15**

Change the downward pull of your right hand movement to an upward movement. This will raise your opponent's center of gravity, and his heels will rise off the ground as he loses his balance. Shift your weight to your right leg. Step forward with your left foot and place it in front of your opponent's left foot. At the same time, keep your right hand raised over your head while holding your opponent's wrist. Pull your right hand back to pass over your head. As you step, lower your body down slightly and move forward quickly (fig. 4-7-12).

Turn your body back, so that your opponent is behind you. Shift your weight to your left leg and move your right leg back to block your opponent's right leg. Lower your body down to form a left-side bow stance, and at the same time pull your right hand slightly forward (fig. 4-7-13).

Continue to grip your opponent's right wrist with your right

hand and pull forward and down toward your left toes. At the same time, use your left hand to grip your opponent's right wrist and help the right hand pull your opponent down (fig. 4-7-14). With both hands gripping your opponent's right wrist, pull him down in a curving path from your right shoulder toward your left toes. This movement, called "shaking a suit of armor," will cause your opponent to trip over your right leg and fall down (fig. 4-7-15).

Note: It is common to combine these two skills as follows: after the elbow strike in the first skill (fig. 4-7-9), step to the right with your left foot and turn your body to the right and back (fig. 4-7-12); then continue with the remaining movements of the second skill.

8. 野马奔腾 Wild Horse Galloping

Posture Name

"野马奔腾 — *ye ma ben teng*" means a skill that creates a powerful and quick movement forward. Wild horses are strong and powerful. In full gallop, they are hard to control. In this posture, imagine that you are a wild horse just starting to run and that your fists are hooves stamping down and kicking up. The movements of this posture should be so quick and powerful that any defense against them is impossible. This posture includes two main skills. The first is a downward punch; the second, an upward punch. The full force of your body should be used in both punches. All parts of the movement should be smooth and coordinated.

Movement Name and Description

侧身进立身直栽 — *ce shen jin li shen zhi zai:* Step forward with your body turned to the side, straighten your body, and punch straight down

Continue the movement from figure 4-7-6.

Keep your weight on your left leg. Raise your body and place your right foot in front of your left foot with only the toes of your right foot touching the ground. Empty your chest and withdraw your stomach slightly. Make a right fist and raise it to the level of your mouth. At the same time, turn your right forearm counterclockwise until the little finger faces toward your mouth. Keep your left palm facing down in front of your stomach. Look forward (fig. 4-8-1).

Shift your weight to your right leg. Step forward with your left foot and turn your body slightly to the right. Make a left fist and raise it to shoulder level and move forward a little bit. At the same time, drop your right fist down to chest level. Your left fist should be in front of your right fist and slightly higher. Both fists should face up. Both arms should be bent, as should both legs (fig. 4-8-2).

Straighten your arms and legs. Step forward with your front foot and stamp the ground with your back foot. This will cause your body to charge powerfully forward. At the same time, turn both fists over so that they face down. Punch forward and down with both fists. Look at an angle forward and downward (fig. 4-8-3).

Drop both arms down and withdraw your left foot until it is in front of your right foot. Keep your right heel raised off the ground. Make a vertical circle with your left fist back toward your body and then up and forward until your left fist is at mouth level. As you make this fist circle, turn your left forearm until your left

4-8-1

4-8-2

4-8-3

4-8-4   4-8-5   4-8-6

thumb faces forward and your little finger faces your mouth. At the same time, withdraw your hip and stomach, and then step right and a little bit forward with your left foot. Put your right fist face down close to your navel. Look forward (fig. 4-8-4).

Shift your weight to your left leg and step forward with your right foot. Turn your body slightly to the left. Turn your right forearm and raise your right fist to shoulder level with your right fist facing up. Move forward a little bit. At the same time, drop your left fist down slightly to the right at elbow level. Bend both arms and legs slightly as though they were shrinking together (fig. 4-8-5).

Step forward with your front foot and stamp your back foot to cause your body to charge powerfully forward. At the same time, turn both fists over to face the ground and throw a right punch forward and down. Look in the direction of your punch (fig. 4-8-6).

Application

If your opponent punches at your chest with his right fist

Step back slightly with your left foot. Make a right fist and raise it up from your stomach to your chest and then to a point just in front of your mouth. At the same time, twist your right forearm until your palm faces to the right and the little finger of your right fist is in front of your mouth. Your right forearm should cross and

touch the right side of your opponent's right forearm. To avoid the direct force of your opponent's attack, withdraw your chest slightly and expand your back to create additional space in front of your chest (fig. 4-8-7). A side-by-side force will be generated in your right forearm. This movement sequence is called "using a side-by-side force to defend against a straight force."

When your right forearm touches your opponent's right forearm, you should make sure that your touch is soft and does not become a hard block. Your touch should be designed to feel your opponent's movement, to dodge and surround him and to adhere. As soon as you touch your opponent, step forward quickly with your left foot to the right side of your opponent's right foot. Use the inside of your left knee to touch the outside of your opponent's right knee. Raise your left arm and make a left fist with your palm facing up. Place your left forearm lightly on your opponent's right elbow or arm. Withdraw your chest a bit and lower your body slightly. Feel your arms and legs withdrawing together. This will cause a downward pressure on your opponent's right arm (fig. 4-8-8). If you feel your opponent try to raise his arm to resist the downward pressure of your force, relax your body and rise up slightly. This will cause your opponent to rise up, and his root will be shaken.

Look at your opponent's chest and direct your mind through your opponent's body to a distant point behind him (fig. 4-8-9). Sink your body slightly and twist your left forearm and fist clockwise as

4-8-7

4-8-8

4-8-9

4-8-10

though your arm were a heavy drill burrowing into your opponent's chest at the point of your gaze. At the same time, twist your right forearm and fist counterclockwise and use your right fist to follow the path of your left fist. Push hard against the ground with both feet. This will cause a heavy, powerful, and quick force to extend from your body to your left fist (fig. 4-8-10). This movement is called *ma xi ti*—"a horse washes its hooves."

If your opponent raises his arm or blocks your attack from the side (fig. 4-8-11)

Twist your left fist counterclockwise and drill it upward to hit your opponent's chin. Release your force quickly, smoothly, and continuously from your feet to your legs, your waist, your back, and finally to your left arm (figs. 4-8-12a, 4-8-12b). This movement is called *ma fan ti*—"a horse kicks back."

4-8-11   **4-8-12**

If your opponent has a chance to use his left hand

If your opponent attacks your head or chest with his left hand, turn your left forearm over and press your opponent's right arm down.

Use the inside of your right forearm to touch your opponent's left forearm or elbow. Withdraw your stomach and chest. Shift your weight to your right leg and keep your left heel raised off the ground (fig. 4-8-13).

Turn your body slightly to the right. Remove your right forearm from the touchpoint and move it down and then back and up. This movement should trace a heavy, powerful curve that will open your opponent's chest and ribs. At the same time, move your left foot back slightly and let only the toes of that foot touch the ground. This movement will raise your opponent's center of gravity, and his heels will lift off the ground as he loses his balance (fig. 4-8-14).

Step forward with your left foot. Turn your body to the right continuously. Twist your right fist counterclockwise and punch down at your opponent's chest or ribs. In this very powerful punch, the force should be released from your feet through your legs to your back and then to your fist. Imagine that your punch can pass through your opponent's body and into the ground behind his body (fig. 4-8-15). This punch is called "a plant punch."

Because this posture is used to fight at very close range, the key point is to maintain the touchpoints so that you can constantly sense all changes in your opponent's movement. It is also important to adhere, follow, and change with your opponent's movements. Your movements will gain power to the extent that you control them from your waist and let your body follow the motion of your waist.

4-8-13   4-8-14   4-8-15

9. 饿虎扑食 Hungry Tiger Pounces on Its Prey

Posture Name

"饿虎扑食 — *e hu pu shi*" imitates the movements of a tiger as he hunts. A hungry tiger will fight harder than a well-fed one. Imagine that you are a hungry tiger and that your opponent is the prey. Feel confident that whether he is big or small, you will overwhelm him. The force for this commonly used skill must come from your feet and legs and be released through your hands. Your whole body must be well integrated, and you should move forward very quickly as though pouncing.

Movement Name and Description

进步冲双掌前撞 — *jin bu chong shuang zhang qian zhuang*: Step forward, both palms ramming forward

Continue the movement from figure 4-8-6.

Drop both arms down. Take a half step back with your left foot and then step back immediately with your right foot so that it follows the movement of your left foot. Your right foot should still be in front of your left foot. Keep your right heel off the ground when your right foot comes to rest. Withdraw your hips and stomach slightly. Turn your hands so that both palms face toward your body. Look forward (fig. 4-9-1).

Push against the ground with your left foot and spring forward with your right foot in a long leap. Raise both hands up to chest level. At the same time, turn your forearms until both palms face forward (fig. 4-9-2). When your right foot steps forward, keep pushing off with your left foot, so that the force from your left leg will push your body forward powerfully and quickly. This will increase the length of your forward movement.

At the same time, empty your chest and tighten your back. Focus your mind on the *Jiaji* point at the center of your upper back.

4-9-1　　　　　　4-9-2　　　　　　4-9-3

4-9-4

This will cause a quick, powerful, and spring-like forward force that resembles the leap of a hungry tiger toward an unsuspecting sheep. These two movements should be executed as one single forward lunge (fig. 4-9-3). When you spring forward, your left foot should follow your right foot, and the big toe of your right foot should push against the ground, so that you get force to keep your balance. After you spring forward, keep about sixty to seventy percent of your weight on your left leg. Look forward (figs. 4-9-4a, 4-9-4b).

The key point for proper execution of this posture is that the hard and soft forces complement each other and are seamlessly combined. In the first part of the posture you should be soft so that you can dissolve your opponent's force, but you must also be hard internally so that you do not become weak. In the second part of the posture, your external movement should be hard so that

you can make a powerful strike, but you must combine this with internal softness so that you do not hurt yourself while striking.

Application

If the opponent punches your face with his right fist

Use your right wrist to meet your opponent's right wrist (fig. 4-9-5). Turn your right wrist over to grab his wrist and then pull down to the right side of your body. This is called *chen cai jin* or "heavy stamp-down force." It will cause the opponent to lean forward (fig. 4-9-6).

Follow this movement by stepping forward with your left foot to your opponent's right side. Pull your opponent's right wrist with your right hand to the left side of your body. Release your opponent's wrist. This will cause your opponent to lean slightly to the right. Your weight should be on your right leg, and the toes of your left foot should touch the ground lightly in front of your right foot. Sink your body down slightly and relax your waist. At the same time, empty your chest and bend your arms and legs as though to pull some-thing back toward your body. Turn your palms so that they face toward your torso and put them in front of your stomach. Look at the right side of your opponent's ribcage. This movement is called *xu li (xu jin)* or "storing force"

4-9-5

4-9-6

4-9-7

4-9-8

(fig. 4-9-7). In the Chinese classics, it is said that: "*xu li* is like bending a bow."

Raise your palms to chest level and turn them outward to face your opponent. At the same time, push against the ground with your right foot and step forward with your left foot. Strike at your opponent's ribs as though you were a tiger springing to attack a sheep (fig. 4-9-8). Your legs, arms, and body should stretch out simultaneously. This is called *fa jin* or "releasing force." The classics say: "*fa jin is just like shooting an arrow.*"

If your pull down does not succeed in making your opponent lean forward and lose his balance completely, he will have a chance to use his right arm against you.

If your movement is not perfect, your opponent's best defense against your strike is to push your right arm. If he does this, you should step back a half step with your right foot, relax your arms and drop your hands, letting your palms face your body. Drop your center of gravity down slightly. This will cause your opponent's push to meet only emptiness, and he will begin to lose his balance. This movement allows you to repeat "storing force" *(xu li)* (fig. 4-9-9). When you use this movement, you should maintain the touchpoints between you and your opponent so that you can know immediately if he is about to make any change in the direction or timing of his advance.

When you have completed "storing force," you can do "releasing force." Continue to push off with your right foot to increase your forward power. Step as far forward with your front foot as you can. Raise your hands to chest level. Turn your palms to face your opponent and strike at his chest or stomach. Your power should originate from your back foot and move through your leg, back, arms, and finally your palms. All movements should be smooth and should finish at the same time. Keep your mind on the *Jiaji* point (fig. 4-9-10). Do not let your back become completely straight.

4-9-9

4-9-10

Keep it rounded like the surface of a ball. It is said that "if the back is not covered (rounded), your power cannot reach its maximum force." All parts of your body must work together, and the internal and external components must be fully coordinated. This will give you the high-speed power of a hard spring.

If your opponent attacks you with his right hand, you can grip his right wrist and pull him down to the right and move his balance (fig. 4-9-11).

In this situation, you are on the right side of your opponent. Imagine throwing your opponent's wrist to the right quickly by releasing his wrist from your right hand. At the same time, repeat "storing force" (fig. 4-9-12); that is, empty your chest, withdraw your stomach, and bend your arms and legs as though pulling something back toward your body. Turn your palms so that they face toward your torso and put them in front of your stomach. Look at the right side of your opponent's ribcage.

Then execute "releasing force" (fig. 4-9-13) by raising your palms to chest level and turning them outward to face your

4-9-11

4-9-12

4-9-13

opponent. At the same time, push off with your right foot and step forward with your left foot to move close to your opponent. Strike at your opponent's ribs like a tiger pouncing on its prey. Your legs, arms, and body should stretch out simultaneously.

10. 周仓扛刀 Zhou Cang Shouldering the Big Sword

Posture Name

"周仓扛刀 — *zhou cang kang dao*" refers to a powerful skill. General Zhou Cang, a tall and powerful man, was General Guan Yu's assistant. It is said that General Guan's weapon, called Qing Long Yan Yue Dao or more simply Guan Dao, was a long-handled sword weighing eighty-two *jin* or almost ninety pounds. Between battles, General Zhou always carried this sword on his shoulder for General Guan.

In this posture, imagine that you are General Zhou and that your opponent is General Guan's big sword. Think of your opponent's arm as the sword's handle. Your goal is to straighten out your opponent's arm and carry it over your shoulder as you might a large sword.

There are two main skills used in this posture. The first one, called *wan xin zhou,* is an elbow strike to the center of your opponent's chest. The second is a downward press applied to your opponent's arm as it extends over your shoulder. To use this skill, you must first straighten your opponent's arm and lock his elbow. Your turn must be nimbly executed.

Movement Name and Description

问心肘转身扛臂 — *wan xin zhou zhuan shen kang bi*: Elbow strike to the heart and turn around to press arm down over the shoulder

Continue the movement from figure 4-9-4.

Withdraw your hips and body slightly. Touch the ground with your right toes and raise your body up slightly. Stretch your right arm out until your wrist is at face level and your right palm faces your face. Move your left hand to the left side of your abdomen with your left palm facing down. Look forward (fig. 4-10-1).

Turn your right hand over and imagine gripping your opponent's right wrist and pulling it down (fig. 4-10-2). Raise your left hand and move it forward until it is to the left and in front of your right hand. The heel of your left hand should be opposite the tiger mouth of your right hand. Look at your left hand (fig. 4-10-3).

Imagine using your left hand instead of your right hand to grab your opponent's right wrist. Move your left hand from the right to the left side of your body. At the same time, withdraw your abdomen and hips. As soon as your left hand meets your right hand, bend your right arm and step forward with your left foot. Strike forward and down with your right elbow. With this strike, your right elbow should trace a circle that begins with a movement down and toward your torso and then up and forward toward your opponent and finally slightly downward again. Place your left hand on your right wrist. Your right hand should be in front of your chest. Following your elbow strike, shift your weight forward to form a left bow stance. Look straight ahead (fig. 4-10-4).

Imagine that the tip of your right elbow is an axle and that your right forearm can rotate around it. Stretch your right arm forward as your right forearm rotates around the imaginary axle. At the same time, make a right fist and throw a forward punch from the front of your chest. Imagine that your arm is a hammer as you hit your opponent's face with the back of your right fist. Put your left hand in front of your lower abdomen with your left palm facing the ground and the tiger mouth of your left hand facing your body. Push your left palm slightly down. This push should be coordinated with your right punch. Use your back and waist

4-10-1

4-10-2

4-10-3

4-10-4

4-10-5

4-10-6

4-10-7

4-10-8

to release your power. Look at the point of contact between your right fist and your opponent's face (fig. 4-10-5).

Maintain a left bow stance, and change your right fist to an open palm. Turn your right wrist counterclockwise until your palm faces out. Bend the fingers of your right hand as though to grab something. At the same time, move your left hand directly forward

and turn it up until your left palm faces the sky as if it were holding something up. Step slightly forward with your left foot and turn your left toes to the right to form a side bow stance. Turn your body slightly to the right also. Look straight ahead (fig. 4-10-6).

Bend your left hip so that your body will move slightly down. Turn your body to the right and move your left shoulder forward. Shift your weight forward to your left leg and turn your right foot on the ball of the foot to form a sitting stance. Look up and to the left of your body (fig. 4-10-7).

Use your left heel as though it were an axle to turn your left foot and your body to the right and then fully around 180 degrees. Make fists with both hands as though to grab something tightly. Then pull your hands down toward the front of your abdomen. Keep your weight on your left leg. Imagine that your head is being gently suspended from a point directly above your body. Raise your right heel, letting only the toes of your right foot touch the ground. Imagine lifting something up on your left shoulder. Look forward and down (figs. 4-10-8a, 4-10-8b).

Application

If your opponent punches your chest with his right fist

Use your right wrist to meet your opponent's right wrist. At the same time, step back with your left foot (fig. 4-10-9).

Turn your right hand over to grip your opponent's right wrist, and then pull down and back to the right side of your body. At the same time, step back with your right foot but only slightly so that your right foot remains in front of your left foot. This will cause your opponent to lean forward (fig. 4-10-10).

Withdraw your hip and abdomen slightly. Continue to pull your opponent down and to the right. Then suddenly change the direction of your pull to the left side of your body. At the same time, exchange the grip on your opponent's right wrist from your

right to your left hand and pull to the left side of your body as you push down on your opponent's wrist. This will shake your opponent's root and cause him to lose his balance (fig. 4-10-11).

Bend your right elbow and move your right hand close to your right shoulder. Raise your right elbow up and strike forward and down at your opponent's chest. At the same time, maintain your grip on your opponent's right wrist and push it down. The downward force of your right elbow strike and the downward force of the push

4-10-9

4-10-10

4-10-11

4-10-12

by your left hand should be well coordinated. As you strike forward with your elbow, step forward with your right foot. The force for this strike should originate from your waist (fig. 4-10-12).

If your opponent blocks your right elbow strike with his left hand (fig. 4-10-13)

Stretch your right arm forward. When your opponent touches you with his left hand to block your elbow strike, imagine that your

4-10-13   **4-10-14**

right elbow is an axle and that you are using it to turn your right forearm up. At the same time make a fist with your right hand, and using your right arm as though it were a hammer, hit your opponent in the face with the back of your right fist (fig. 4-10-14).

If your opponent punches your face with his left fist

*Note: The pictures for this application show the movements from the side opposite to the side shown in the form movement description.

Use your left wrist to meet your opponent's left wrist and step back and to the right with your right foot (fig. 4-10-15).

Shift your weight back to your right leg. Withdraw your abdomen and hips. Step slightly back with your left foot and touch the ground with your left toes. At the same time, turn your left hand over to grip your opponent's wrist and pull down (fig. 4-10-16).

Step forward with your right foot and let your body drop down slightly. At the same time, hold your opponent's left elbow with your right hand and push down on it. Simultaneously, pull up on

his left forearm with your left hand and press his left hand back slightly toward his body. The combination of the downward force created by the push of your right hand on your opponent's elbow and the force of your left hand pulling his arm and pressing his left hand back will cause his left arm to straighten and his left elbow to become locked (fig. 4-10-17).

If your opponent uses force against the push of your right hand, just follow the direction of his force and push your right hand forward a little bit. Then remove your right hand from his elbow. This will cause his body to rise slightly up. Immediately drop your body down and step forward with your right foot, placing it close to your opponent. Turn your body counterclockwise. At the same time, move your right shoulder forward until it is under your opponent's left armpit, as though you wanted to carry his arm on your shoulder. Move your right hand down along your opponent's left arm until your right hand reaches your left hand. Then grip

4-10-15   **4-10-16**   **4-10-17**

4-10-18   **4-10-19**

your opponent's left wrist with your right, so at this time, both your hands grip the opponent's left wrist (fig. 4-10-18).

Continue turning on your right foot until your body faces 180 degrees back. Shift your weight onto your right leg and touch the ground with the toes of your left foot. This will cause your body to move back and sink down slightly. Use both hands to pull down on your opponent's left wrist. Raise your left shoulder up slightly. This move, called "carrying a big sword on your shoulder," will tightly lock your opponent's left elbow (figs. 4-10-19a, 4-10-19b). If you feel your opponent push against you with his left arm, step to the left with your left foot and continue turning your body to the left. This will increase the force of your elbow lock.

11. 栽花移木 Plant Flower and Move Tree

Posture Name

"栽花移木 — *zai hua yi mu*" means to plant a flower in the earth and move a tree from one place to another. In order to plant a flower, one has to hold the plant and put it into the earth. This movement is similar to a downward punch, so the title of this posture uses "plant a flower" as a metaphor for the punching technique employed. To move a tree, one first has to pull the tree up by its roots, then hold it and finally use considerable force to move it to its new location. Whereas planting a flower requires care, moving a tree requires power.

In this posture, imagine that your opponent's arm is the stem of a flower and his hand is the root. Your goal is to push his hand down with a punch forceful enough to give the impression that his arm is being inserted into the earth. Then imagine that your opponent is a big tree that you want to hold up and move to another place.

This posture is comprised of two main skills. The first is a downward punch. This punch is not aimed at your opponent, but rather involves holding his wrist and pushing it down toward the

ground as though you wanted to insert his wrist deeply into the earth. The second skill involves reaching around to the back of your opponent's shoulders and throwing him down backward. You should first imagine holding him up as though to pull the root of a tree just out of the ground. Then you should move him backward and down.

Movement Name and Description

栽捶势抱肩反搬 — *zai chui shi bao jian fan ban:* Downward punch and turn around to hold shoulders and move backward

Continue the movement from figure 4-10-8.

Drop both arms and shift your weight forward, letting your right foot fully touch the ground. Step forward with your left foot and make sure both knees touch each other. Turn the toes of your left foot to the right, and then turn your waist clockwise to the right (fig. 4-11-1).

As you turn your body, shift your weight onto your left leg. Raise your right heel off the ground and rotate on the ball of your right foot so that your right foot follows the turn of your body. Raise your right arm and stretch your right hand out with your right palm facing to the right and then forward, and your right thumb pointing to the ground (fig. 4-11-2).

Turn your right hand over until your palm faces down. Stretch your left hand out and then bend your left arm at the elbow until the left tiger mouth faces your body and your left palm faces down. Turn your body to the right in a continuous motion. Move both hands together and make loose fists at chest level. The tiger mouths of both hands should be opposite each other. Make a swing step to the right and back with your right foot. Look down and to the right (fig. 4-11-3).

Continue your swing step to the right and back with your right foot. Turn your left foot on the heel as your body turns around. Push both hands down and to the left as though you were holding

4-11-1   4-11-2   4-11-3

4-11-4   4-11-5   4-11-6

something in both hands and trying to insert it into the earth. Shift your weight to your right leg to form a right bow stance (fig. 4-11-4). Pay close attention to your footwork at this point. Your steps should be adjusted continually to follow the movement of your body as expressed in the injunction "steps change to follow body."

Turn your right toes to the left about ninety degrees. Turn your right hand until your right palm faces up. At the same time, place your right hand over your left. Turn your body slightly to the left. Keep your weight on your back leg to form a sitting stance (fig. 4-11-5).

Turn your left hand over until your left thumb faces the ground. Imagine gripping something with your left hand. Straighten your body and raise your right hand to head level. As your body keeps turning to the left, swing your left foot to the outside. Raise both hands slightly and look forward and down (fig. 4-11-6).

4-11-7   4-11-8   4-11-9

4-11-10   4-11-11   4-11-12

Imagine that your right hand is gripping something and then push down with your right hand in front of your body and to the left. At the same time, raise your left hand up and back. Shift your weight onto your left leg slightly and turn your head to the left. Look in front and to the left of your left foot (fig. 4-11-7).

Continue to shift your weight onto your left leg to form a left bow stance. At the same time, push your right hand forward and down until it is in front of your abdomen. Pull your left hand back slightly (fig. 4-11-8).

Straighten your body and shift your weight back onto your right leg to form a sitting stance. Drop both arms and look forward. Then raise your right hand to face level and stretch it out in front of you. Focus your mind on your right hand to prepare to meet an attack. Look forward along your right wrist (fig. 4-11-9).

Step back and to the left with your left foot. Turn your right hand

4-11-13

4-11-14

over and imagine gripping your opponent's right wrist and then pulling to the right and down. At the same time, move your right foot slightly back and touch the ground with your right toes. Look down at your right hand (fig. 4-11-10).

Straighten your body and raise your left hand to face level. Shift your weight onto your right leg. Look forward and to the right (fig. 4-11-11).

Step forward with your left foot to form a sitting stance. Raise your right hand up from under your left hand in a cover move and let your hands cross as you make this move. Straighten your body slightly and look at your right hand (fig. 4-11-12).

Move your left hand down a little bit and then stretch it out in front of you and raise it slightly upward in a curving motion until it is higher than your shoulder. At the same time, move your right hand slightly back. Your palms should face each other. Look straight ahead (fig. 4-11-13).

Imagine using your left hand to hold something and then pull it down and to the left in a curving motion. At the same time, raise your right hand up and push forward. Turn your body slightly to the left. Withdraw your abdomen and hips a little bit. Look forward, to the left, and down (fig. 4-11-14).

Application

If your opponent wants to grip your chest with his right hand

Step to the left and back with your left foot. Raise your right hand to meet your opponent's right wrist (fig. 4-11-15).

Turn your right hand over to grip your opponent's wrist and

4-11-15   4-11-16   4-11-17

4-11-18   4-11-19   4-11-20

pull it to the right and down. As soon as you pull his wrist down, use your left hand to grip your opponent's right elbow and push down and pull back. Withdraw your hips and empty your chest. Stamp the ground with your right toes to create a reaction force in your body (fig. 4-11-16).

Move both hands to follow your opponent's forward motion and to make his arm become straight. At the same time, step back with your right foot and then turn your right foot around until the right toes point back. Shift your weight onto your right leg to form a bow stance. Move both hands continuously and pull forward and push slightly down. At the same time, release your left hand from your opponent's elbow and move it close to your right hand. The tiger mouths of both hands should be opposite each other. At this point, move your left elbow forward to press down on your opponent's right elbow. Then pull with both hands and quickly and powerfully

push your opponent's right arm forward and down as though you wanted to insert his arm into the ground (fig. 4-11-17).

If you sense that your opponent wants to bend his arm and pull his body back forcefully, and you feel that it will be difficult to maintain your position, follow your opponent according to the principle of "follow by bending and straightening." Release your right hand from your opponent's right wrist and immediately grip it again in the opposite direction. To do this, you must change the direction of your right tiger mouth so that it faces in the same direction as the fingers of your opponent's right hand. Sit back on your right leg and turn your body around clockwise with your right foot turning back. Then, turn your left foot and move your left hand back to your opponent's elbow. Use your left thumb to press the right *Quchi* point on the outside of his right elbow (fig. 4-11-18).

Step forward with your left foot and place it to the right of your opponent's right foot. Shift your weight onto your left leg. Push your right hand forward and then vigorously down as though you want to put his arm into the ground behind his right foot. At the same time, push your opponent's right elbow slightly up and to the right with your left hand. This will cause the force he directed against you to meet only emptiness, and as a result, he will lose his root (figs. 4-11-19, 4-11-20).

If your opponent punches your face with his right fist

Step back and slightly to the left with your left foot. Raise your right hand to meet your opponent's right wrist (fig. 4-11-21).

Turn your right hand over and grip your opponent's right wrist. Then pull strongly down and to the right. Move your right foot back slightly and touch the ground with your right toes (fig. 4-11-22).

Raise your right hand up quickly in a small cover move. This changing of direction must be accomplished smoothly so that your opponent leans forward and then backward. His root will be shaken and his balance lost. At that moment, move your left hand to his

4-11-21   4-11-22   4-11-23

4-11-24   4-11-25

right elbow and close your fingers around his elbow in a tight grip. Push your left hand to the right slightly to lock his right elbow. At the same time, step forward with your left foot (fig. 4-11-23).

Pull your opponent's right elbow up and to the right with your left hand. At the same time, release the grip of your right hand. Turn your right hand around under your opponent's right arm and immediately grip his right wrist or forearm and push his right arm up. Simultaneously release your left hand from his right elbow and then stretch it out behind him and place it on his left shoulder (fig. 4-11-24).

While pressing firmly with your left middle finger on the left *Jianjing* point of your opponent's left shoulder, pull his shoulder to the left. Turn your body to the left. Continue to push your opponent's right arm up and to the right with your right hand. The movement of both hands should be fully coordinated. This

combination of forces is called *bao jian shuai*—holding shoulder and throwing—and it will cause your opponent to spin around and fall down (fig. 4-11-25). The movements of your arms and legs must also be smoothly coordinated. Finally, your steps must be very nimble and must change fluidly to follow your continually changing hand techniques.

12. 醉卧苍松 Sleeping Off the Wine Under a Pine Tree

Posture Name

"醉卧苍松 — *zui wo cang song*" is a skill that involves a hard, arm-breaking movement. There is a well-known painting of a man lying under an old pine tree. The man, having drunk too much, leaned on the old pine on his way home and fell asleep. The picture conveys a sense of complete relaxation.

In this posture, imagine that you are the drunken man and your opponent is the pine tree. You want to lean on him and relax your full weight on him as though to lie down and sleep. When you lean on him, your whole body weight should bear down on his arm.

The main skills used in this posture are the step in from the side and the turn of your body back to pull and lean on your opponent's arm.

Movement Name and Description

侧身上转身搬靠 — *ce shen shang zhuan shen ban kao*: Step forward with body turned to the side and turn around to pull and lean on arm

Continue the movement from figure 4-11-14.

Step forward with your left foot to form a left bow stance. Open your left tiger mouth and stretch your left hand forward with your left palm facing up. Imagine touching the inside of your

4-12-1   4-12-2   4-12-3

4-12-4   4-12-5

opponent's right wrist. At the same time, drop your right hand in front of your abdomen. Look at your left hand (fig. 4-12-1).

Raise your right hand with your right palm facing the ground. Stretch your right arm to the left and forward and then move it to the right and forward in a curving line until it reaches the level of your shoulder. Imagine moving your right hand from the front of your chest to the right side of your opponent's neck. Look forward and to the right (fig. 4-12-2).

Move your left hand up and then to the right while simultaneously moving your right hand down and then to the left. Both hands should move in a clockwise circle, and your left hand should be over your right. At the same time, turn your body slightly to the right and look forward (fig. 4-12-3).

Continue to turn your body to the right and let your hands continue in their circles until your right hand is outside of your

left thigh and your left hand is at the level of your head. At the same time, turn your left foot on its heel to the right. Look at the outside of your left foot (fig. 4-12-4).

Turn both feet to face back. At the same time, put your right hand in front of your left hip and keep your left hand moving in a clockwise circle down and to the right. As you do this, shift your weight to your right leg to form a right bow stance. Look at a point in front of your right hand (fig. 4-12-5).

Application

If your opponent throws a center punch to your chest or stomach with his right fist

Raise your right hand and use your right palm to meet the inside of your opponent's right wrist. Step to the left with your left foot. At the same time, grip your opponent's right wrist with your right hand and pull him to your left side. As soon as he moves in this direction, raise your left hand so that it is close to your right hand. Your left palm should face up and forward, and the left tiger mouth should face to the left and back. Put your left upturned palm on the inside of your opponent's right wrist. Then change your grip on your opponent's right wrist from your right to your left hand (fig. 4-12-6).

Step forward and to the left with your left foot. Shift your weight onto your left leg. Grip your opponent's right wrist and pull toward the right side of his body. This will cause his body to lean to the right. At the same time, move your right hand in front of your left shoulder and raise it up and forward along your opponent's right arm until your right forearm is on the right side of his neck (figs. 4-12-7, 4-12-8). This movement can also be done as a quick, hard strike. To do this, instead of just putting your right forearm on your opponent's neck, use the edge of your right palm to chop his neck with a sharp and sudden movement.

Then push up with your left hand and move it in a clockwise

4-12-6   4-12-7   4-12-8

4-12-9   4-12-10   4-12-11

circle to the right. This will cause your opponent's right elbow to straighten and will tighten the pressure on his right shoulder as his body leans forward. At the same time, open your right hand and use your right palm to push your opponent's neck down and to the left in a clockwise circle. When you push with your right hand, you should stretch it out and around his neck as though to push his neck from the left side. This will cause his body to rotate clockwise toward the left side of your body. Keep pushing his head to the left until his head is under your left ribcage. Shift your weight slightly forward to form a left bow stance. Relax your waist and stretch slightly forward. The circling of your hands must be perfectly coordinated. The effect of all your movements will be to lock your opponent's right arm and neck so tightly that he will have no chance to counter your attack (fig. 4-12-9).

Push your left hand up and to the right. At the same time, press

your right hand down and push it continuously to the left. This will cause your opponent's right shoulder and neck to be pressed under your left hip. Move your left hip slightly forward to lock his neck firmly (fig. 4-12-10).

Turn your body clockwise toward the back and let your feet turn back also. Shift your weight to your right leg to form a right bow stance. At the same time, release your right hand from your opponent's neck and raise it up to join the left hand in gripping your opponent's right wrist. Push down and to the right side of your body with both hands on your opponent's right arm so that his arm moves forward and down (fig. 4-12-11). This is called "making a shoulder depart." (Actually fig. 4-12-11 does not illustrate this movement to completion, because a complete movement would seriously hurt my partner's arm.) To get more effect from this skill, you can step to the right with your right foot and turn your body to the right as though leaning your body on your opponent's head when you push down on his right arm.

Please pay great attention when you practice this skill. It is very easy to break your partner's shoulder. Never apply this skill quickly and hard!

13. 猛虎出洞 Fierce Tiger Leaping Out of Its Lair

Posture Name

"猛虎出洞 — *meng hu chu dong*" describes a vigorous attack as when a tiger leaps out of its lair to hunt down its prey. In this posture, imagine that your hand is a tiger and that an open spot in your opponent's defense is the opening of your lair. In striking forward through the opening in your opponent's defense, your hand mimics the movement of a tiger leaping out of its lair.

The posture includes two main skills. The first involves seizing your opponent's throat, and the second involves stepping toward

your opponent, tucking in your hand, and then ramming your opponent with your palm. In this posture, your hand must find an open space in front of your opponent's throat or chest and go through it suddenly and powerfully to attack the vulnerable spot.

Movement Name and Description

上掐嗉进步掖撞 — *shang qia su jin bu yie zhuang:* Choke and step in to tuck and ram with palm

Continue the movement from figure 4-12-5.

Step forward with your left foot and turn your left toes to the right. Your knees should touch each other. Straighten your body. Relax your shoulders and let your arms drop down naturally. Look forward (fig. 4-13-1).

Relax your right hip and swing your right foot around clockwise. At the same time, shift your weight onto your left leg and touch the ground with the toes of your right foot. Turn your body around. Raise your right arm until it is level with your chest. Your right palm should face to the left. Imagine touching your opponent's right forearm to block his punch. Look forward along your right hand (fig. 4-13-2).

Raise your left hand over your right hand and let your hands cross each other (fig. 4-13-3). Then separate your hands, with the left hand pulling to the left and the right hand pulling to the right. Both hands should push down slightly as they move. At the same time, drop your body slightly and raise your head slightly. Look forward and down (fig. 4-13-4).

Step forward with your right foot and let your left foot follow naturally. Raise your right hand and stretch it out straight ahead. At the same time, open the tiger mouth of your right hand and bend your thumb and fingers as though to seize your opponent. Do not change the position of your left hand. Keep your weight about evenly distributed on both legs (fig. 4-13-5).

Shift your weight back and take a half step back with your right foot. Keep your right heel raised off the ground. Bend your right

4-13-1   4-13-2   4-13-3

4-13-4   4-13-5   4-13-6

arm and move it back until it is in front of your chest with the palm facing up. At the same time, bend your left arm and raise your left hand until it is in front of your left shoulder with the fingers pointing back and the palm facing up. Withdraw your chest and abdomen slightly. Look forward in front of your right arm (fig. 4-13-6).

Turn your waist and let your right arm follow the turn by moving in an arc from the left, to the back, and then to the right. As your right hand moves to the right, turn it over and stretch it forward. Your right palm should face the ground with your fingers pointing forward. Look forward (fig. 4-13-7).

Keep your weight on your left leg. Step forward with your right foot and then shift your weight forward to form a right bow stance. At the same time, let your left palm follow the movement of your right hand and hit the back of your right hand. Imagine, though, that you are hitting your right foot. Look at the back of your right

hand and imagine that you can see through that hand to the ground (fig. 4-13-8).

Bend your right wrist so that the fingers of your right hand point up and your right palm faces forward, as though to push forward. Turn your body slightly to the left. At the same time, push your left hand forward and down and then pull it back until it is in front of your left hip. Imagine that you are using your left hand to plow a ditch in the ground. Straighten your body and shift your weight back to form a half riding horse stance. Look forward and far away (figs. 4-13-9a, 4-13-9b).

4-13-7

4-13-8

4-13-9

Application

If your opponent throws a punch to your chest with his right fist

Instead of dodging back to evade the punch, move forward to get close to your opponent. Step forward with your right foot and raise your right hand to block the punch. The force of your block should follow your opponent's movement. Use your right palm to meet the inside of your opponent's right forearm, and then stroke his arm and push it down and to the left and back. This is called *heng shun jin*—side-by-side and following force (fig. 4-13-10).

When you block your opponent's right punch, he will use his left hand to attack you. Using your left hand this time instead of your

4-13-10

4-13-11

4-13-12

4-13-13

right, continue to control your opponent's right arm by pulling and pushing it down (fig. 4-13-11). At the same time, release your right hand and use it to block your opponent's left hand. Meet the inside of your opponent's left forearm with your right palm and then stroke and push his right arm down and to your right and back. Be careful not to oppose his force directly. Instead, direct your force across his. This is called using side-by-side force to defend against straight-ahead force, and it will cause your opponent to lose his balance and change or forego his attack (fig. 4-13-12).

Turn your waist slightly to the right so that the force of your right hand is a little bit stronger than the force of your left hand. This will cause your opponent to lean to the right. As soon as this happens, release your right hand from his left arm and immediately stretch your right hand forward toward his throat. Use your right thumb, index finger, and middle finger to clutch his Adam's apple. At the same time, step forward with your right foot to enter his *zhong men,* the center "gate," between his legs (fig. 4-13-13).

In this skill, you must take care to coordinate the movement of your left hand with that of your left foot and the movement of your right hand with that of your right foot. Also, you should keep most of your weight on your back leg. When you step forward with your front foot, the back foot must follow and move forward, too.

This skill will be especially effective if your movements are sudden and quick.

If your opponent punches your lower chest with his right fist

Step forward with your right foot and let your right toes touch the ground. Raise your right arm and bend it at the elbow. Put your right forearm across and over your opponent's right forearm with your right palm facing up and the fingers of your right hand pointing to the left (fig. 4-13-14). The touchpoint between your arm and your opponent's arm should be light so that you can feel any change in the speed or direction of his movement without his being able to determine these characteristics of your movement. Maintain the touchpoint, but do not use force.

Raise your left palm over your left shoulder. Move your right hand to the left and then back in a circle as though grinding something. Turn your right palm over and move it around your opponent's arm until your right palm is under his right forearm with your right palm facing the ground. At the same time, step forward with your right foot and place it between your opponent's legs (fig. 4-13-15). Continue to raise your left hand and let your left palm face the sky. Lightly maintain the touchpoint between your right hand and your opponent's forearm. Your left palm should face up as though holding something. This will allow your right hand to acquire a balancing force. Keep your weight on your back leg and let only the ball of your front foot touch the ground. This will allow you to change your movement forward or back quickly and easily.

Follow your opponent's movement, and let your force come from your waist. Withdraw your chest and abdomen slightly. When your opponent's right fist extends beyond your right arm, he will lean forward. At that moment, stretch your right arm out toward him and place your right palm directly on his chest (fig.

4-13-14   **4-13-15**   **4-13-16**

4-13-17   **4-13-18**

4-13-16). Your middle finger should point to the *Tanzhong* point at the center of his lower chest. Lower your body slightly.

Shift your weight forward by stepping slightly forward with your right foot. At the same time, use your left palm to hit the back of your right hand. Imagine that your left palm is pursuing your right palm and then hitting your right foot. Be sure that the movements of your foot and hand are coordinated. Your right palm should hit your opponent's lower chest or ribs, and your left palm should hit the back of your right hand. By combining the force of both hands and your right foot, this strike will cause a powerful forward and downward force in your right palm to the opponent's chest (fig. 4-13-17). The most important point to keep in mind during this sequence is that all the movements must be coordinated.

As soon as your left palm hits the back of your right hand, move your left hand down and pull it back until it is in front of your left

hip. At the same time, shift about sixty to seventy percent of your weight to your left leg to form a half riding horse stance. Imagine plowing a ditch on the ground with your left hand. Turn your body to the left, with your left hand pulling back. This movement will lend a powerful forward and upward force to your right palm (figs. 4-13-18a, 4-13-18b).

The last two movements should be done smoothly and without interruption. During this sequence, the direction of your hitting force changes, and this change will cause your opponent to jump up and then fall down.

14. 风轮飞旋 Wind-and-Fire Wheel Spinning Swiftly

Posture Name

"风轮飞旋 — *fang lun fei xuan*" is a quick and powerful skill. *Fang lun* refers to a wind-and-fire wheel, a magic weapon described in ancient Chinese mythology. When it is thrown out for attacking, the wheel flies fast and rotates powerfully with wind and fire.

In this posture, imagine that your arm is a wind-and-fire wheel and that it can repel an attacker by its powerful rotation. The posture includes two main skills. The first, the shoulder strike, should be done with a quick and powerful small circular movement; the second, hooking hand and chopping palm, should be done with a big circular movement. The movements involved in both skills resemble a rotating wheel.

Movement Name and Description

肩撞进勾手削掌 — *jian zhuang jin gou shou xiao zhang:* Step in with shoulder strike, hooking hand and chopping palm

Continue the movement from figure 4-13-9.

Shift your weight to your right leg to form a right bow stance. Drop your right hand and let your right palm face to the right. Raise

your left hand to the right side of your head, with your left palm facing out and the fingers of your left hand pointing up. Imagine moving your right hand back. Look forward (fig. 4-14-1).

Gather your right fingers together so that your right hand forms the shape of a hook. At the same time, step forward with your left foot and shift your weight onto your left leg. Imagine raising your right hand slightly. Look forward (fig. 4-14-2).

Relax your right shoulder and raise your right arm toward the back of your body so that your right fingers point to the sky. Imagine touching the back of your head with the fingers of your right hand. Move your right foot forward to follow the movement of your left foot, and touch the ground with the toes of your right foot. At the same time, drop your body slightly and look forward. Imagine that your left hand is pushing back along the right side of your head. This will create a powerful straight-ahead force as your right shoulder moves forward in a shoulder strike (fig. 4-14-3).

Shift your weight to your right leg and straighten both legs to raise your body up. Drop both arms. Step to the left with your left foot and raise your right knee up in front of your chest. Stretch your arms and waist forward. Stretch your right hand out in front and to the right of your body with your right palm facing out and down, and the fingers of your right hand pointing forward and slightly down. Imagine that you are placing your right hand on something. At the same time, raise your left hand and stretch it out until it is at head level. Your left palm should face out and slightly forward. Coordinate the movement of both hands so that the palms push outward together. Look forward and down (fig. 4-14-4).

Step forward with your right foot. Lower your body. Move your left hand to the right side of your head with your left palm facing out and the fingers of your left hand pointing up. Drop your right hand down to the right side of your body and make a "hook-hand" by gathering your fingers together and pointing them up and to the right. Look down at your right hand (fig. 4-14-5).

4-14-1 **4-14-2** **4-14-3**

4-14-4 **4-14-5** **4-14-6**

Change the right "hook-hand" to a flat palm. At the same time, raise your right arm up and turn it clockwise until your right palm faces up. While raising your right arm, straighten your legs slightly so that your stance becomes more erect. Keep your right leg weighted and bent. Step forward with your left foot to form a sitting stance. At the same time, drop your left hand down until it is in front of your left knee with your left palm facing down. Look at a point in front of your left hand (fig. 4-14-6). Continuously raise your right palm up, push your left palm down, and raise your body slightly (fig. 4-14-7).

Step back and to the left with your left foot. Drop both arms down in front of your body. Look forward and down (fig. 4-14-8).

Raise your right hand in front of your head, with your right palm toward your face. Take a small step back with your right foot until it is in front of your left foot. Look at your right hand

4-14-7   4-14-8   4-14-9

4-14-10   4-14-11   4-14-12

4-14-13

(fig. 4-14-9). Imagine meeting your opponent's punch with your right wrist.

Turn your right hand over and shift your weight forward to your right leg. Turn your body slightly to the right and pull your right hand down and to the right. Turn your head to the right and look at your right hand (fig. 4-14-10).

Raise your right hand until it is over your head. The right palm

should face up and forward. At the same time, move your left hand to the right until it is in front of your right hip. The movement of both hands should be coordinated. Look straight ahead (fig. 4-14-11).

Step forward with your left foot but keep your weight on your right leg to form a sitting stance. Raise your left arm up and stretch it out at shoulder level. Your left palm should face to the left, and the left tiger mouth should face down. Imagine that you are gripping the inside of your opponent's right arm with your left hand. At the same time, move your right hand in a counterclockwise horizontal circle above your head, starting from the front of your head, then to the left, the back, and finally to the right. Look up and to the left (fig. 4-14-12). Imagine that you are peering directly into the eyes of your opponent. The curvilinear movements of both arms should be smoothly coordinated.

Continue to move your right hand in a counterclockwise circle and follow the movement of your right hand by turning your body to the left. With this movement, push your left hand down and to the left and turn your right hand over so that the palm faces first up and then to the left. At the same time, chop down and to the left with your right hand at shoulder level. While both hands are moving in a slanting circle, straighten your right leg slightly and take a small step back with your left foot. Touch the ground with the toes of your left foot. Look to the left and down in front of your left foot. Imagine chopping your opponent down to the level of your left foot (figs. 4-14-13a, 4-14-13b). The movements of your body must be fully coordinated and should occur simultaneously. The power for the chop comes from your legs and extends through your waist and back to your arms and hands.

Application

If your opponent punches your face with his right fist

Raise your right hand to meet your opponent's right wrist (fig. 4-14-14). Turn your right hand over to grip his wrist. Pull his wrist

4-14-14   4-14-15   4-14-16

4-14-17   4-14-18

down and to the right. This will cause him to lean forward (fig. 4-14-15).

Step diagonally left and forward with your left foot. At the same time, put your left hand on the outside of your opponent's left elbow and push it to the right and slightly back. This will cause him to lean further to the left. At the same time, drop your body down slightly and move forward to close the distance between you and your opponent (fig. 4-14-16).

Follow your opponent's punching movement by pushing his right arm backward with your left hand. Keep moving your left foot forward until it is on the right side of your opponent's body. Lower your body and move your right shoulder forward until it touches the right side of your opponent's ribcage (fig. 4-14-17).

Move your right hand back and form a right "hook-hand." The fingers of your right hand should point to the sky. Step forward with

your right foot, and let the toes of your right foot touch the ground. At the same time, imagine raising up your right "hook-hand" from behind. This will cause your right shoulder to acquire a powerful force as it rams forward in a shoulder strike (fig. 4-14-18).

If the opponent kicks you with his right foot

Step to the left with your left foot and then step back with your right foot until your right foot is in front of your left foot. Relax your waist and turn slightly to the right. Stretch your right arm down and raise your left hand. Let the fingers of your right hand point to the ground and the right palm face out. Touch your opponent's right foreleg with your right palm (fig. 4-14-19).

When your right hand touches your opponent's right foreleg, step forward quickly with your right foot. At the same time, change your right palm to a "hook-hand," insert it under your opponent's right leg, and then hook it up. Simultaneously drop your body down slightly and drop your left hand for protection (fig. 4-14-20).

Move your right hand back and then up in an arc. At the same time, turn your right forearm clockwise under your opponent's right foreleg until your right palm faces up. Simultaneously step forward with your left foot, raise your body up, and put your left hand in front of your body to block your opponent's right hand (fig. 4-14-21).

Straighten up, keeping your weight on your right leg. Open your

4-14-19

4-14-20

4-14-21

4-14-22

right hand and continue moving it up until it reaches shoulder level. If your opponent tries to get close enough to grab you, step back slightly with your right foot, turn your right forearm back, and raise it up. This will cause your opponent to lean back and jump back on one leg in an effort to keep his balance. At that moment, push forward while continuing to raise your right forearm (fig. 4-14-22). Imagine throwing his right foot far out behind his body.

It is most important that you maintain the touchpoint between your right hand and your opponent's right leg. If you feel that he wants to move his leg forward, move your right hand back and up. If you feel he wants to withdraw his body, move your right hand up and push forward. Continue your efforts to destroy his balance and cause him to jump onto one leg so that you have a chance to throw him powerfully and far with your rotating movement.

If your opponent punches you with his right fist

Meet your opponent's right wrist with your right wrist, and at the same time step back and to the left with your left foot (fig. 4-14-23).

Turn your right wrist over to grip your opponent's right wrist and pull it down and to the right. At the same time, move your right foot slightly to the right and shift your weight onto your right leg. This will cause your opponent to lean forward and lose his balance (fig. 4-14-24).

Instead of using a pull-down force with your right hand when your opponent begins to lose balance, raise your right hand as though to hold something and stretch it out and up to the right. At the same time, step forward with your right foot. This sequence is called *ti jin,* or "raise-up" force, and it will cause the heel of

4-14-23　　　　4-14-24　　　　4-14-25

4-14-26　　　　4-14-27

your opponent's rear foot to leave the ground (fig. 4-14-25). The direction of your right hand's movement should change quickly, suddenly, and smoothly.

If you feel that your opponent's body is becoming tense while your right hand moves up and to the right, change the direction of your arm movement so that your right hand moves back and slightly up. At the same time, raise your left hand up in front of your body and grip the inside of your opponent's right biceps or elbow. Release your right hand from your opponent's right wrist and make a horizontal counterclockwise circle starting from the front of your face and continuing to the left and then to the back of your head. Straighten your body, and drop and push your left hand to the left. It will cause the opponent to lean to the right. Keep your weight on your right leg. Look directly at your opponent's eyes (fig. 4-14-26).

Pull your left hand down and to the left. At the same time, continue moving your right hand in a counterclockwise circle from the back of your head to the right of your head with your right palm facing up. In a continuous movement, chop with the edge of your right palm at the left side of your opponent's neck. It is important that the circling movement of your right hand and the pull by your left hand be fully coordinated. Your body should follow the movement of your hands by turning to the left. All your movements must be coordinated and your force integrated in order to turn your opponent's body around and shake his root. The chop by your right palm must be powerful and quick (fig. 4-14-27).

15. 猿猴入洞 Monkey Jumping in Its Lair

Posture Name

"猿猴入洞 — *yuan hou ru dong*" is a quick and nimble skill. *Yuan hou* means "monkey." *Ru dong* means "to jump in a lair." Monkeys are nimble, alert, quick, and smart animals. In a famous story, many monkeys lived on a beautiful mountain. There was a waterfall on the mountain. One day they played near there and one monkey asked what was behind the waterfall. Someone suggested leaping through the waterfall to find out, but no one wanted to try it. Then someone said that if there was a monkey who could do it, they would respect him as a king. So one monkey said he could do it. He was quick and nimble enough to leap through the waterfall, and he discovered a big and beautiful lair hidden under the waterfall. This monkey became the Monkey King, and the lair became the monkeys' new home. Later the Monkey King acquired many notable abilities and performed great deeds.

Like the Monkey King's movements, the skills used in this posture should be quick and nimble. Think of your target as the monkeys' lair, your opponent's defense skills as the waterfall, and your hand as the monkey. Your attack skills should be nimble and

quick like the skills the Monkey King used to jump through the waterfall and into the lair.

This posture is comprised of two main skills. The first is *ye na* or "holding wrist and pulling in." Here, think of the lair as your armpit. Your goal is to lock and control your opponent with your hand and then pull your hand back. When you do this, imagine that you are going home. The second skill is "holding wrist, and turning body back with wrist strike." Here, think of your opponent's chest or ribcage as the lair and your quick, nimble wrist strike as the Monkey King leaping into the lair.

Movement Name and Description

掤拿势转身腕打 — *ye na shi zhuan shen wan da:* Grip wrist and tuck back, and turn body back with wrist strike

Continue the movement from figure 4-14-13.

Turn your body to the right. Drop your arms down to your sides. At the same time, shift your weight to your left leg and step forward with your right foot. Touch the ground with the toes of your right foot to form a sitting stance. Look forward and down (fig. 4-15-1).

Raise your right hand to waist level and then raise your left hand immediately to grip your right wrist. Look at the back of your left hand (fig. 4-15-2). When your opponent grips your right wrist, imagine that you are putting your left hand on his right hand.

Relax your right wrist and open your right palm. Rotate your right wrist clockwise, simultaneously bending your fingers as if to grip something. Step back with your left foot. Continually increase the strength of your grip. Use your right index finger, and then your middle finger and ring finger to lead your right arm in a clockwise circle back toward your body until your right hand is under your left armpit. At the same time, turn your left foot to the left and let your body follow in a turn to the left. Look at your left armpit (fig. 4-15-3).

Keep your weight on your left leg. Move your right hand under your left armpit and then insert it back past your armpit and upward. At the same time, place your right foot to the left side of your left foot. Your knees should touch each other. This will cause your body to turn to the left. Stretch your right arm up as you continue to turn. Your body will also stretch upward as it follows the movement of your right hand. Put your left hand beside your right elbow. Look at the tip of your right middle finger (fig. 4-15-4).

Keep your body straight and stretch your right arm up. Shift your weight onto your right leg. Drop your left hand down in front of your right shoulder. Continue to turn your body to the left. Turn your head to the left and look forward. At the same time, drop your right hand down in front of your left shoulder. Cross your hands and while lowering them, separate them so that they come to rest at your sides. Bring the fingers of each hand close together to form "hook-hands." Move your left hand forward and up in a curve until it is at shoulder level. The fingers of your left hand should point to the ground, and your left wrist should face up. This will generate a powerful upward striking force in your left wrist. At the same time, move your right hand backward and up in a curve until it is a little bit higher than your waist. The fingers of your right hand should point up. This will generate a strong pull-back force. Simultaneously raise your left knee and ram it upward. Look forward (fig. 4-15-5). The three forces, one from each hand and one from your left knee, should be smoothly coordinated.

As your left foot lands on the ground, drop both arms. Then raise your left hand in a small circle and move it to the right side of your right ear, with your left palm facing out. At the same time, turn your left foot on the heel about ninety degrees to the right. Bend your left leg and lower your body. Step forward with your right foot behind your left leg. This will cause your legs to cross each other in a movement called a "back step" or a "sneak step." The purpose of this movement is to prevent your opponent from

4-15-1

4-15-2

4-15-3

4-15-4

4-15-5

4-15-6

4-15-7

sensing that you are taking a step. Keep your left hand moving to the right and your body turning to the right (fig. 4-15-6).

Turn your feet to follow the turn of your body and form a riding horse stance. Look to the right. Move both arms back and cross them in front of your chest. Bring the fingers of both hands together to form goose-head fists, and then stick them to the sides of your body (fig. 4-15-7).

4-15-8

Application

If your opponent grips your right wrist (fig. 4-15-8)

Put your left hand on the back of your opponent's right hand. Relax your right wrist and use the fingers of your right hand to lead the hand and turn your right wrist in a clockwise direction until your right palm touches the outside of your opponent's right wrist and your right hand grips his right wrist. Point your right index finger forward slightly (fig. 4-15-9). This will create pressure on your opponent's right wrist and cause him to bend his knees and drop down.

Rotate the fingers of your right hand around your opponent's right wrist in a clockwise direction. This will give you complete control of your opponent's right wrist. At the same time, shift your weight onto your right foot and step back with your left foot. This will generate a powerful and very painful force on your opponent's right wrist. In an attempt to reduce this pain, your opponent will kneel down on the ground (fig. 4-15-10).

If you grip your oppon-ent's right wrist but cannot gain complete control of him, relax your right hand, bend your right wrist and right elbow, and insert your right hand under your own

4-15-9

4-15-10

4-15-11

right armpit. At the same time, step slightly back with your left foot and turn your body to the left. Let your hand lead your body as it turns to give additional power to your hand. This coordinated movement will generate a more powerful grip and create a stronger pull on your opponent's right wrist. It will also cause him to lose his balance and fall forward and down (fig. 4-15-11).

If you cannot make your opponent fall forward in the above skill, he may shift his weight back slightly and try to use his left hand to attack you.

Turn your body to the left and circle your right hand through the space under your left armpit (fig. 4-15-12). Raise your right hand until it is over your head. At the same time, place your right foot to the left side of your left foot and turn your right foot back. This movement will cause your body to turn around and will raise your opponent's center of gravity (fig. 4-15-13).

Continue turning your body counterclockwise. Make a goose-head fist with your left hand by bending your left wrist downward and gathering the fingers and thumb of your left hand close together. Your left wrist can then be used to deliver a wrist strike, also called *wan da*. Place your left hand in front of your stomach (fig. 4-15-14). Then, move your goose-head fist forward and up to strike your opponent's ribs or chin. At the same time, if you are close enough to your opponent, you can raise your left knee and

4-15-12

4-15-13

4-15-14

4-15-15

4-15-16

ram it into his right ribcage. Alternatively, you can kick him (fig. 4-15-15).

If your opponent withdraws his body to avoid your attack

When your left foot lands on the ground after your knee strike, make a cross back insert step with your right foot (fig. 4-15-16). Change the grip on your opponent's right wrist from your right to your left hand. Turn your body to the right. Turn both feet back and form a riding horse stance. Move your right hand down to the left side of your body (fig. 4-15-17). Make a right goose-head

4-15-17

4-15-18

fist or use the back of your right palm to hit your opponent's right ribcage. Look his right ribcage as you strike (fig. 4-15-18).

16. 朔风扑面 **Cold Wind Caresses the Face**

Posture Name

"朔风扑面 — *suo feng pu mian*" describes a skill which is soft and smooth outside but hard and quick inside. *Suo feng* means "a very cold wind." The winter winds of northern China are always very cold and strong. People say that when such a wind "caresses" one's face, it feels as though the skin is being cut with a knife. In this skill, your hand should be like the cold wind, apparently soft and flowing but actually hard and strong when it hits your opponent's face. This hand skill is also called *pu mian zhang* or "prey-face palm."

When you strike your opponent's face, the movement of your hands and arms should be soft and smooth. Their impact on his face, however, should be very hard.

Movement and Description

将手势搂腰盖掌 — *luo shou shi lou yao gai zhang*: Pull hand, hold waist, and cover palm

Continue the movement from figure 4-15-8.

Shift your weight to your left leg and move your right foot back until it is in front of your left foot. Touch the ground with the toes of your right foot. Turn your body to the right and stand erect. Raise your right arm up and stretch it out in front of your face with your palm toward your face. Look straight ahead (fig. 4-16-1).

Turn your right wrist over. Bend the fingers of your right hand as though to grip something and then pull down and slightly to the right with your right hand. At the same time, lower your body slightly and stamp the ground with your right toes. Look at the back of your right hand (fig. 4-16-2).

Open your right hand to form a palm and then move it in a curving path up and forward until it reaches the level of your face. The fingers of your right hand should point upward and forward. Imagine pushing your opponent's face with your right palm. At the same time, step forward quickly with your left foot. Stretch your left hand out at waist level and imagine putting it on the lower part of your opponent's back. Look forward and down (fig. 4-16-3). When you change the movement of your right hand from pulling

4-16-1

4-16-2

4-16-3

4-16-4

down to pushing forward and up, you should feel as though your legs are springs. This will lend great force to your attack. Your right hand should follow this force as it pushes forward.

Shift your weight onto your left leg to form a wide bow stance. Push your right hand forward and down, and at the same time pull your left hand back until it is just in front of your abdomen. When you pull your left hand back, twist your left forearm until your palm faces up. The force from both hands should be coordinated as though you want to break something. Look forward and down (fig. 4-16-4).

Application

If your opponent punches your face with his right fist

Step back slightly with your left foot and turn your body slightly to the right. Raise your right hand to meet your opponent's right wrist (fig. 4-16-5).

If, when your wrist touches your opponent's wrist, you feel as though his punch is continuing to move forward, turn your right wrist over his in a firm grip. Pull his hand back and down with your right hand. At the same time, shift your weight to your left leg and step back with your right foot so that it is slightly in front of your left foot. This will cause a powerful force that pulls your opponent forward and causes him to lean forward and lose his balance (fig. 4-16-6).

When you feel your opponent begin to lean forward, release your right hand immediately and put your right palm on your opponent's face. At the same time, move your left hand to the lower part of your opponent's back and put the middle finger of your left hand on his *Mingmen* point (fig. 4-16-7).

Step forward with your left foot and place it behind and to the left of your opponent. Put your right middle finger on your opponent's forehead at his *Shenting* point, your right palm on his

4-16-5   4-16-6   4-16-7

4-16-8   4-16-9

nose, and the heel of your right hand on his mouth. Then push his head back and down. At the same time, pull his back toward you and up with your left hand. In this movement, your hands should be applying force in opposite directions (fig. 4-16-8).

The pull of your left hand will cause your opponent's center of gravity to rise, and his root to be broken. The downward push of your right hand will easily throw him to the ground. You must be very careful when practicing this skill. If your right hand pushes down too quickly and directly, you can easily injure your opponent's waist.

If you feel your opponent push back against the downward push of your right hand, relax your right hand and raise it slightly. At the same time, move your left hand slightly higher on your opponent's spine. This will cause his force to meet only emptiness. Then move your left hand down to his *Mingmen* point again and repeat the coordinated push and pull of your right and left hands,

respectively. This time it should be easy to throw him down (fig. 4-16-9). Occasionally, it may be necessary to repeat this sequence several times.

✪ Closing Form: 华陀问脉 Hua Tuo Feeling the Pulse

Posture Name

"华陀问脉 — *hua tuo wan mai*" is a skill that involves gripping another's wrist. Hua Tuo was a famous Chinese doctor who lived about 1,800 years ago. His medical skill was great and he saved many lives, including the life of the great warrior General Guan. He also made a significant theoretical contribution to the field of Chinese medicine. In traditional Chinese medicine, the major diagnostic skill involves assessing the patient's pulses. In this posture, the main skill is to take hold of your opponent's wrist, like a doctor feeling a patient's pulse Then, you twist his wrist and bend it backward.

This posture is also the closing-form posture. It includes a turning-around skill and a closing-form movement. The turn of your body and the twist of your opponent's wrist should depend on the reaction you sense from your opponent when you grab him. You should adjust the direction and speed of your movements to ensure that you attain the desired effect and gain complete control of your opponent.

The closing-form movement is very important for your practice. It will help you conclude your practice in a comfortable way and produce an internal feeling of cooling down. To do it well means to practice completely.

Movement Name and Description

回身走拧腕归原 — *hui shen zou ning wan gui yuan:* Turn around, twist wrist, and return to starting position

Continue the movement from figure 4-16-4.

Keep your weight on your left leg. Turn your left foot on the heel to the right. Turn your body clockwise to follow the turn of your left foot. Let your right foot turn naturally on the toes as your body turns. After your body turns around, your weight should still be on your left leg to form a sitting stance. Relax your arms and lower them to your sides. Look forward and down (fig. 4-17-1).

Shift your weight forward to your right leg to form a bow stance. Raise your left hand and let your left palm face to the right. Imagine gripping your opponent's elbow with your left hand. Turn the toes of your right foot, followed by your body, slightly to the right. Look at your left hand (fig. 4-17-2).

Turn your left palm up slightly. Bend the fingers of your left hand and imagine gripping something and then pulling your left hand back. At the same time, raise your right hand up to ear level and bend the fingers of your right hand as though to grip something. Simultaneously step forward with your left foot to form a sitting stance. Withdraw your left elbow slightly and look forward and down (fig. 4-17-3).

Shift your weight onto your left leg to form a bow stance. Pull your left hand back continuously until it is under your right arm. At the same time, push your right hand forward and then down in a curving arc until it is at stomach level. Look down in front of your left foot (fig. 4-17-4).

4-17-1

4-17-2

4-17-3

4-17-4

Relax your shoulders. Bring both arms back in front of your chest and then slowly drop them down slightly. The tips of your index fingers should touch each other. At the same time, step forward with your right foot and place it beside your left foot. Look at the touchpoint of your index fingers (fig. 4-17-5).

Make the tips of both middle fingers touch each other, and move your gaze to this touchpoint. Then make the tips of both thumbs touch each other, and move your gaze to this touchpoint. At the same time, relax your legs. This will cause your legs to bend more deeply and your body to drop slightly down (figs. 4-17-6a, 4-17-6b).

Focus your mind on your ankles. This will cause your ankles to straighten up slowly. Then focus your mind on your knees, causing them to straighten up slowly. Finally, focus your mind on your hips. Then they, too, will slowly straighten up (fig. 4-17-7).

Continue to straighten your body until you are standing erect.

4-17-5   4-17-6

4-17-7   4-17-8

Then focus your mind on your shoulders. This will cause them to relax and drop down. Next, focus your mind on your elbows, causing them to relax and drop down. Finally, focus your mind on your wrists so that they, too, relax and drop down. As a result of all these adjustments, your hands will slowly separate. Raise your head slowly to look forward. Move your hands to the sides of your body and let your palms touch your legs (figs. 4-17-8a, 4-17-8b). Adjust your breathing to achieve slow, smooth, and deep breaths.

Application

If your opponent punches your chest with his right fist

Take a small step back and to the left with your left foot, and put your right foot in front of your left foot with the toes of your right foot touching the ground. At the same time, raise your right hand with your right palm facing up until it is over your opponent's right wrist. Then bend your right wrist, like a hook, with the fingers of your right hand pointing to the left. Put the lower edge of your right palm on top of your opponent's right wrist and slightly move your right palm so that it traces a curve from right to left on his wrist. Turn your body slightly to the left to generate a *heng jin,* or side-to-side force. At the same time, withdraw your chest slightly and raise your left hand in natural way (fig. 4-17-9).

Put your left palm on your opponent's right elbow and then grip his elbow. Place the thumb of your left hand at the *Quchi* point on the outside of your opponent's elbow, and grip the inside of his elbow with the fingers of your left hand. Then pull his right arm back and to the right. At the same time, keep your right hand in contact with your opponent's right wrist and rotate your right hand counterclockwise around his forearm until you can grip his right wrist with your right hand. Simultaneously shift your weight to your right leg and turn your body to the right. As you turn, empty your chest slightly. This is called *hanxiong,* and it will help

4-17-9   4-17-10   4-17-11

4-17-12   4-17-13   4-17-14

you avoid your opponent's punch and allow you to execute the whole movement more smoothly (fig. 4-17-10).

Grip your opponent's right wrist with your right hand. Put your fingers on the *Maimen* area at the inside of his right wrist and grip tightly as you raise your right hand a little bit and pull slightly back so that the tiger mouth of your right hand faces up. Turn your body slightly to the right. At the same time, step forward with your left foot (fig. 4-17-11).

Continue to exert pressure on your opponent's *Quchi* point with your left thumb and pull his elbow back slightly. Continue also to grasp his *Maimen* with the fingers of your right hand, and raise your right hand until it is at the level of your right ear. Turn your head to look a few yards behind your opponent's right heel (fig. 4-17-12).

Shift your weight onto your left leg. Continue to put pressure

on your opponent's *Quchi* point with your left thumb as you pull his elbow slightly back. This will cause his elbow to bend. At the same time, add more force to the fingers of your right hand as they dig into his *Maimen* area, and push his right hand backward and then down quickly. This will create pain in his right wrist and elbow, causing him to bend his knees and lean backward from his waist. In this position, he will find it very difficult to move against you (fig. 4-17-13).

Continue to shift your weight to your front leg and push your opponent's right hand down. This will bring the weight of your whole body to bear on his right shoulder and elbow; move them in opposite directions until he falls down (fig. 4-17-14). If you can, move your right foot behind your opponent and to his right. This will greatly increase the power of your downward push.

If your opponent grips your right shoulder from behind with his right hand (fig. 4-17-15)

Step forward with your left foot and turn it back immediately to the right. Let your body follow the turn of your left foot by turning clockwise 180 degrees. As your body turns, turn your right foot on the toes. Relax and drop your right shoulder and slightly withdraw your abdomen and right hip. Raise your left hand in a natural way. Look at your opponent (fig. 4-17-16).

Grip your opponent's right elbow with your left hand. Dig your left thumb into his *Quchi* point, on the outside of his elbow (fig. 4-17-17). Then step forward with your right foot and pull his elbow back and to the right (fig. 4-17-18).

Turn your body to the right and keep pulling your opponent's right elbow around with your left hand in a clockwise circle. This will cause him to lean forward. At the same time, grab his right wrist in your right hand. Clutch the *Maimen* point on his right wrist with the fingers of your right hand. Simultaneously step forward with your left foot. Look at your right hand (fig. 4-17-19).

4-17-15   4-17-16   4-17-17

4-17-18   4-17-19   4-17-20

4-17-21   4-17-22

Look behind your opponent's body as you continue to pull his right elbow back with your left hand. Shift your weight forward onto your left leg. At the same time, raise your right hand until it is level with your right ear (fig. 4-17-20).

Shift your weight onto your left leg. Continue to put pressure on your opponent's *Quchi* point with your left thumb and pull his

right elbow slightly back. This will cause his elbow to bend. At the same time, add more force to his *Maimen* area with the fingers of your right hand, and push his right hand backward and then quickly down. This will cause pain to his right wrist and elbow. His knees will bend, and his body will bend backward from the waist. From this position, it will be very difficult for your opponent to counterattack from this position (fig 4-17-21).

Continue to shift your weight to your front leg and to push your opponent's right hand down. This will cause his right shoulder and right elbow to move in opposite directions as the full force of your body bears down on him and causes him to fall down (fig. 4-17-22). If you can step forward with your right foot and place it behind your opponent and to his right while executing this movement, you will intensify the downward force being applied to his body.

CHAPTER FIVE

The Practice of Applications

Basic *gongfu* training and application training are the two major aspects of traditional Chinese martial arts instruction. Basic *gongfu* training, in which the main training exercises are stretching training, strength training, post-standing, and form practice, builds a foundation of basic skills; and application training develops fighting skills. The twofold goal in internal martial arts basic *gongfu* training is to condition the body so that it can execute all martial arts skills and to modify the internal components—*shen, yi,* and *qi*—so that they conform to martial arts principles and skill requirements.

Because the first goal is relatively easy to understand, emphasis in training is usually placed on the second goal, which is best achieved by form practice. Many forms have traditionally been included in martial arts practice. A lengthy period of practice is usually required to master form training before advancing to application training. It is generally agreed that if you do not have a good foundation, your application skills will never reach a high level of mastery.

Given that the principles and features of the internal martial arts are very different from those of other martial arts, internal martial arts application training is also distinctive. Unfortunately, over the last hundred years, most groups have not provided their students with comprehensive application training. There are several reasons for this lapse, but the primary one is that basic *gongfu* training was considered so important that little time was

devoted to the practice of fighting skills. This exaggerated focus on basic *gongfu* training to the relative exclusion of application training was widespread, and much knowledge was lost forever. Even in martial arts groups that are currently known for the fighting skills inherited from past generations, practitioners do not have high-level fighting abilities. Although they know many forms, these martial artists lack expertise in the application of the movements they so intensively practice.

✪ Application Training

In most martial arts groups, the main application training is *chai shou* or "take partial skills from forms," which means to take each skill from a form separately to practice and understand its application in detail. This training provides knowledge in how to fight using the skills developed through form practice. In *chai shou,* each skill is discussed in detail. Masters analyze the direction, angle, timing, force, and methods for changing and connecting all skills. Then according to this analysis, students practice single skills first in solo practice and then in two-person practice with a helper. A wide variety of methods and training steps is used across the many different martial arts groups and styles.

Unlike the training methods in other martial arts styles, the skills of form training in the internal martial arts are different from the skills of application training, and the purpose of basic *gongfu* or form training is different from that of application training. The movements practiced in form training are different from the analogous movements practiced for fighting. In form practice, for example, movements should always be large in order to train the internal capabilities. In application training, however, the movements should be small to have maximum effect.

Accuracy of movement is emphasized in form practice because correct movement increases awareness and flow of the internal

components. The emphasis in application training, on the other hand, is on the ability to change and vary movements and skills smoothly and quickly. The ability to change movements focuses on how to change from one skill to another; while variation concerns how to apply a given skill in different ways from one situation to the next. Each skill has many variations, and all possible variations should be mastered in training if fighting ability is to improve. Usually these variations are not discussed directly in form training, and students who devote many hours to form practice are often dismayed to discover that their skills cannot immediately be applied to fighting situations.

It is important for you to understand what benefits the different training methods can bring and what you want to accomplish in your practice. Form training cannot yield an understanding of applications; application training like *chai shou* is necessary. The traditional application training process will help you understand how to use the skills developed through your form practice.

In application training, masters need to explain how each movement from the form can be used in real fights and, especially for high-level internal skills, masters need to offer their bodies as targets so that students can practice applying each movement. This allows masters to check if students really understand the skills. With such understanding, students can then progress to mastery through continued and specialized practice.

Although some of the steps in application training differ among groups, they can generally be divided into two basic types: a fixed skill application step and a variation skill application step. Each step uses different training methods. In the fixed skill application step, masters explain each movement of a skill in great detail and then describe how the skill can be correctly applied, especially in terms of correct angle and timing. Without correct angle and timing, no skill can be well executed. After detailed explanations, students should practice each skill with a partner to gain a feel for

the correct application. This is called "feed training" because your partner "feeds" or presents you with some movements and you react by applying the appropriate skill.

In the variation skill application step, masters explain all possible variations of each skill. The most common variations involve applying the skill from different sides and at different heights. Some variations require significant changes in the basic movements. Students should practice each skill variation separately and develop an understanding of the underlying meaning of each skill. Finally, students should be able to devise their own variations.

✪ Assessing the Opponent

The ability to assess and test your opponent's skills quickly is a critical aspect of real fighting. Unlike the martial arts competition fighting today, in which contestants often know each other at least by reputation and in many cases often having multiple opportunities to compete with each other, in real cases opponents often have little, if any, knowledge of each other's skills. There is rarely time to find out about the opponent's level of experience or expertise before the fight begins. You must instead be able to get the information you need from a quick look and a few touches. Judging the opponent is called *liang di* and it is the first step in the development of correct fighting techniques.

Each person has a unique combination of abilities, *gongfu* level, body conditioning, habits, and personality. Some of these characteristics can be known from observing your opponent, some from testing his skills, and some from simply touching him. Observation can provide information about the opponent's size and body condition. You may be able to estimate how quick and powerful he is from watching him move. From observing his standing posture or his way of walking, you may be able to discern his skill level and his nimbleness and stability. Testing

him by presenting him with a variety of challenges can provide information about aspects of his personality—for example, whether he is patient or impetuous. Touching helps you assess his *gongfu* level. Does he really understand, for example, how to change force? Accurate judgments of your opponent's characteristics will always give you an advantage in fighting situations. It is said that if you know both yourself and your opponent well, you will never be in danger in a fight. On the other hand, you need to be careful to hide your abilities from your opponent.

✪ Finding the Proper Distance

Knowing how to find and maintain a proper distance is very important for effective use of your fighting skills. You need to know both the safe distance and the best skill distance. The safe distance is the distance at which your opponent cannot defeat you with his skill movement, and the skill distance is the distance at which you can beat him with a skill movement of your own.

In fighting, you must first determine the safe distance that is necessary to maintain between you and your opponent. To make this determination, you need to know how quick your opponent is and what kind of skills he likes to use. Before attacking, you should protect yourself by maintaining this safe distance. As long as you keep this distance, you can stay relaxed and adjust your movements easily and well. If you are not sure what the safe distance is, you should start by standing quite far from your opponent and then move closer to him only as you become more confident about your ability to make an accurate assessment. You should move quickly and nimbly to maintain the safe distance if your opponent tries to approach you. Once you know your opponent's capabilities, you may want to let him get close to you for your own purposes. You may, for example, want to lure him toward you so that you can launch an attack.

Skill distance refers to how close you need to be to your opponent for your skill to have maximal effect. In real fighting, it is common to be a half step too far from your opponent. This occurs because your opponent will quite naturally step back as you move toward him, and this will put him just slightly out of ideal range. You should anticipate this and adjust your steps accordingly. This requires that you practice footwork carefully and consistently.

In the internal martial arts, skill distances are typically very short. It is said that if you want to beat your opponent, you must be close enough to seem as if you want to kiss him.

In fact, an effective balancing of safe distance and skill distance is difficult. It is necessary to practice your body movements in order to dodge your opponent's attack instead of merely stepping back. This is a useful way to keep a short safe distance. Also you should pay attention to your opponent's forward motion. You should take advantage of his forward motion to achieve and maintain your skill distance more easily. There are many types of training for your eyes and footwork in order to improve these skills. After long practice, you can develop a good intuitive feel for how to keep optimal distance.

✪ Determining Timing and Direction

Timing and direction are closely related. These terms refer to when and from what angle your force should be released in a fight. The basic principle of internal martial arts is that you should never release your force directly against your opponent's force. Most often, the optimal time to release your force is just at the moment when your opponent is about to finish one skill and begin the next. This moment has been described as the time when the opponent's "old force has just passed and his new force has not yet arrived." At this time it will be most difficult for your opponent to change his movement.

The most common direction for releasing your force is diagonal to the direction of your opponent's movement. Diagonal force is effective not only to defend against the release of his force but also to upset his balance and more easily to gain control over him. In many cases, it may be even more useful to follow his direction rather than to move against it with crossing force, but this is usually not easy to do.

In general, determining the correct timing and direction for skill release is very difficult and requires extensive training. Push hands is the most common training method for increasing this ability because it provides deep and detailed practice in how to apply all skills. Push hands practice allows you to develop a feel for each application and to master it thoroughly.

✪ Moving Forward, Backward, and Sideways

Basically, your body can move forward, backward, or sideways. Usually when you move forward in a fight to get close to your opponent, you should lower your posture. This will make your body more stable and integrated and will make it more difficult for your opponent to defend himself. When you move backward to increase the distance from your opponent, you should raise your posture. The higher posture will allow you to see your opponent more clearly and will make it easier to defend yourself against his attack.

Sideways movement is very important and useful in many situations, but it is difficult to do well. Because sideways steps feel less natural and are less common than forward and backward steps, they must be carefully practiced. In training, sideways movement is always combined with forward or backward movement to create diagonal action. If you move forward in a straight line to get close to your opponent, it is very likely that your force will meet his force

directly. This violates an important principle and will reduce your chances to win. If you move backward in a straight line to leave your opponent, it will be easy for him to follow you and difficult for you to change the timing or direction of your movements. You will not be able, for example, to shift your movement quickly or easily from backward to forward. Two important points to keep in mind when moving sideways are first to keep your body erect in order to maintain your balance, and second, to feel ready at all times to move quickly back toward your opponent.

✪ Protecting Your Body

The ability to protect yourself is as important in the traditional Chinese martial arts as the ability to cause damage to your opponent, and there are many methods for developing this skill. In centuries past, martial artists had to be prepared to respond to difficult challenges at a moment's notice, so the ability to protect oneself was crucial and became the focus of intensive training. Martial artists today do not face a similar situation and usually do not include daily practice of self-protective skills in their training.

Two aspects of these skills are: how to protect yourself when you hit your opponent with intense force and how to protect yourself when your opponent hits you. As your practice progresses, especially as your internal power increases, you will be able to release ever larger amounts of force. Then the question becomes one of how much force you can release without hurting yourself. Iron palm is the most common practice for protecting yourself in this circumstance. Practices like iron shirt are useful for the second goal of making your body strong enough to withstand powerful strikes from your opponent. These practices are a vital part of your training. Although different training methods are used in different groups, the basic principle is the same: the body's ability

to endure strong attacks is increased by repetitively hitting hard objects over a long period of time.

While these methods were traditionally included in internal martial arts training, they were practiced in a unique way. Because sensitivity is a critical component of internal martial arts practice, great care is taken to ensure that training exercises like iron palm and iron shirt do not interfere with the development of this ability. Exercises that harden the body can all too easily reduce sensitivity. The tradition of internal martial arts values strong bodies but also requires that practitioners maintain softness of movement and relaxation at all times. These qualities are fundamental to all internal martial arts skills and applications and must not be sacrificed in the pursuit of developing a hardened body.

A common misunderstanding is that thick, rough, and calloused skin is indicative of good training. Actually in the internal martial arts, correct practice can make your skin softer. A martial arts adage warns that if you meet a person whose hands are very soft, you should be careful. Exercises that strengthen the skin and limbs usually involve hitting a bag filled with sand or made of iron. Such practice in the internal martial arts should involve light hitting, the use of *qi* force, and post-training herbal washes.

✪ Practicing Applications

Although dummies are often used in the training of application skills, the most common and useful method of training involves the use of a partner or "helper." The helper is said to "feed" his partner mock attacks that allow the partner to practice each fighting skill and to develop a heightened awareness of movement, timing, direction, relaxation, and sensitivity.

Three points of central importance in two-person training are: *deng zhao,* which means to wait until your opponent launches his skills; *jie zhao,* which describes how to make the first contact with

your opponent's incoming skills; and *huan zhao,* which describes how to respond to your opponent's incoming skills. The most important aspect of *deng zhao* training is to anticipate and adjust to your opponent when he launches an attack. Focusing on his shoulders, for example, will help you anticipate and respond to a punch about to be thrown. In *jie zhao,* the important feature is the timing and angle of your movement when you first touch your opponent. When your opponent throws a punch, for example, it will be easier for you to intercept his hand if you raise your hand up to his elbow and then move it down along his forearm to his hand, rather than trying to catch his hand directly. For *huan zhao* practice, the most important goal is to combine defense and attack skills. Unlike the external martial arts—in which defense and attack skills are used separately, first defense and then attack—most skills in the internal martial arts include both defense and attack elements and apply them simultaneously. The key points in *huan zhao* practice are to understand and use the *yin-yang* principle properly and to keep all movements smooth and curvilinear.

There are three stages in helper practice, though they need not be clearly demarcated. The first stage involves researching each skill in detail. You should understand each movement and think about how it can be applied in every possible case. Then your helper should simulate each case and "feed" or present it to you. You should practice every skill repeatedly until you are very familiar with it and can execute it well. In this stage, the helper should not change his movements in response to your execution of each skill. This ensures that you can pay close attention to applying your skill correctly and not to what your partner might do next.

In the second stage, you should combine several skills, and your partner should present you with more complex combination moves. In each presentation, more changes will be required of you. Your focus should center on footwork and body movements.

The third stage of two-person practice more closely resembles

real fighting. Your partner should present you with the kind of challenges you might encounter in a real fight so that you can practice responses to deal with these challenges. This is the most difficult stage of partnered application training because many of the skills practiced can lead to serious injury. A person assigned to act as protector can offer some help but this may not be sufficient, so you must be very careful. It is advisable first to practice all moves slowly and to learn how to control your force. Gradually, you will know the points at which the greatest harm can occur. When you practice controlling and gripping skills, for example, you should know at which point to release your control so that you can avoid hurting your partner. To practice punching and kicking skills, it may be necessary to augment helper practice by hitting a wooden training post. When practicing with your partner, you need to control your force to avoid hurting him, but you can use the same skill to hit a post hard and experience what a real attack should be like.

✪ Are You Ready for Fighting?

We have discussed many technical aspects of training, and with diligent practice you will experience improvement. Does this mean, however, that you can successfully engage in a real fight? Unfortunately, the answer is a resounding "no." There are still many things for you to learn.

You need to prepare yourself mentally to face a fight. Because a hard fight typically involves an element of cruelty, you are likely to feel nervous at the prospect of combat, and this nervousness will change the way you move. It is said that applying as much as fifty percent of one's skill in a real fight is a notable achievement. To do so requires psychological training.

Psychological factors are very important in real fighting. You need to learn how to bear a real attack with equanimity and

resolve. Most martial artists today engage in competitions meant to test their skills rather than in serious fights intended to harm or destroy an opponent, but psychological factors are still important. You should train yourself so that you can remain stable and relaxed and not let your opponent's intensity influence or control you. Second, you should learn to use psychological factors to your own advantage as tools for subtly influencing your opponent. The way you present yourself, for example, can inspire fear in your opponent or lure him into underestimating your skill. Changing the rhythm of your movements is often helpful in undermining your opponent's confidence and confusing him about your abilities.

To increase your chances of success in a fight, keep your mind relaxed and clear. It is easy in a fight to lose your focus, become nervous, and forget your skills. Physical and mental preparation can help you overcome these common tendencies. Pay attention to your strongest and weakest points and to those of your opponent. Try to attack your opponent's weakest point and to conceal your weakest point from him. Use your strong points to the fullest.

If your opponent has some good or special skills, look for a chance to defend against them rather than a chance to dodge them. Attack is said to be the best defense, and dodging cannot eliminate the problem. If your opponent charges forward to catch your leg, for example, and you move back to dodge his attack, your attempt is likely to fail because steps backward are usually slower than steps forward. You will be better able to defend yourself if you move forward instead of backward because forward movement will make it easier to maintain your balance and to destroy the rhythm of your opponent's movement.

Patience is important, especially when you compete with people whose skills are close to or even better than yours. Recognize that your task is not easy and that your only chance to win rests on the possibility that your opponent will make a mistake. Wait patiently and vigilantly for him to give you that chance. Waiting, however, does

not mean doing nothing. You must keep yourself as safe as possible from his attacks and then find a way to give him some trouble.

Wen, ling, song, jing, and *jue* are qualities necessary in fighting, and these concepts have both psychological and physical aspects. *Wen* refers to stability of mind as well as body, and this trait can be a manifested by not rushing the execution of your skills. It is easy in the heat of competition to speed up your movements; your mind, too, can easily begin to race. Once you become hurried, you are likely to forget what you should do, so it is important to slow down and let your responses flow at a measured pace. *Ling* means "to move in a nimble and lively manner"; *song* denotes relaxation; and *jing,* a sense of stillness or quiet. *Jue* means "to make decisions resolutely" and to execute them without hesitation. If you have a chance to win the fight, you must apply your skill directly and with confidence. Chances are quickly lost and may not come again.

In application training, you should never judge your ability by whether you can use a given skill; instead, determine whether your attempt applies a principle correctly. Sometimes a lower-level skill or even a skill that is technically inappropriate for a particular situation can be used if it adheres to principle. If your skills follow correct principles, you will make progress. Do not be ashamed, frustrated, or angry if you lose a fight or fail to use a skill successfully. Your focus should always be on how to learn from your experience so that you can improve your skill.

Training and practice can provide basic knowledge and develop competence, but to become a good fighter, you need a lot of experience in situations of real combat. If you use what you learn in fighting to fine-tune your training and what you learn in training to improve your fighting, you will, little by little, become good. Keep practicing and try again and again—you will achieve your best.

About the Author and Translators

Lu Shengli

Author Lu Shengli has spent his entire life cultivating the skills of the internal styles of taijiquan, xingyiquan, baguazhang, and other traditional martial arts. Starting in the 1970s, he studied internal martial arts with master Luo Shuhuan and grandmaster Wang Peisheng. He has taught in Beijing since 1984, where he is a martial arts instructor of the Beijing Wu Style Taiji Quan Association and an instructor at the Beijing Information Technology Institute.

Zhang Yun

Translator and editor Zhang Yun, from Beijing, China, is a student of Luo Shuhuan and Wang Peisheng and lives near Pittsburgh, Pennsylvania. He has taught internal martial arts in the United States since 1989 and is the President and head instructor of the Yin Cheng Gong Fa Association, North American Headquarters. He has published more than fifteen articles and is the author of *The Art of Chinese Swordsmanship: A Manual of Taiji Jian*.

Susan Darley

Translator and editor Susan Darley, Ph.D., has studied taijiquan with Zhang Yun since 1995. She assists Zhang Yun in teaching classes and seminars and writing books and articles.

About North Atlantic Books

North Atlantic Books (NAB) is an independent, nonprofit publisher committed to a bold exploration of the relationships between mind, body, spirit, and nature. Founded in 1974, NAB aims to nurture a holistic view of the arts, sciences, humanities, and healing. To make a donation or to learn more about our books, authors, events, and newsletter, please visit www.northatlanticbooks.com.

North Atlantic Books is the publishing arm of the Society for the Study of Native Arts and Sciences, a 501(c)(3) nonprofit educational organization that promotes cross-cultural perspectives linking scientific, social, and artistic fields. To learn how you can support us, please visit our website.

TABLE OF CONTENTS

The author Lu Shengli and Great Master Wang Peisheng
in San Francisco, 1993

僅以本書獻給我的師爺武學大師王培生先生

This book is dedicated to my grandmaster,
great martial artist Wang Peisheng.

Photo and Illustration credits: the photographs in this book were taken by Zhao Zeren, Zhang Yun, Lu Shengli, Kenneth Stinson, and Taotao Zhang. The illustrations and lineage charts were drawn by Zhang Yun.

Published by Blue Snake Books,
an imprint of North Atlantic Books
Berkeley, California

Cover and text design by Brad Greene
Printed in the United States of America

Combat Techniques of TaiJi, XingYi, and BaGua: Principles and Practices of Internal Martial Arts is sponsored and published by the Society for the Study of Native Arts and Sciences (dba North Atlantic Books), an educational nonprofit based in Berkeley, California, that collaborates with partners to develop cross-cultural perspectives, nurture holistic views of art, science, the humanities, and healing, and seed personal and global transformation by publishing work on the relationship of body, spirit, and nature.

PLEASE NOTE: The creators and publishers of this book disclaim any liabilities for loss in connection with following any of the practices, exercises, and advice contained herein. To reduce the chance of injury or any other harm, the reader should consult a professional before undertaking this or any other martial arts, movement, meditative arts, health, or exercise program. The instructions and advice printed in this book are not in any way intended as a substitute for medical, mental, or emotional counseling with a licensed physician or healthcare provider.

North Atlantic Books' publications are available through most bookstores. For further information, call 800-733-3000 or visit our websites at www.northatlanticbooks.com and www.bluesnakebooks.com.

Library of Congress Cataloging-in-Publication Data

Lu, Shengli.
    Combat techniques of Tai Ji, Xing Yi, and Ba Gua : principles and practices of internal martial arts / Lu Shengli ; translated and edited Zhang Yun and Susan Darley.
        p. cm.
    Summary: "A comprehensive introduction to the essential fighting techniques of Taijiquan, Baguazhang, and Xingyiquan, presenting authentic training material that has survived the cultural revolution"—Provided by publisher.
    ISBN 1-58394-145-2 (trade paper)
    ISBN-13: 978-1-58394-145-4
    1. Martial arts—Psychological aspects. 2. Tai chi. I. Title: Combat techniques of Taiji, Xingyi, and Bagua. II. Title.
    GV1102.7.P75L82 2006
    796.815—dc22   2006034663

5 6 7 8 DATA 20 19 18
Printed on recycled paper
North Atlantic Books is committed to the protection of our environment.
We partner with FSC-certified printers using soy-based inks
and print on recycled paper whenever possible.

COMBAT TECHNIQUES OF TAIJI, XINGYI, AND BAGUA

Principles and Practices of Internal Martial Arts

LU SHENGLI

鲁勝利

Translated and Edited by

ZHANG YUN AND SUSAN DARLEY

Yin Cheng Gong Fa Association

BLUE SNAKE BOOKS

Berkeley, California

nèi jiā quán shí zhàn jì fã zhī li lùn yǔ shí jiàn

内家拳實戰技法之理論與實踐

COMBAT TECHNIQUES OF TAIJI, XINGYI, AND BAGUA

Principles and Practices of Internal Martial Arts

Yin Cheng Gong Fa
Traditional Chinese Martial Arts Training System

D1218166